Lights Out

The Electricity Crisis, the Global Economy, and What It Means to You

Jason Makansi

BICENTENNIAL
1807
WILEY
2007
BICENTENNIAL

John Wiley & Sons, Inc.

Published by John Wiley & Sons, Inc., Hoboken, New Jersey.
Published simultaneously in Canada.

Wiley Bicentennial Logo: Richard J. Pacifico.

For general information on our other products and services or for technical support, please contact our Customer Care Department within the United States at (800) 762–2974, outside the United States at (317) 572–3993 or fax (317) 572–4002.

Wiley also publishes its books in a variety of electronic formats. Some content that appears in print may not be available in electronic formats. For more information about Wiley products, visit our Web site at www.wiley.com.

Library of Congress Cataloging-in-Publication Data:

Makansi, Jason.
    Lights out : the electricity crisis, the global economy, and what it means to you / Jason Makansi.
        p. cm.
    Includes bibliographical references and index.
    ISBN 978-0-470-10918-2 (cloth)
    1. Electric utilities—United States. I. Title.
    HD9685.U5M326   2007
    333.793'20973—dc22   2007008125

Printed in the United States of America

10 9 8 7 6 5 4 3 2 1

This book is dedicated to Munzer and Nellie Makansi, my dad and my mom, who both seem to get younger with each passing year.

Contents

Preface

The day I started writing this book was the day the lights went back on in our house after a very hot and humid four-day electricity outage. It was late July in St. Louis when the storm literally blew down our street, toppling hundred-year-old trees and, with them, hundreds of power lines. We were among the lucky ones. We suffered minimal storm damage and a loss of power that was, in some cases, almost a week less than some of our neighbors. Fast forward six months to early December. As I complete the first comprehensive draft of the book, 500,000 customers are still without electricity following a brutal winter storm that swept across the region. I can't image a more appropriate (or unfortunate) way to book-end a manuscript called *Lights Out*.

Two difficult outages in one year and the accusations are flying. Investigations have been initiated. And St. Louis is not alone. Major electricity outages have hit metropolitan areas such as Chicago, Detroit, Seattle, and New York. The same is true for entire geographic regions such as the blackout of 2003 in the northeastern United States and parts of Canada, the 2006 blackout that affected many cities across Europe, and those outages that are common occurrences throughout the developing world. This demonstrable increase in what utilities call "reliability events" began in the mid-1990s. What is causing this string of outages, the effects of which range from catastrophic to inconvenient, is one key issue that I address in this book.

My friends and neighbors have a simpler question: Who's to blame? How could such a serious outage happen twice in one year? I don't want to remind them that another serious one occurred last summer, although it did affect different parts of the city. The root cause of most, if not all, widespread service interruptions is a combination of extreme weather events and deficient utility operations and equipment and work processes that lead to malfunctions. Mother Nature and Father Utility conspire to ruin your day, or week, as the case may be.

That's the simple version—the version easiest to see and understand. However, as with most things, the reality is much more complicated. It is often hard to determine where Mother Nature ends and Father Utility begins. In most areas of the United States, dear old dad isn't acting alone but is instead working at the direction or under the oversight of the regulator, or state public utility commission (PUC). Electric utility service comes courtesy of a two-headed beast—the utility service provider and the state regulator.

Less reliable service is not the only big issue looming over electricity delivery, just the one with the greatest direct impact on our lives. Electricity production is the second largest influence on global climate change. Automobiles are the largest. Our electricity service is expected to become more dependent on global energy supply lines that feel less and less secure as the government fights its War on Terror. The business of electricity service has shifted from one driven by engineers to one driven by financial engineering. All of these issues are intricately woven together. The resulting tapestry reveals an industry in peril and electricity consumers mostly ignorant of the dangers that lie ahead.

I want to accomplish three primary objectives with this book. One of the most important is to explain how we've arrived at our current predicament, and why it is vastly different from state to state as a result of some dubious deregulation and competition programs launched in the late 1990s. (A note to all of the free-marketers out there: I'm not against competition. Far from it. I am saying—and most other experts are saying it, too—that the seeds of deregulation's failure were contained in the way the programs were conceived.)

But the past isn't as important as the future. The second objective I have for the book is to lay out the electricity roadmap before you—one I believe will take us to a better place. It is obvious that we're not now headed anywhere that we want to go. In fact, electricity's present map is not a pretty map at all. The road we're on is all too familiar, and where we're headed is pretty much like where we've already been—only more so. Let me assure you. We don't want to stay on this course. We need something different, hopefully something better. In the last section, I propose a strategy that charts what I believe is a much better course.

My third objective is to galvanize you to action. I hope that this book motivates you to speak up, to take the small steps that we can all embrace in order to build momentum and drive our electricity-driven society toward change. It comes down to this: It is up to us to ensure that our neighborhoods, our cities and states, our nation, and the economy that drives it do not deteriorate because we no longer have the most robust and reliable electricity system in the world.

This book follows my book *An Investor's Guide to the Electricity Economy* (Hoboken, NJ: John Wiley & Sons, 2002). After *An Investor's Guide* hit the shelves, I decided to put my money where my mouth was. I started an investment fund. My partners and I worked to monetize the information in the book by focusing specifically on the electricity production and delivery value chain. Since then we've experienced real change in society, in the business world, and in the electricity sector specifically. Electricity is the largest business sector in the country, with larger-than-life characters and wild mood swings. Just before I finished the first book, Enron imploded, and the rest of the electricity industry tumbled down after it; the effects of 9/11 were still taking shape; and the "new millennium" for the energy industry could not have gotten off to a more inauspicious start.

As I put the finishing touches on this book, the Republican majority has been swept out of Congress, the Bush administration is under relentless attack over the Iraq war, and the U.S. electricity business has almost completely retreated from the globalization that characterized the 1990s. China and India have ascendant economies, becoming an increasing consumer of the world's commodities, many of which we consume in great abundance for our electricity needs. Electricity service disruptions seem to be rampant. A million customers were without power in the Seattle area following a severe windstorm in December. This power disruption marked the first time since 1953 that the *Seattle Times* was unable to publish, and only the third time in the paper's history that it wasn't able to put out a paper. As you will see, everything—from local publishers to national elections to distant economies and global weather systems—is inextricably related. As this book unfolds, I'll attempt to connect the dots for you.

One thing has not changed in these past five years. As a nation, we do not pay enough attention to our electricity service. It is something that is missed only by its absence, as in when your service is disrupted. We do not fully realize the breadth of impact of our electricity production and consumption—we are 3 percent of the world's population and we produce and consume 25 percent of the world's electricity. We do not see that the supply lines for virtually everything needed for our electricity infrastructure are expanding across the globe. When we think of electricity at all, it is only in terms of our local electric utility, not in terms of the diverse energy sources needed to generate it, the long transmission lines needed to move it, the vast network needed to distribute it, and the emissions and discharges that result from the entire process.

I wrote this book to call attention to these other, less savory aspects, of electricity. I am a consultant to the industry, and electricity has been my career. I see our industry backsliding, rather than moving forward. I see our leadership in the technology, once unchallenged, now seriously eroded. I see our industry leaders neglect the least valuable and most nettlesome component of the value chain, our transmission system. It is only 10 percent of the "value chain," but it is the linchpin between supply and demand. Transmission experts describe it as a "third-world grid."

I believe we're headed for real trouble in that part of our economy, the electricity infrastructure, which supports and enables the rest of it. Power delivery is at the heart of our modern, increasingly digital society, and electricity is its life blood. When disaster strikes, it is the electricity system that must recover first and fastest because it powers every other layer of infrastructure—fuel delivery, water systems, telecommunications, mass transportation, banking, and health care. In the modern world, electricity is not optional.

Our industry's leaders think we're back to the good times. We're embarking on a massive power plant construction program. Private investment funds are pouring into our industry. The economy has done well over the last four years. You can hear the charge: "More is better!" I'm going to throw some metaphorical cold water on these people, hopefully to jolt them out of their stupor. In this pursuit, you may also get "splashed." If we're going maintain our economy—let alone grow it—then each of us has to acknowledge our own role in the electricity production and delivery value chain, that of responsible consumer.

Acknowledgments

I am grateful to my wife, Kristina, who plays such a key role in making my prose less dense and more approachable for those readers outside the electricity business—and for helping this graphically challenged author with illustrations. Also, I wish to thank Robert Schwieger, the editor, publisher, and chief bottle-washer and cook for *Combined Cycle Journal*. He had been my boss ("captain") for 18 years at *Power* and *Electric Power International* magazines and the myriad publications and industry events that we launched together. He is also a career-long mentor and friend. Bob read and commented on the draft manuscript when he had far better things to do over Christmas. Bob essentially gave me the opportunity to build the career that I enjoy today.

Finally, it is important for all of us to acknowledge the men and women who actually work on, in, and around the electricity infrastructure. They are the ones who keep the lights on; our entire society benefits from their hard work, often under adverse circumstances.

Part One

THE WORST-CASE SCENARIO

L iving without electricity is visceral, maybe even surreal. You begin to feel the difference in everything you do, in almost every step you take. In a very real sense, the lack of electricity drains the lifeblood out of you. You certainly begin to feel a loss of control, and for good reason. The vast majority of us are not in control of our electricity service. It's bad enough to recount your movements in an electricity-less world. Most of us have been through a recent and lengthy outage. It feels like the worst-case scenario. But when you envision a future influenced by the issues that I mentioned in the preface, you begin to realize that the worst case in the years ahead could be *worse.*

In this section, we walk through what happens in an outage so that you can experience how electricity pervades modern existence. Then we learn how today's system works, from the extraction of the raw energy source to the electricity-consuming appliances in your home. After that, we experience more than a century of colorful industry history condensed into what I hope is an engaging and fun approach. Finally, we return to the worst-case scenario theme and show how a system that is breaking can be fixed.

Chapter 1

Night of the Living Dead

You are into day three without electricity at your residence. The heat wave is scorching and you have no air-conditioning. Friends up the street who really can't stand the heat booked what they claim was one of the last rooms available at a hotel still connected to the grid. All the food in the refrigerator is fast becoming fodder for the dumpster. The security system has exhausted its last electrons of backup battery power.

The line last night at the only Mickey D's still able to serve up burgers was brutal. The land-line phones in the house have been down since the storm blew through because they are all remotes that require an electrical connection. You've resorted to burning gasoline in your car to keep the cell phone charged up and your body cool, but you are wondering if you can refill the automobile's tank because half the local stations can't run their pumps. You're taking quick showers, careful to use as little hot water as possible, knowing that the water heater's controls are also electronic and don't work without power.

In the initial hours of the outage, you learned to live without Internet and cable television. These aren't essentials, you think to yourself, although your kids have a different opinion and have spent most of the day moving from one Wi-Fi hotspot to another. Meanwhile, more gasoline is consumed.

You go upstairs to use the bathroom and discover that the water tank on the toilet isn't filling back up. That's weird. The cold water supply to the sink and the bathtub are also low. Check with the neighbors. Same issue. Is there a connection to the electrical outage? Perhaps. The city water system may have lost one or more of the pumps that keep the water pressure high enough to reach the upper floors of homes. Or the water flows had to be redirected because of pump outages, a water main broke from being overloaded, and less water is now in the system. Indeed, in the morning you read that a water main broke less than a mile from your home.

Many of the neighbors have fled to relatives or friends who live in outlying areas. They've been told of the news reports presaging no relief from the heat wave. On the first night or two, there was some comfort, even gaiety, as neighbors gathered on front porches to share storm stories while curious others walked by with their dogs and kids. You were busy keeping chins up in the face of adversity and just thankful that no one in the neighborhood was hurt. Now, it's the third night without power. The neighborhood is eerily quiet. No lights, no security systems. The city's a mess, with thousands of trees down. Police, firefighters and even the National Guard are working to locate individuals who may be at risk of heat stroke. You live in a historic city neighborhood where gang-related petty crime is always an issue, but now everyone's talking about looting. How long before the frustration turns to anger, anger turns to opportunity, and gangs of marauding youth begin plundering the homes?

At the office the next day, power is available. The high-rise office building has a backup generating system in the basement and is connected to the grid in such a way that it can get electricity from more than one source. You do some Internet research on your local utility or electricity service provider. You find that the utility's customer satisfaction indices have slipped this year compared to last. You also discover that there have been controversies between the utility and the

Public Service Commission (PSC), which regulates the utility, about expenditures for distribution system improvements. Not sure how all this relates to your particular situation, you push it to the back of your mind.

You leave work early. Even though the air-conditioning works fine at the office, the last time you slept without air-conditioning on such hot evenings was when you first got out of college and had no money. You can barely type or write in between yawns.

At 3:30 in the morning of day four, you wake to the blaring siren of your security alarm. The power's on—at least on your side of the street. Lights all over the house are on, ceiling fans are whirring, the siren is still screaming and you are completely disoriented. The whole scene is jarring. But the lights are on! Once daylight breaks a few hours later, you move on to the tasks of cleaning up and throwing out. Things begin to return to normal, although it will be another four days of darkness for your friends right across the street.

But for now, it's over. That's it. The worst-case scenario is behind you, isn't it? You wish.

Lurking in the Shadows

Most of us don't think about electricity at all unless it isn't there. But your service, whether at home or at your business, is merely the last link in a long electricity production and delivery "value chain" that is getting longer, going global, governed by vacillating regulations, and subject to all sorts of new threats and vulnerabilities.

Your electricity comes through a distribution circuit, connected to other distribution circuits, which are fed by the transmission system (those long high-voltage wires that go off into the horizon), which is fed by the power plant, which gets its energy from either water in the form of a hydroelectric dam, wind, coal, natural gas or uranium, which can come from places as close as America's heartland or as distant as Iran, Nigeria, Russia, Australia, Venezuela, or Kazakhstan. The large power stations that generate electricity serve various classes of customers: industrial, commercial, and residential. After electricity is first generated, it is greatly increased in voltage to make the long trek over the transmission line more efficient, and then stepped down in voltage as it is taken off the grid for delivery to an end user.

Coal, uranium, and natural gas account for more than 90 percent of the electricity generated in the United States. Renewables make up the rest—with hydroelectric at around 8 percent, wind at 1 percent, and a variety of other sources making up the rest. Today, most of this raw energy is sourced in North America. However, over the next 20 years, things are likely to be different. I like to portray the production and delivery value chain as a "supply line." Unlike in the past, your electricity doesn't really come from a nearby utility. It can come from hundreds, or even thousands, of miles away. These supply lines can be fragile.

Twenty years ago, a worst-case scenario blackout was a much simpler event because the supply line was tighter. A vertically integrated electric utility, highly regulated, was responsible for the entire electricity supply and delivery chain of events. In many cases, these electric utilities also had some control over the coal, natural gas, and nuclear fuel used in their power stations.

In the 1980s, the nation began a protracted experiment with deregulation of the electricity industry. Deregulation was a social, political, and economic trend that affected trucking, telephones, airlines, banking, natural gas, and health care. In the 1990s, under the banner of globalization, large swaths of the rest of the world also began to dismantle state-owned energy enterprises, such as electric utilities, and began to create market-oriented businesses.

Today, and for the last five years, the electricity industry is in what I've called in my speeches to the industry a "quasi-deregulatory quagmire." Depending on where you live, and how vigorously your state pursued competition and deregulation, the vertically integrated supply chain has been busted apart. Some states imposed no competition in the first place. Some started down the path but reverted to regulation. Other states went so far down the competition path that no amount of political maneuvering can "put the genie back in the bottle." In many other countries, deregulation proved to be little more than political rhetoric or window-dressing.

The triple forces of deregulation, market-oriented institutions, and globalization have resulted in many of the consequences that will be described later in this book. However, one of the most important is that the transmission function in this country somehow got lost and ignored during most of the deregulatory fervor. As a result, this country now has what many transmission experts call a "third-world" grid. It's a clever sound bite, but most people will understand the phrase. Certainly, after two major outages this year, my friends and neighbors get it loud and clear.

We have to be careful about how we use the word *grid*. Some industry experts use it to refer only to the transmission function. To others, the grid means all the lines, wires, and circuits between the power station and the electricity meter attached to your home. In other words, it includes the transmission and the distribution functions. In this book, we use it to refer to the latter—all transmission and distribution functionality—and use the phrase *transmission grid* to mean only the transmission assets.

Thirty years ago, we in the industry described our transmission grid system as "gold plated." That means that utilities usually spent more than they needed to ensure that the system was robust and probabilities of massive failures were as close to zero as possible. The reliability of your service used to be something akin to a social guarantee. Regulators benchmarked, or compared, their utilities to others, based on reliability. Today, utilities are trying to maintain some semblance of reliable service on the backs of a deteriorating transmission grid and in the face of a more competitive world for electricity supply.

Many of the much-vaunted positive benefits of deregulation, like lower electricity prices, more reliable service, and new consumer and demand-management technologies, could only have occurred with improvements, constant upkeep and greater integration of the transmission system. Ironically, just the opposite has occurred. Transmission has become the weak link in the supply chain, and many of those positive benefits have yet to materialize. All those ultra-modern, next-generation services deregulation was going to bring to your front door were, unfortunately, dependent upon an increasingly "brittle" transmission grid. Imagine driving a brand-new Maserati over a road littered with potholes.

We're supposed to be balancing electricity supply with electricity demand nationwide, or at least regionally through competition. Low-cost power in the Midwest is being shipped to New England where costs are typically higher. Areas with great reserves of coal, prime sites for new coal-fired units, could generate power economically, and it could be shipped to high-cost regions.

However, because the transmission grid got lost in the deregulatory shuffle, the ability to move this power around to meet these market-oriented expectations did not expand. And, because the utilities and regulators were focused on other parts of the system, the basic infrastructure was actually allowed to deteriorate.

Are you one of those people who would like to see coal-fired generating plants shut down, replaced with renewable energy? One reason you won't see this happen in a big way is that the country lacks the transmission infrastructure to bring wind energy from high-wind areas (usually where few people live) to the places where electricity demand is highest (such as big cities).

So the number one vulnerability in our electricity system is *a deteriorating transmission grid*. While the government and industry have studied the problem and have been taking steps to fix this, progress is slow, and too few of the industry's resources are focused on it.

At the Heart of It All

When you are in the middle of an electricity outage, it's easy to understand how interconnected is our infrastructure. Phones don't work, trains don't run, elevators stop between floors, water pumps quit pumping, compressors that move fuel like natural gas stop turning, computers no long whir, and so on (see Figure 1.1). Electricity is to modern society like blood that runs through the body. It touches everything. It powers everything in some way. If you viewed our infrastructure as a pyramid, electricity would be the base, the bedrock, the foundation upon which everything else depends.

To understand the predicament we may find ourselves in a decade or two from now, imagine inverting that pyramid to where everything from the base down is dependent on the unstable apex.

Fear at the Heart of the Future

Once you thoroughly survey the entire supply chain, transmission isn't the only weak link. When was the last time you thought long and hard

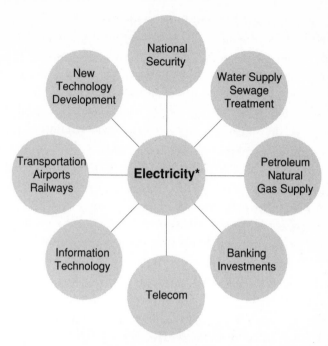

Figure 1.1　Electricity is fundamental and central to modern life.
Note: There is no Strategic Electricity Reserve as there is for oil upon which to draw in case of a true national emergency.

about freight trains? Many Americans believe that our era of dependence upon the railroads ended long ago. But today, more than 50 percent of our electricity comes from the conversion of coal at power stations, and much of that coal is shipped over long distances by rail—from Wyoming to Georgia, for example. Electric utilities east of the Mississippi have been complaining about poor rail service, and are therefore having a difficult time maintaining coal inventories.

Several decades ago, these fuel supply lines were shorter. There are two reasons why coal is hauled greater distances today. Coal from the western United States, primarily the Powder River Basin (PRB) in Wyoming and parts of Utah, is cheaper and has less sulfur than coal from traditional eastern sources concentrated in Kentucky, West Virginia, Illinois, and Ohio. The tradeoff is, however, that it is also a poorer quality coal that burns less efficiently and increases the discharge of carbon dioxide and other pollutants.

Most of our coal-burning plants are getting old. Over the last 10 years, almost all of the new power plants built are fueled by natural gas. That's because the natural gas industry was working off of a supply surplus, or "bubble," created, in part, when natural gas use was banned from power stations between 1979 and 1986. That bubble has been depleted (it took close to 15 years), and now immediate supply is scarce and prices have skyrocketed. In fact, prices have gone up so much that many gas industry experts believe that market forces will force us to import substantial quantities of natural gas from overseas as liquefied natural gas (LNG). Forecasts by the Energy Information Administration (EIA) and others show that we could be importing up to 25 percent of our natural gas consumption by the year 2025.

The list of our potential major LNG suppliers around the world doesn't match up to this country's "best friends" in the rarefied air of geopolitics. Many are our arch enemies, like Iran (the world's second largest holder of natural gas), our former Cold War adversary Russia (with by far the world's richest natural gas holdings), or countries that have given us trouble over the years (Algeria, Indonesia, Libya, and others) and those that are becoming more worrisome by the day such as Nigeria.

If you haven't been keeping up with the electricity industry, you wouldn't know that we're in the permitting stages for a fresh round of construction of large nuclear power units. The dirty secret of nuclear power isn't unsafe reactors, catastrophic accidents, or the potential for nuclear grade materials to find their way into terrorist hands. Those are controversial aspects, to be sure. It is that most of our nuclear fuel is imported. Thankfully, it has largely come from two long-time friends, Canada and Australia. As we'll see later in the book, a significant amount also comes from converting fuel-grade nuclear material from Russia.

With these examples, let's summarize the second vulnerability to the electricity metered into your home or business: *lengthening supply lines*. Under the old regulated electric utility model, the route from energy source to electricity meter attached to a building probably averaged a few hundred miles. In 20 years, if it continues to be more economical to import energy sources, a large fraction of our electricity supply will be "sourced" several thousand miles away, even halfway around the globe. We're even starting to talk in this industry about importing coal, even though we sit on the world's richest coal reserves, enough to generate all of our electricity for several hundred years. It's all about short-term economics, unless we change our national will.

As the supply lines lengthen, it is best to understand them as a taut rope being pulled on both ends. The forces pulling on one end are global economics and geopolitics. The force on the other end is like a powerful vacuum cleaner: Our insatiable demand for energy of all forms has been sucking the supply out of the world. This is okay as long as we're the premium destination for this energy, the ones who can pay the best price or guarantee long-term contracts. This is a global game of tug-of-war that we're playing, and the rules and the players are rapidly changing.

It's Not Just about Us

The economies in China and India have been growing at 7 to 15 percent annually for years. Those two countries represent one-third of the people on the planet. The United States represents 3 percent of the world's population and our businesses cheer and applaud when economic growth tops 3 percent per annum. "That giant sucking sound," the celebrated description by Ross Perot referring to the probable movement of labor to Mexico following passage of the North American Free Trade Agreement (NAFTA), is, in the world of energy, moving away from North America and toward Asia.

There is going to be tremendous competition for the planet's energy resources in the coming years. One thing is certain: We're going to have to pay much more for our share, or our share is going to go where the demand is much higher. However, one sentiment I do not share is this half-baked notion that we're running out of energy. I've been at this business for 25 years. As long as I can remember, we've been "running out." During that entire time, we've had a "10-year supply of natural gas," a "250-year supply of coal," a "30-year supply of petroleum." While I recognize that our planet inherently has a finite amount of resources, in the energy business it's not a matter of resource availability, it's a matter of what price the market will bear to extract those resources.

Resource availability isn't the problem and it isn't going to be—at least for a very, very long time. Our problem is the fragility of our supply lines. Whether energy for electricity is sourced as LNG from the Middle East, uranium from Australia, coal from Wyoming, or electricity from thousands of miles across the country, electricity supply lines are extending beyond the horizon. It is more than shortsighted to think that what happens in China or India has no effect on your electricity.

Just-in-Time Inventory

The number three vulnerability of our electricity system stems from a peculiarity of electricity as an energy form: It cannot be stored; at least, not as electricity. Actually, it can be stored in tiny quantities as electrons in devices called capacitors, which, thanks to advancing technology in microelectronics, are getting larger (called *ultracapacitors*) and more robust. However, for large quantities, it must be stored in another form, such as the chemical energy in a battery, the mechanical energy in a flywheel, or the hydraulic energy of a reservoir of water at a high elevation.

As a country and as an industry, we store vast quantities of petroleum in what is known as the Strategic Petroleum Reserve (SPR). Large volumes of natural gas are stored in underground caverns around the country to balance seasonal demand and supply. Vast reserves of coal are located in mines, a natural means of energy "storage."

We have nothing like this for electricity. We do have facilities called pumped storage hydroelectric plants, which function as bulk electricity storage. However, only 2 percent of our electricity-generating assets are represented by such facilities. In other countries, such as Japan, the United Kingdom, Europe, and South Africa, the percentage is more like 4 to 10 percent.

It seems odd, doesn't it, that we have so little storage for that part of the infrastructure that supports and enables the rest of it? Odd, short-sighted and, I believe, dangerous. Storage technologies are under development rapidly; but so far, few in the industry or in the political arena have given them much attention.

Whither the People

While stored electricity is in short supply, it's in much better shape than our supply of trained and skilled workers. At least for now. And while electricity storage is an issue of physics (a topic scientists and engineers can get their minds around), the supply of workers is an issue of people (a topic even scientists and engineers can't figure out). The supply of trained and skilled workers depends on the creation of incentives.

Electricity is often viewed as a mature or "smokestack" industry. Some have called it a dying industry. Whatever you call it, you can't call it popular. Recent graduates are eager to begin glamorous careers in higher-paying fields such as computer science, electronics, bioengineering, pharmaceuticals, and health care. Meanwhile, the electricity-sector worker is aging and getting ready to retire. The numbers are staggering. For every two workers about to retire, the industry has *less than one* to replace them with. Ninety percent of the engineers and scientists around the globe will come from India and China, according to recent speech by a high-ranking official from the Department of Energy. I just read a report that states the nuclear power subsector alone will require 90,000 trained workers and engineers in the coming years. Ninety thousand! I don't know where those workers are coming from, and neither does anyone in the industry. They are not yet loitering in the halls of academia, judging from reports on college majors.

The fourth major vulnerability, then, is *the lack of specialized workers to maintain and operate the infrastructure.* In the end, this will primarily prove to be an issue of escalating cost, but it will still greatly impact affordable, reliable service. Like energy resources, labor shortages are temporary dislocations, not a situation of "running out." The question is, will we have the right people at the right time? Right now, it doesn't look good.

National Security

During the run-up to year 2000, we learned a great deal about the vulnerabilities of the infrastructure given the impending year 2000 (Y2K) crisis. Experts analyzed and very capably planned for and prevented massive computer failures resulting from the "date" issue affecting a good deal of computer code. The electricity industry, in particular, performed in stellar fashion.

Y2K taught us about how everything is interconnected. That knowledge is now providing the foundation for understanding and protecting ourselves from security threats, which can range from the catastrophic (terrorist attacks) to the mundane (disgruntled workers who hack into the system and do mischief—or windstorms that blow through the neighborhood).

Not only is our electricity grid "third world" in quality, it actually is weakly interconnected. What this means is that the grid is not built to move large increments of electricity long distances. Instead, it is interconnected primarily to move emergency levels of power from one region to another in the event of a widespread outage.

In some ways, a weakly interconnected grid may be beneficial when it comes to security. Disconnected systems cannot all fail together. However, the Y2K studies revealed that there are a handful of major substations in our "national grid" that, if taken out, could likely cause the entire eastern or western parts of the U.S. electricity system to falter. We had a taste of this during the great Northeast Blackout of 2003. The root cause of the failure turned out to be tree limbs along important grid supply lines near one of the substations critical to the systems in the Northeast and Midwest.

Because electricity is the life blood that flows through the rest of the infrastructure, the security of these substations, as well as other parts of the grid, are paramount to national security. Much of the work in this area has "gone underground" since 9/11, and isn't available for public scrutiny. However, it is clear that the gears of the federal government are grinding painfully slowly to take steps to protect such vital facilities. *The fifth vulnerability, therefore, is the interconnection of the grid from a national security perspective.*

Degrading Our Surroundings

Every segment of the electricity production and delivery value chain has associated environmental and ecological impacts. When you think through them, there seem to be no good options for supplying electricity, only less bad ones. Minimizing the impacts on our surroundings adds substantially to the cost of the product and the service.

Today, the most troublesome impact of coal-fired power stations is the massive amount of carbon dioxide (CO_2) that is discharged, contributing to global climate change. Nuclear power's "Achilles' heel" is the safe long-term management (disposal or recycle) of what is known as high-level nuclear waste. The renewable energy sources wind and solar seem attractive until you acknowledge the intermittent nature of those sources. The wind doesn't always blow and the sun doesn't always shine. Long transmission lines require right-of-ways that often must cut through pristine areas. Even many long-time environmentalists are against some of the planned wind farms because of either the NIMBY (Not in my backyard!) effect or because of concerns for bird migration patterns, offshore ecosystems, or just because the 100-foot-tall turbines might ruin their view. It is ironic that large wind farms now may suffer from NIMBY just like nuclear power plants. Finally, there's that lingering EMF (electromagnetic field) issue that slid off the radar screen. That will probably reemerge as soon as new or upgraded transmission lines start being proposed.

Today's natural-gas-fired power plants are typically more efficient than other types of power stations, but they still emit substantial quantities of CO_2. An interesting, little-known aspect of natural gas is that it is almost completely composed of methane (CH_4). Methane is known to be a global warming agent that is more than 20 times as potent as CO_2. Natural gas pipelines, extending hundreds, even thousands of miles, supply the fuel. Leakage occurs along these lines. They are small leaks to be sure, but not insignificant when you consider that every CH_4 molecule that leaks into the atmosphere is like 20 molecules of CO_2! Estimates are that anywhere from 2 to 10 percent of the methane escapes as natural gas is being delivered to the consumer.

So far I've briefly touched on only the most pressing long-term environmental issues associated with each option. Many others, shorter term in nature, are described in later chapters devoted to these options. Nevertheless, it is clear that *our sixth vulnerability is environmental impact.*

Never Say Never: The Worst Case Could Always Be Worse

Let's return to the scenario that we opened with. It's day four and no electricity. The storm has not only damaged distribution equipment, but also caused one or two power stations to shut down. A utility one state over did not experience the storm and has reserve capacity. However, only a minimal amount of that reserve could be transmitted to your location because the transmission lines are weak and are not even able to safely carry the load for which they were originally designed.

Your local utility has two "reserve" power stations that are fueled by natural gas. However, it has contracted to have those plants supplied by LNG under short-term contracts under which the utility has to pay the highest market prices for the fuel because the long-term economics are better. Plus they need those plants so infrequently. The supplier included provisions in the contract that allow the price to escalate based on demand at the time of shipment. An LNG tanker bound for your utility suddenly reverses course when the shipper learns that a firm in China is willing to pay more for the LNG. Either pay up or lose the shipment. The utility decides it will not be held hostage to the vagaries of the global LNG market because that will ruin its balance sheet that quarter. And while the global LNG market may be uncertain, there are some sure things in this life: Wall Street does not like ruined balance sheets.

In the meantime, supply is dwindling at the utility's primary coal-fired power plants. Inventories held in the coal yard adjacent to the power units have been allowed to run low because the financial planners see little need for tying up money in excess inventory when it could be put to better use in other short-term investment instruments. With few alternatives, the utility runs the coal units even though there are some maintenance issues that need to be addressed. It is less efficient than usual and so is consuming even more coal, drawing down the inventories that much further. The next unit train of coal destined for the plant is held up by electrical issues along the railroad. Because the units are being "run harder," one of them experiences a "forced outage."

The utility issues warnings, sanctioned by the state and local government officials, about how much electricity each household can use over the next several days. Run the refrigerator, but unless it is a health emergency, do not run the air conditioners.

Because your utility now competes directly with the utilities adjacent to it, they no longer come to each other's aid in emergencies like this outage. The utility contemplates "airlifting" skilled workers from Asia, but finding ones that speak enough English (so that they understand our safety criteria, for example) is difficult. Plus, the expense is staggering, to say nothing of the bureaucratic challenges of getting security clearances and visas. In exploring this solution, the utility finds that many skilled American workers are now employed in Asia because the money is better and the work, designing and building new infrastructure with advanced technologies, is more gratifying than operating and maintaining the antiquated systems in the United States.

Day four becomes day five, the day that the looters showed up in your neighborhood. Day five becomes day six, when a voltage surge caused by an inexperienced worker cascades to create new equipment failures. Day seven begins a long week during which brownouts are frequent and electricity use is rationed on a daily basis—as it is in third-world countries.

I am only imagining what it might be like in the future, but you can easily get the point. It's getting to be a perilous journey between the source of energy and the electrons at your meter. The trained and expert professionals needed to assure that it's all done safely may not be around. You may think that I'm taking liberties in conjuring up these scenarios. But in December 2000, no one would have believed that Enron could implode by December 2001. On September 10, 2001, few people believed that two 110-story buildings could be felled by airplanes commandeered by hijackers armed with box cutters.

The economic costs of electricity outages are astronomical (see Table 1.1). That's why the most vulnerable businesses maintain sophisticated capability to recover from electricity service disruptions (a field called *business continuity*). The cost to you and I may be more difficult to estimate, but we know it is high, whether gauged by pain in the wallet or psychological damage.

Table 1.1   The Costs of Outages for Selected Commercial Customers

Industry	Average Cost of Downtime Per Hour
Cellular communications	$41,000
Telephone ticket sales	$72,000
Airline reservations	$90,000
Credit card operations	$2,580,000
Brokerage operations	$6,480,000

In later chapters, we'll spend more time on the frequency and severity of electricity outages. There are good reasons why *Power* magazine, one of the industry's most prominent trade publications, reported late last year through its Power News service that one of the largest grid operators in America, PJM, calls the need for new transmission an "emergency," and that "time is of the essence to avoid reliability problems." The North American Electric Reliability Council (NERC), now responsible for the reliability (and reliability standards) for the nation's grid, reports that "the transmission system in North America requires additional investment to address reliability issues and economic impacts." In fact, you almost can't read a report on the U.S. electricity industry that doesn't decry the state of the nation's transmission grid either overtly or covertly.

It does seem like we'll be experiencing more nights of the living dead without electricity. As the issues become clearer, a better strategy also comes into focus. This is what we'll see in following chapters.

Chapter 2

The Production and Delivery Value Chain

O ur electricity system can be considered one huge machine. All of the pieces and parts are intimately connected. They must be operated in concert with each other, completely synchronized, or the machine grinds to a halt. The machine is dynamic. That is, the state of any part of the machine depends on the state of the machine as a whole.

With the institutional and business structures that prevailed up to the 1980s, the national "machine" consisted of regulated regional and local utilities, each with its own vertically integrated submachine, weakly interconnected (to move emergency levels of power from one region to another) with each other. Under today's business and financial structures, different owners and operators are responsible for the different parts of the machine.

The tool that we will use to understand the parts is called the *production-and-delivery value chain* shown in Figure 2.1. It's a popular technique to understand most any industry. In the most fundamental sense, the diagram in Figure 2.1 shows that an energy source has to be extracted first as coal, natural gas, or uranium or harvested as wind, solar, or water. That energy is converted into electrical energy. Then the electricity is transmitted long distances and distributed to individual consumers, and finally each consumer uses and manages the electricity in various ways, including lighting systems, home entertainment, microwave ovens, home-heating controls, motors, compressors, and so on.

Burn It, Convert It, Move It, Distribute It, and Then Consume It

In agriculture, you might call it "farm to market," or plant it, grow it, harvest it, ship it, buy it, and eat it. In the petroleum and natural gas industries, it could be extract it, refine it, distribute it, pump it, and burn it. In electricity, it's burn it, convert it, transmit it, distribute it, and consume it. More instructive for my purposes (we'll come back to this idea many times), I think of the value chain in terms of the "left" being the production side and the "right" being the delivery side of the chain. Transmission is the linchpin between the two. The left side nominally is production, the right side delivery. In Figure 2.1, you can see that transmission is in the middle between electricity generation (burn it and convert it) and distribution and consumption.

"Burn it" refers to the burning of a fuel to generate steam (ignoring for the moment renewable electricity sources). The "turn it" part simply means that a machine, usually called a *turbine*, of some sort turns a generator, which produces the electrons. An energy source is needed to "turn it." That source can be high-pressure steam, water, hot high-pressure air, or wind. In the case of high-pressure steam, the energy source needed to heat the water to create the steam can be a fossil fuel such as coal, petroleum, or natural gas. Or it can be uranium as in nuclear fuel. A few plants even have generated the steam using solar energy; but

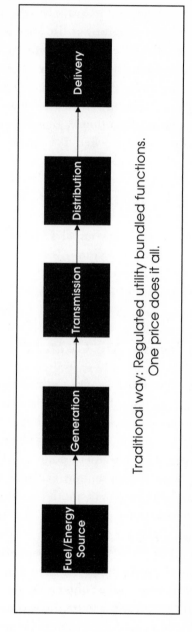

Figure 2.1 The production-and-delivery value chain.

this has proven to be mostly impractical. (In later chapters, we'll get familiar with other ways to use solar.)

After the electricity is generated and it leaves the power plant, it is stepped up in voltage using a transformer. In essence, voltage is what moves the electricity down the wire. Large power stations are usually located far from population centers; so long transmission lines are needed to move the electricity. Then the voltage is stepped back down in what are called *substations* (also a collection of transformers, with measuring and protection devices mounted on them). Branch lines from the substations go in different directions to where the population centers are.

Electricity leaving the power plant can be anywhere from 765 kilovolts (kV) to 235 kV. Once the wires branch even more, the distribution system begins. Usually, the definition of a distribution voltage is 135 kV or below. Once it gets to the small transformer on a utility pole outside your home or in your alley, the electricity may be as low as 13 kV. From here, it is metered into your home or business and distributed through your electrical wiring to the various devices that require electricity.

Circuits Are Circuits

The best way to understand distribution is to think about it in terms of your household electrical system. The essential similarity is that distribution is a collection of circuits—electricity is distributed in a loop and individual users feed, or take power, off the loop. The essential difference is that the voltage is higher on the utility poles and lines than in your house. In both cases, however, the circuit principle has to be noted. In your home, you go to the basement and flip a circuit breaker when you work on your electrical system. That means that multiple electricity using devices, outlets and lights for example, are cut off. When you lose a distribution circuit, lots of devices are without power.

However, when the electricity is cut off from one loop, it continues to flow into another loop somewhere. This circuit characteristic is what makes electricity so unpredictable. The fact is, you really don't know where the electricity is flowing. All you know is that it takes the *path of least resistance*. The path of least resistance depends on what's going on at any moment in every other path it could take. Circuits need to be fed by multiple paths, so if one source of electricity fails, it can be substituted by another. All of this has to be done without overloading the lines. After all, you usually don't run your clothes dryer on the same circuit that runs your computer equipment!

Storage, or the lack thereof, is the other thing that makes electricity so unique. As we have seen, electricity isn't stored in large quantities, at least not as electricity. Very few people on this planet truly appreciate how difficult it is to control the flow of electricity, especially without storage. Do you let your utility know when you are about to turn off your air conditioner, a major consumer of the juice, and allow that electricity to flow to another circuit, another neighbor or another business down the road? No? No one else does either. And that's why demand fluctuates moment to moment and is a function of individual decisions such as, "I'm going to turn off my air conditioner and open the windows for a while."

If You Don't Know Your Demand . . .

The production and delivery value chain can also be thought of as *supply and demand*. Until recently, the utility hasn't been able to monitor the system in a way that allows it to accurately estimate demand. Therefore, they have difficulty determining the supply that needs to go into the system.

The cornerstone of economics is matching supply with demand at a certain price. Until very recently, this has essentially been conducted based on the law of averages in the electricity industry. Utilities and suppliers analyze patterns of behavior daily, weekly, monthly, and seasonally. They know that the demand will be a function of weather. They know that demand will be a function of population and economic growth over time. *What they don't know is the demand in real time.*

Don't panic! They aren't guessing. They use several techniques to match supply with demand. One, they rely on the principle, which doesn't work on Wall Street, that past behavior is some guarantee of future performance. Two, they do communicate in real time about the status of the grid and its many parts. Three, they rely on design margin. Four, they classify power-generating plants in certain ways so that they are available when they are needed. Five, they've designed the circuits so that the system can still operate even if one or more major transmission lines, power plants, or substations trip off line.

The first thing to understand is that the supplier looks at the patterns of demand. We all know that we're creatures of habit. Most people have to get up around the same time, crank up the coffeemakers at the same time, push down the toaster knobs, and turn on the microwaves. Different parts of the system experience what is known as a peak load at different times. Most peak loads occur between 7:00 and 9:00 AM, right before the peak loads on the highways. Then another peak hits around dinnertime, after rush hour. In the meantime, offices close down, and factories reduce output for the second and third shifts. The peak load shifts around the system and the supply is shifted accordingly.

Matching Supply with a Moving Target

Here's how the supply shifts to meet this demand: Power plants are classified for different duties. Some power plants, such as the large nuclear and coal-fired plants, are called *base load plants*. They run at full or close to full output all the time, with one-to four-week seasonal breaks to inspect and repair systems so that, hopefully, nothing breaks when it starts back up and has to run another four to twenty-four months. These plants have what we call *high-capacity factors*. These are the hours that they run in a calendar year divided by the total hours in the year. Nuclear power stations, or *nukes*, typically operate at 90 to 100 percent capacity factors, coal plants are more like 70 to 90 percent. They are also, expectedly, the plants that exhibit the lowest operating costs.

Next are *intermediate load plants*. Electricity demand is largely dependent on the weather. During mild weather seasons—spring and fall—demand is light; during the winter and summer, demand is high. Intermediate load plants run more during heavy demand seasons. They may also run during the week and shut down or operate at partial load during the weekends. Intermediate-load power plants may have capacity factors between 30 and 50 percent.

Finally, there are *peaking power plants*. These plants are characterized by fast startup times but also by high operating costs. You probably know that your car is least efficient when it is starting up and warming up. The more stop and go driving you do, the worse it is for your car. It is the same for power plants. This concept goes back to the idea of cycling we touched on earlier. Peaking plants get beat up because just when they get really warmed up, they are turned off. A "peaker" might run for three hours in the morning, shut down, and then two hours in the evening, every day in the summer. Thermal stresses (swift changes in temperature), whether in your car or in a power plant, are pure hell on metal components. Talk about burnout!

Could You Have at Least Called?

As I mentioned, no one calls the utility to tell them they'll be shutting down appliances or industrial equipment. Now let's look at the demand side. A refinery, paper mill, steel mill, or other "continuous" manufacturing process that runs 24/7 is an electricity supplier's dream customer. It buys a big chunk of capacity, its demand does not fluctuate much and it needs its supply to be guaranteed. It is a steady customer, day in and day out. By contrast, you, dear reader, are the supplier's nightmare. Your loads fluctuate by the hour, and are often at the whims of your behavior.

But what about those large electricity-consuming customers that do turn things on and off? Like an electric arc furnace at a steel mill? Big customers that turn on and off big electron-eating systems literally wreak havoc on the entire electricity grid. The supplier loves the load, but hates having to get the grid to recover when that load trips off line. Remember that the whole system is connected and it is "live" responding dynamically to events up and down the transmission line. When your individual house load turns off, there's nary a blip on the grid. When an electric arc furnace goes down, it can screw up the delicate balance between voltage and load in the circuit it is feeding from, as well as all the other circuits connected to it.

Some electricity consumers are so large that they are treated as wholesale customers. That means two things: They have huge appetites and, therefore, are able to get bulk/wholesale prices, and/or that they connect to the grid at higher distribution voltages. The difference between these electron-guzzlers and you is important when it comes to the deregulated and market-oriented business models used today. Distinct customer classes need distinct business models.

No Degrees of Separation

In order for this whole complicated system to keep operating, someone must tend to the grid itself. It takes power to move power. Some electric generating capacity must be dedicated to the reliable function of the grid itself—either operating or in standby position. In other words, although most of the electricity generated is drawn off the system and used by a consumer, about 10 percent of it has to be maintained in a ready position to regulate grid voltages. Some older power stations, by their very location, have to run to maintain the stability of the grid. Utilities call these "must-run" stations.

If that steel mill's arc furnace shuts down and the voltage goes haywire, the grid dispatcher must be able to call immediately to a plant somewhere to increase or decrease its load to restabilize the voltage. Usually, this is a must-run plant that is humming along and that can increase its capacity quickly.

Take Us to Your Leader

Is it any wonder that for much of the industry's history, it was thought that the best way to orchestrate this system is to have one conductor, that is, one utility organization responsible for the entire value chain? That's not the way it is today. However, it is next to impossible to say whether it is better or worse without getting lots of people all fired up. For better or worse, today the production and delivery chain is disaggregated, and many different entities are responsible for different parts as shown in Figure 2.2.

Depending on which state you live in, there can be multiple "conductors" of the electricity grid orchestra. My state, Missouri, is still highly regulated. There are two large electric utilities, which serve the major metropolitan areas of Kansas City and Saint Louis, and then smaller utilities, coops, municipal plants (munis), and small investor-owned

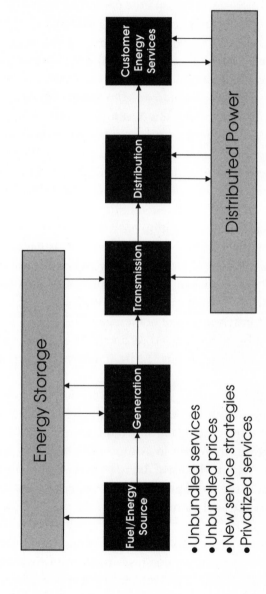

Figure 2.2 The new electricity value chain.

utilities (IOUs), serving the hinterlands. For the most part, each utility is still largely responsible for the entire value chain.

In the other states I have lived in for long periods of time, including New York and Pennsylvania, this isn't the case. New York and Pennsylvania pushed deregulation and competition hard. Electric utilities were forced to sell most or all of their power plants so that they could no longer control the "source" of the commodity. The transmission system in New York was converted into a separate business and market entity, called the *NY-ISO* or New York *independent system operator*. Most electric utilities in that state are now mostly distribution businesses or "wires." They are analogous to an automobile dealership. They provide the product and manage the "customer experience" with the product. New power plants built over the last 10 years are owned and operated by many independent and privately held companies. So-called "merchant" power companies acquired the divested utility power stations.

In Pennsylvania, the disaggregation process unfolded a bit differently. An entity called the *Pennsylvania New Jersey Maryland Interconnection* (PJM) had already been in place to economically move wholesale power around the three states to the advantage of all. This proved to be a convenient platform for creating a market-based transmission business, now called PJM. Utilities in Pennsylvania were not forced to sell their power plants, but they may have been encouraged to do so. The result is that many large utility power stations are owned by independent, privately held companies.

Pennsylvania did push retail competition harder than others. That meant that customers, even homeowners, were given a choice of which electricity supplier they wanted. The distribution utilities were obligated to "wheel" that power over their lines and systems, for fair payment of course. This is not unlike the early days of phone competition, when AT&T was obligated to carry Sprint and MCI to customers. Your telephone bill carries a fee paid by those long-distance service providers to use the AT&T network.

California, Illinois, Texas, Michigan, and Pennsylvania can be considered the states that pushed competition and deregulation the hardest, with New York, New Jersey, Connecticut, Maryland, and Massachusetts the second tier. With the exception of Texas, these were, coincidentally enough, also the states with the highest electricity prices to consumers. The consequences are the same: The parts and pieces of the value chain are disaggregated. Multiple business entities and owner/operators are responsible for them. Where there may have been a handful of primary electric utilities ten years ago in a given state, today there are dozens of participants now working within that same system. This has provided a wealth of opportunity for lots of smart people to build successful new businesses while at the same time causing a whole new set of headaches. As for the question of whether it is better or worse—if you've got a strong opinion, join the crowd. So does everyone else.

Fortunately, the electricity crises in California and the Northeast/Midwest Blackout of 2003 prompted the federal government to address some of the regulatory, financial, and institutional gaps lingering in the industry. You can review the salient elements of the Energy Policy Act of 2005 in the feature box "The Energy Bill: Fine Print, Invisible Ink."

The Energy Bill: Fine Print, Invisible Ink

To much fanfare, Washington passed a comprehensive energy bill, The Energy Policy Act of 2005, in August of that year, around the second anniversary of the Blackout of 2003. In it are clues as to the future direction of the electricity industry. Big legislative efforts like this take a long time to play out, sometimes decades. Congressional bills "authorize" activities, which must then be executed, and appropriated. But count on this bill having a huge impact on the architecture of the electricity industry over the next 5 to 10 years.

The bill provides load guarantees, cost-sharing, and production tax credits for new clean coal and nuclear plants. With respect to nuclear, what the bill did not do was address speeding up activities for long-term nuclear waste management or consolidate the permitting and licensing steps necessary to get a new nuclear unit built. Most of the benefits in the coal area are directed at one type of technology: coal gasification. Why?

(continued)

Probably because GE is the 900 lb. gorilla of the industry (some things haven't changed in a century), has an army of lobbyists, and is the one company that can supply most of the parts of a coal gasification power plant. Does this ability to dominate sound familiar?

The bill also repeals the Public Utility Holding Company Act of 1935 (PUHCA), which we just discussed in the preceding chapter. This sets the stage for additional activity in electric utility mergers and acquisitions, although new combinations have to pass other litmus tests for market power administered by the Federal Energy Regulatory Commission (FERC).

Transmission is the sector that will likely be most transformed by the bill, however. FERC has been given authority to site transmission lines in what would be called "national interest transmission corridors." FERC is also charged with providing transmission investment incentives and to assure cost recovery for reliability investments in the grid. Incentives are also provided so that utilities can sell transmission assets and defer the gain on the sale. Finally, the bill gives FERC oversight of a self-regulating reliability organization to enforce mandatory rules on all market participants.

One aspect that is unique to this bill is the support shown for advanced electricity metering. Advanced metering is a technology that puts some control for demand in the hands of the consumer and helps them to more wisely manage their electricity appetite. How? Simply by connecting price with demand. Advanced meters allow consumers to see what the price point per kilowatt hour might be at any time of the day.

These transmission and delivery topics notwithstanding, it is important to know that the bill was originally designed in 2001 to focus on energy production, rather than consumption and conservation, and it surely does that. This also is a source of the insecurities that we'll be discussing in the next section. Before 9/11, electricity was one of the biggest crises that the newly elected President Bush had to deal with. The California electricity market had imploded, and markets everywhere became nerve-wracking. Electricity trading had been discredited. Enron had sneezed, and President Bush was busy distancing himself from his good friend and major campaign contributor, Enron CEO Ken Lay, a.k.a. "Kenny-boy." Meanwhile, Vice President Dick Cheney focused on being the behind-the-scenes architect for the administration's new energy policy.

Although it is dangerous to generalize (and to tread into the ideological quagmire), it is generally safe to assume that Republican administrations, especially ones from Texas with deep ties to the oil patch, will emphasize production. Democratic administrations tend to emphasize environmental concerns and conservation. The draft of the energy bill from 2001, albeit tweaked and red-lined until it was hardly recognizable, was the starting point for the 2005 bill. Unfortunately, it interpreted the California crisis incorrectly. The market was truly being gamed. But consumers (once again) were given no means of adjusting their behavior in the face of this emerging electricity marketplace. In fact, retail electricity rates were fixed to "protect" consumers, while wholesale rates were allowed to fluctuate with the "market." This caused a huge distortion that allowed the traders to game the system, putting the monkey on the backs of the utilities who either ended up declaring bankruptcy or were forced right to the edge of the bankruptcy precipice.

The problem wasn't supply; the problems were market manipulation and the inability of consumers to respond to the market. Fixed prices and blatant manipulation do not a "free" market make. We've already touched on the left side of the value chain (production) and the right side (consumption). The energy bill mostly focused on the left side, without a corresponding emphasis on the right side. In the next section, we'll explore this issue and how this affects the production and consumption aspects of the value chain in more detail.

Markets: The Not So Invisible Hand

How do these markets that we keep talking about work? It is not easy to explain, especially since there is no one market. The markets in individual states and around the world function in different ways. And, depending on the location, only some classes of customers are actually exposed to real competition. Because regulators had a big role in designing these markets, it is difficult to say where the market begins and the regulation ends.

In any case, the first rule to understanding this whole big complicated system is to divorce the physical assets of the electricity system infrastructure from the market. The "market" is a separate institutional layer. Like other commodities, contracts for electricity supply are bought, sold, swapped, traded, hedged, and bartered. Prices are quoted on exchanges, and there is a level of transparency in pricing, volumes, and the like. This is perhaps the most important new element today, because pricing had been completely invisible to almost all ratepayers, the exception being large industrial consumers and the new class of electricity traders. This is the part of the business that gave competition and deregulation a "black eye" following the 2000–2001 California crisis.

In theory, electricity prices are set "by the market." That is, the market entity, usually the ISO (remember this stands for the *independent system operator*), functions as an intermediary between demand, organized by the distribution utilities that "touch" the end users and are, therefore, "in touch" with demand, and supply, the companies/plants that actually generate the electricity. Suppliers bid into the market, and the market entity dispatches the plants into the system based on those prices. There can be a day-ahead market, a real-time market, and other markets defined by increments of time. Like other markets, the discrepancies between the contractual obligations and the actual physical transfer of electricity is cleared, settled, or "trued up" after the fact. The same increments of electricity supply can be bid on and traded many times before the electrons ever end up at their destination—before the supply is ever "delivered." So, in practice, markets are a combination of bilateral contracts between buyer and seller and collective retail supply, all handled by the same physical assets.

Another part of the market "theory" is that by disaggregating the different parts of the supply chain, companies in the industry could then focus on specific functions and drive down costs. If you live in an area with more aggressive competition, you may see breakouts on your electricity bill for fuel, generation, transmission, distribution, and other services.

From the consumer side of the equation, electricity markets mean choice, that is, choice of supplier. Retail and wholesale customers in competitive markets can "choose" a supplier. In turn, suppliers can advertise and promote themselves to buyers. Just like you can "choose" your supplier of gasoline, and change filling stations, in theory you should be able to choose an electricity supplier. While it is true that an electron is an electron is an electron no matter where it came from, some suppliers have attempted to differentiate themselves in the market by advertising their electrons as being cheaper, produced more efficiently, or even by being greener.

So Much Bottled Water

I remember, as the industry was transforming to a more competitive model, that executives occupied much of the air time at industry meetings by comparing this industry to others. Some thought it would be like banking—with a few large nationally based banks having a mostly regional consolidation. Others thought it would be like natural gas, as another energy "utility." Still others preferred the telecommunications model. This is an interesting one because cell phones and wireless communications were disrupting the usual order. My pick was bottled water.

That's right. Bottled water. Here was a product, at the retail level, much like electricity. Electrons are electrons. H_2O molecules are H_2O molecules. Some argue that they can distinguish among bottled waters. I can't. Of course, if you add additional elements, chemicals, or flavors into the bottled water, it is no longer just bottled "water." And then even I can tell the difference. At any rate, in both cases, retail suppliers had to convince customers that their "product" was better when in fact, it's really pretty hard (i.e., impossible) to distinguish between different electrons or H_2O molecules. Cheaper might work—or, in the case of water, more expensive might work—but how much cheaper could it be if the same physical assets, the same transmission service, and so on, is being used to deliver it?

If all electrons are the same, then another way to distinguish yourself as a supplier is through service. Indeed, changing the customer experience with electricity quickly became the rage with many distribution utilities and new market entrants. The issue here was that most customers didn't know how to benchmark their original service to determine how their new service was different. What do you compare it to? Monopolistic utilities didn't provide much information about how much better they were doing than others. They had a monopoly. There was no need.

Summary

To recap, the elements of competition and markets in the electricity production and delivery value chain are these:

- Disaggregation of fuel, generation, transmission, distribution, and services
- Customer choice in supplier and distinguishing the product/service
- Bidding of supply into a market entity based on demand, which sets prices
- Marketers and traders who buy and sell bulk electricity
- Distinction between the retail market and the wholesale market
- Merchant electricity generators whose output and price follows the needs of the market (rather than on a long-term contract)
- Aggregation of many small electricity buyers into large purchasing entities to improve negotiating position, increase volumes, and moderate prices

Ten years ago, there were no real markets for electricity in the United States. Today most electricity consumers are at least exposed to markets with one or more of the elements bulleted previously. However, the realities are that very little of the total electricity produced and delivered is based on a fully competitive value chain.

Perhaps no one has summed up the current state of the electricity business better than Leonard Hyman, lead author of *America's Electric Utilities: Past, Present, and Future* (Arlington, VA: Public Utilities Reports, 2005). In his most recent edition, he writes:

> *In a way, the industry participants consist of profit-maximizing non-utility generators, regulated utilities that seek to earn a reasonable and steady return, public power agencies that try to earn profits necessary to maintain financial stability while striving for low prices, non-profit monopolistic regional transmission organizations whose operations affect the costs and profitability of other participants, energy service companies that attempt to maximize profits while working on a slim margin, and consumers that might want reliable service or low-priced service or steadily priced service or combinations thereof.*

Later, Hyman concludes, "The restructuring artists left the consumer out of the picture from the beginning, when they decided to concentrate on the wholesale market. More than a decade later, the customer still remains an afterthought." The legacies of restructuring, the hodgepodge of participants, all with different business motivations, are a potent source for the insecurities we encounter later in this book.

Chapter 3

Around the World, Around Town

During the 1990s, a phalanx of management consultants held the hands of utility executives as they faced the brave new world of deregulation and competition. I found myself having lunch with one of these consultants and he casually remarked: "In the California market, a unit of electricity could be 'traded' more than 30 times before the electricity was actually physically delivered." My salad almost came out of my mouth. What is he talking about? He sensed my awe and tried to comfort me with this advice: "Engineers like you need to separate the physical assets from the market."

That's good advice as we get into the history and industry background, context for understanding where this industry needs to go and your role in it. The physical infrastructure, the assets on the ground so to speak, has been developed over more than a century. However, the electricity trading market has developed only recently with its inception dating to about 1992. Most industry experts would likely agree that it is still not a mature market, or that it is a highly fragmented market with different rules in different regions. It still lacks a "center of gravity," the way Wall Street is for the stock market, the way the Chicago Board of Trade is for the commodities market, and the like.

With some hindsight, I believe what my lunch companion was really trying to tell me was to separate the electrons from the dollars. The physical assets make and move the electrons, the electricity. But the institutional and financial structures overlaid on top of the physical assets make and move the money. The critical link between the two are the legislative or regulatory structures that, throughout history, rise and fall in an attempt to keep the electricity flowing while changing the pockets into which the money flows.

Here's a kinder, gentler, image: Think of a square dance, in which regulators, investors, electricity companies, and you, the consumer, are latching arms, releasing them, and then latching the arm of the next person. Let's see how this dance has been performed in the nineteenth century as a overture to how the dance should be conducted in the rest of this century.

A Map of Our Town

The modern era of electricity delivery and supply is widely regarded to have started more than a century ago. Collapsing more than 100 years into a chapter would be a disservice to the historians who have examined this rich legacy in microscopic detail. (See the bibliography at the end of the book.) Plus, when you study the history books, you realize that a straight story is hard to come by. Still, context is necessary.

So, let's a take a whirlwind trip around an imaginary town (Figure 3.1) where the principal cast of characters reside and where the major events have taken place. We begin on Pearl Street, site of the world's first central electricity generating station. Then, we spend some time on Buffalo Avenue, where George Westinghouse revolutionized electricity delivery; peer into a power station on Harrison Street, and meet the infamous Samuel Insull. Next we skip down Norris Street,

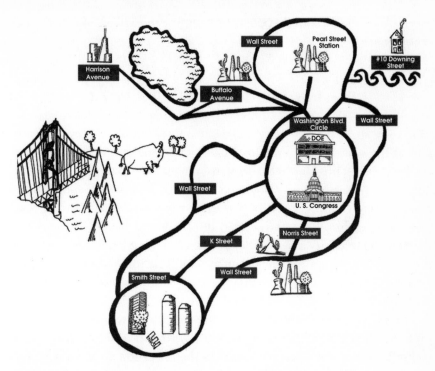

Figure 3.1   A "map" illustrating the history of the industry.

where serious government intervention into the electricity industry began. Then we take a break for lunch.

After that, we check out the ornate offices (too bad we can't see the
alligator shoes in the closets!) on K Street, and stop by modest bureaucratic office buildings on other lettered streets, where regulators, politicians, and lobbyists mingle. Towards the end, we'll detour to Downing
Street to get a global view of the electricity industry, and wind up on
Smith Street, where Enron and its look-alikes captivated, then capsized,
the industry just five years ago.

Unlike most towns, this one is laid out in a grid. Two other things:
There is this tortuous street that cuts through all of the other horizontals
and verticals. It's called Wall Street. Then there is a street, somewhat like
traffic circles, which seem to interrupt the grid. It's called Washington
Street, where traffic is separated by a tree-lined median that looks

lovely from the pavement, but is, in reality, a thicket of ever-changing regulations.

Pearl Street: Where It All Started

Our tour starts here because most accounts of the industry's history start at the world's first centralized electricity generation station located on Pearl Street in Lower Manhattan and built by Thomas Edison in 1882. I consider Edison a boyhood hero, up there with major league baseball players from the 1960s. I named my company after his first generating station. But guess what? Edison got it all wrong. He pursued the type of electricity based on *direct current* (DC), which did not become the dominant design for our production and delivery system. Later, in Chapter 17, which includes a new concept called *distributed generation*, I explain why he could be vindicated in the end.

In the annals of electricity, Pearl Street dead-ended around 1904. At the time, the industry, en masse, made a U-turn. Historians blame it on a technology war that raged at the turn of the last century. Of the two primary types of electricity, AC, for *alternating current*, and DC, Edison fervently backed DC, the kind of electricity Pearl Street station produced. Another character, whom we shall meet shortly, backed AC, which was substantially more efficient for transmitting electricity over long distances. AC also made sense because America's population was expanding outwardly from the big cities during this time. We were becoming a manufacturing and global economic powerhouse. Electricity was becoming a key ingredient in spinning motors, lighting workplaces and homes, driving compressors, powering trolley and subway systems, and so on.

Edison's failure was overshadowed by his many great successes in other areas. But maybe there's more to the story. If you read the history books closely, you'll see that Edison wasn't so interested in building an electric grid. He wanted to sell light bulbs! After all, he is the inventor of record, though disputed by some, of the incandescent bulb, which most of our residential lighting systems still use today. Indeed, it doesn't look much different than it did a century ago.

Edison was stubborn. Biographies of his childhood are replete with accounts of his singular determination. For example, he is said to have tried thousands of materials to serve as a filament for his light bulbs, even hair from a friend's beard! Under history's harsh light, you could say that Edison won the battle but lost the war. That is, he sold light bulbs, but his vision for the *grid* did not take hold.

It was a long battle, and Edison was well-financed. Moguls from the history books such as J. Pierpont Morgan backed Edison to the hilt. Maybe it had something to do with Edison building generators and electric systems to light the homes of the wealthy. Located in what became the financial district of Lower Manhattan, Pearl Street also electrified the office buildings of the big financiers, including J. P. Morgan's. Pearl Street Station, however, also initiated the electricity industry's troubled tango with investors and Wall Street throughout history.

Direct current may, in fact, have been the better choice. For one thing, it is thought to be a safer medium for conducting electricity. For another, we can't know whether technological advances would have accelerated if it had become the de facto "standard" for the industry at that time. Many people still insist that Apple is better than Microsoft. Watching iPods and other Apple devices surge in popularity, you might still believe that Steve Jobs, Apple's founder, will be vindicated. Edison's been dead for a long time, but the last 10 years have, remarkably, seen vast improvements in how one could use DC for transmitting electric current long distances.

During the 1890s, the Pearl Street station, DC-based technical model for generating and transmitting electricity was replicated in several places around the country. But the next 40 years, roughly from 1890 to 1932, belonged to a guy who built transmission capability from Niagara Falls, New York, to Buffalo. Technologically, the next 100 years of grid-based electricity belonged to the guys who backed AC, alternating current.

Buffalo Avenue: Where AC Rules

The dominance of alternating current (AC) got its humble beginnings on Buffalo Avenue in Niagara, New York, and not far from the larger city of Buffalo, where the first long-distance transmission of electricity by AC was conducted.

Westinghouse is another name historians associate with electricity. The technology war between Thomas Edison and George Westinghouse during the 1890s is another version of men behaving badly. It wasn't just fought with formulas, engineering diagrams, and machinery. Dirty tricks, media manipulation, and other tactics still familiar to modern industrial warfare were employed then.

A hydroelectric power station, called the Adams Powerhouse on Buffalo Avenue, exploiting the energy of Niagara Falls, had been operating for several years. The builders and owners of that plant wanted to get the electricity to the city of Buffalo, 26 miles away, where really large numbers of potential customers were located. The plant's owners conducted the equivalent of a talent search between DC and AC. Westinghouse's AC-based system won.

And talk about a public relations bonanza! The 1901 Pan American Exposition, held in Buffalo, became the first to be completely lit by electricity generated from flowing water and transmitted "long distances" by AC from the Adams Powerhouse.

Westinghouse couldn't have done it without help from a relatively obscure Serbian inventor named Nikolai Tesla. You know you've hit the archival skids when you essentially invent the modern electricity grid still used 100 years later and your name is better known as a rock-and-roll group! Tesla is now credited with theories and mathematical formulations that presaged nuclear power, wireless communications, and even chaos theory. His contribution to electricity, though, is the three-phase, or polyphase, alternating current dynamo, an induction motor when it consumes electricity and a generator when it produces electricity driven by a rotating device.

AC versus DC: Still Controversial, Still Hard to Understand

I have a confession to make. I am a chemical engineer by training. I am not an electrical engineer. Once those electrons leave the generator of a power plant, I'm not real clear what happens. It still seems like so much magic to me.

By the same token, I still have difficulty understanding the fundamental difference between AC and DC. I've been at this business for a long time, and I haven't found an explanation that I could use confidently with my kids (my litmus test for a good definition). Therefore, I suspect that many others like me who are "electricity industry" experts either also do not understand the difference or cannot properly articulate it. Many authors, experts, and engineers recount the benefits of one over the other, or they quickly get into the mathematical formulations that describe one over the other. But a definition suitable for the layperson continues to elude me.

Perhaps the best way to think about it is this: DC flows in only one direction, while AC electrons flow in both directions. Electricity from a battery flows in only one direction, so it is DC. Electricity in our transmission grid can flow in any direction. DC requires two energized conductors, while AC requires three live conductors. AC electricity is far easier to increase and decrease in voltage, making it more flexible for transmitting it long distances, and for use by various devices. Technically, DC is most efficient for getting large amounts of electricity from one point to another. AC is most efficient for integrating the greatest number of electricity sources with the greatest number of electricity users.

However, the reason why I stated earlier in this section that Edison may be vindicated is that advances in DC electricity delivery and use now make the old comparisons of dubious accuracy. The fact is, DC can be transmitted at high voltages today over long distances, and many modern devices such as computers and instrumentation use DC.

DC vs. AC is a controversy that, in fact, rages even more so today.

Without getting in the middle of the mudslinging over the patents and timing of the inventions, let's just leave it that Westinghouse obtained the rights to the patents covering Tesla's "polyphase dynamo." Bad behavior often results when someone has something another wants.

In this case, Edison has the rights to the better lighting system, but is saddled with the less efficient means of transmitting electricity. Westinghouse has the better transmission system, but inferior bulbs. Everything comes to a boil at the Chicago World's Fair in 1893. Westinghouse gets the contract to light up the entire fair, and the AC system performs brilliantly for the entire world to see.

The war for the heart of the electricity industry had a softer front as well, a clash of cultures. Tesla was a well-schooled, well-heeled European, and his work reflected his academic training. Edison was a tinkerer. He created through trial and error. The two mirrored the culture clash between "roughshod" America and "reasoned" Europe. Westinghouse managed to harness the latter in the service of the former.

The triumph of AC over DC is an example of what technologists call the "dominant design." In the prenatal years of a new technology, many design pathways exist. All of them tend to have their merits and tradeoffs, but eventually all the stakeholders around the technology—engineers, financiers, customers, et al.—converge upon one of the pathways, at which time an inflection point in growth occurs. Today, many business analysts call the consequences of that inflection point the "hockey stick." The transmission of electricity from Niagara Falls to Buffalo, preceded by the Chicago World Fair, was such an inflection point and we've been riding that hockey stick of growth—an industry based on AC—ever since!

Ironically, AC technology may have won the technical wars, but the business legacy of the AC/DC battle (no, I don't mean another rock group) was two rival companies, Westinghouse and the General Electric Corp. As is typical, both companies found ways to get around patents, or come up with new refinements. Both struggled to dominant this nascent industry in America and around the world. GE emerged as the clear winner, at least in terms of company size and stature. Today, while the Westinghouse name is still a "brand," the company is a shell of its former self. GE, on the other hand, is still the mighty GE.

Harrison Street: Where Financiers Take Over

It takes oil to lubricate a machine, and it takes more than clever inventors and seasoned academics to propel an industry decades into the future. It takes money. Here is where that tortuous street, which we figuratively call Wall Street, first intersects our humble town grid. On Harrison Street in Chicago, one of the most notorious figures in electricity built a power station powered by steam instead of water.

The history books show that Samuel Insull also idolized Thomas Edison. (I hope I meet a different fate!) According to one account, he came to America in 1881 to become Edison's personal secretary, and by 1889, became vice president of Edison General Electric Company. Yes, the precursor to the mighty General Electric Corp (GE) of today. A few years later, J. P. Morgan, that magnate of American industrial finance, took over Edison's power companies, and Insull went to work for Morgan in Chicago.

Like all good investors, Morgan bought low and sold high. After the economic panic of 1893, so history tells us, Morgan's Chicago Edison Co, now being run by Insull, bought up all of its competitors, and become the sole supplier of electricity to the city. He built a new power station along the Chicago River, which suppled water to condense steam, on Harrison Street. Dirty politics and financial shenanigans characterized the city at the time (for many, it has always been this way). It was all tied in with the electrification of the elevated trains and the transit system. Chicago Edison Co. became Commonwealth Edison Co., one of the great American electric utility names.

Insull's special legacy was to control both the big captive customers for the electricity, the transit companies, and the supply of the electricity, the power stations and transmission lines. He also devised special stock and bond sales programs to raise capital. Alas, the empire he built in the Midwest finally collapsed in the early years of the Great Depression. He was blamed for much of the 1929 Stock Market Crash, hounded out of the country, and then extradited back to America, after which he was acquitted of all charges. In 1938 he died of a heart attack.

Later, you'll see how Insull's page of history was taken up by the emperor of Smith Street, right down to that heart attack.

Norris and Washington Streets: Government Takes Charge

Insull wasn't the only electric utility monopolist, industrial tycoon, and pyramid builder (the financial type, not the Egyptian kind) scandalized by hockey stick growth subsequently pummeled by the Great Depression. He was just the most notorious. Maybe he is just the scapegoat. But the history of electricity is not only about the winners of the technological battles, and the rocket-falling-to-earth decline of financiers. It is as much about political ideologies. The Great Depression, the collapse of the utility holding company, and the ruination of the nation's economy also became inflection points for a new political movement. This inflection point begins at the intersection of Norris Street and Washington Street.

With the collapse of the stock market, and many Americans out of work and starving, Franklin Roosevelt changed the political direction of the country. For the next 40 years, government pursued policies that were more socialistic in nature than capitalistic. Our version of socialism did not veer as far as our friends in Europe, or even more so our soon-to-be Cold War adversaries in Russia and China. The last two continued pushing socialism until it became communism.

In electricity, socialism was best represented by the passage of the Public Utility Holding Company Act (PUHCA) in 1935, and the formation of the Tennessee Valley Authority (TVA) in 1933. TVA's creation was one of the first major legislative actions after Roosevelt's inauguration that same year. The first TVA office, headed up by David Lilienthal, was established in Norris, Tennessee. TVA built its first dam and powerhouse there along the Clinch River, both for electricity production and flood control. Thus began the era of "public power," electricity production and delivery owned and managed by government.

New utility structures, called *municipal utilities* and *cooperatives*, were also established and became popular. These were entities either controlled by government (munis, municipal utilities) or "owned by their members" (co-ops, or cooperative utilities). These types of utilities were also allowed special interest rates for borrowing money from the government. Their objective was to electrify the rural areas of little profit, and therefore little interest, to the big utilities.

The privately held utilities, which today are called *investor-owned utilities* (IOUs), didn't go away, of course. But to keep them from reverting to their "evil ways," Congress passed PUHCA, strictly limiting their ability to do business. Around this time, states established *public utility commissions* (PUCs) to oversee and regulate public utilities, which include electric companies. The essential compact, as compared to the wild wholly early decades, was this: A utility could act as a "monopoly" over a defined service territory but in trade, its return on investment and many other aspects of its operations would be determined by the PUC.

Electricity had become a regulated industry. The dominant design had been set, not only in transmission but also in power plants. The steam cycle was established as the most efficient, with coal and oil as the predominant fuels (although hydroelectric plants were still being built). The financiers had been reigned in. A relatively stable business model was established that reigned for four decades, much like the more socialistic direction of the country. It was to be known by many of industry's leaders as the golden years. The other side of town had yet to be built.

But, as I promised, it's time for a break and to stop for some lunch.

G, M, and K Streets: Home of the Regulators and the Lobbyists

You could say that the basic framework of our imaginary town stayed the same, but it got crowded and built up between the mid-1930s and the mid-1960s. Then a tumultuous 10-year period set in, again mirroring general events in the country, roughly from 1968 to 1978. But I'm rushing things.

PUHCA was part of a broader legislative package called the Federal Power Act. The responsibility for executing the tenets of the act fell to a backwater bureaucracy called the Federal Power Commission (FPC), created in 1920 to oversea government's role in constructing new hydroelectric facilities, many of them out West. FPC experienced what we call today "mission creep." As energy and electricity became more and more important to the country, and I might note, to the war effort in the 1940s, FPC was charged with a variety of new responsibilities that can be simply described as managing the interstate flows of energy, principally electricity and natural gas. In 1977, FPC was reorganized into the Federal Energy Regulatory Commission (FERC), and is located on, you guessed it, G street, a short tangent with a cul-de-sac off of Washington Street.

The golden years certainly had their share of mishaps and crises. But they are minor in the scheme of the industry's history. One crisis is worth noting: GE and Westinghouse slowed the fight against each other and began to collude. At least that's what the two giants were accused of and tried for in the early 1960s. Basically, they fixed prices for large steam turbine/generators. But growth in electricity demand was so strong during the post-World War II period, averaging 7 percent per year, that real electricity prices to consumers decreased the entire time. So who cared if the two leaders were fixing prices, carving up the market? Economic growth was robust, and rate payers were sassy and happy.

It was a series of events beginning in 1970 that led to another inflection point and a wholesale change in direction for the industry. In 1969, the heavily polluted Cuyahoga River, which flows through Cleveland, Ohio, caught on fire (Figure 3.2). In 1973, the first Organization of Petroleum Exporting Countries (OPEC) embargo of petroleum shipments to the U.S. occurred. In 1977, the second OPEC embargo occurred. Finally, the accident at the Three Mile Island (TMI) nuclear power plant in Pennsylvania occurred in 1979.

After the spectacle of water catching on fire (!) in the Cuyahoga River, the U.S. Environmental Protection Agency was created, signaling the beginning of environmental regulation at the federal level. The electric power industry proved to be a target-rich environment for the EPA and justifiably so. The embargoes taught us that energy was becoming a global business. These twin forces, globalism and environmentalism, continue to shape our industry today. M Street, another spur off of Washington Street, is where EPA resides.

Once again, the inflection point we are just about to arrive at was girded by a shift in ideology. In the late 1970s, following a decade of relatively low economic growth and rampant bouts of inflation (tied principally to the hangover from the Vietnam War and the run-up in energy prices), socialistic tendencies were receding and deregulation was emerging. It began with the trucking and transportation industries, and over the next 10 years, electricity, natural gas, telecommunications, banking, and health care all would be snared in the rapidly weaving deregulatory web.

The actual start of electricity deregulation, the chink in the armor, the proverbial foot in the door, proved to be the 1980 law, the Public

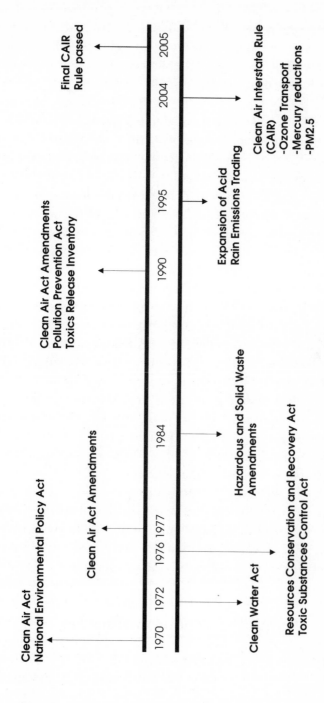

Figure 3.2 Environmental legislation begins to affect electricity industry.

Utilities Regulatory Policy Act (PURPA). The officials in the Carter administration who passed this bill would hardly have known at the time what they had truly wrought. Implementing PURPA fell to FERC. It was barely a crack in the regulated utility structure, but it was enough to disaggregate much of the vertically integrated industry within two decades.

What the Carter administration intended was a policy that encouraged more efficiency in electricity production. It also wanted to promote "the little guy" (small electricity generating businesses) over the big guys (entrenched monopolistic electric utilities). Finally, it intended to change the mix of energy sources used to make electricity. Some of these results occurred. What PURPA really did was open the floodgates that culminated in the second wholesale collapse of the electricity business in 2001.

Fundamentally, PURPA forced electric utilities to buy and transmit electricity from any "qualifying" power production facility. To qualify, these facilities either had to use alternative energy sources, like biomass, wind, solar, and others, or had to meet a rather modest system efficiency goal through a process known as cogeneration. Remember, Carter had just declared the "moral equivalent of war" after the second OPEC embargo. Efficiency was heralded as the path towards energy independence.

Around the same time, 1979, Congress passed the Fuel Use Act (FUA), essentially prohibiting electric utilities from using natural gas to make electricity. Herein lies the loophole that led to the unintended consequences: PURPA allowed a "qualifying facility" to burn natural gas, as long as it met the system efficiency standard. The standard was a token and amounted to little gain in efficiency at all.

The FUA might be one of the shortest legislative acts in history; it was repealed in 1986, coincidentally, the year two sleepy natural gas companies merged and called themselves Enron. Environmentalism, deregulation (overseas called privatization), and globalism were about to converge on what would become the energy capital of the world.

Smith Street: Enron Emerges

In July 2006, the discredited and vilified CEO of Enron, Ken Lay, died of a heart attack just as his trial for fraud and a multiplicity of other misdeeds was about to come to a head. Twenty years before, he was standing at the threshold of a dream. Five years ago, like a king addressing his subjects from the castle, he sat at the energy pinnacle of the world. He was advising the Vice President Dick Cheney on how to solve the California energy crisis, and energy calamities in other parts of the country. President Bush fondly referred to him as "Kenny Boy."

Six months later, December 2001, Enron declared bankruptcy. The lesson Lay learned, like Insull, is that when you sit at the top of the pyramid you just built, the sharp point skewers you.

Not only was the FUA repealed in 1986, but the natural gas industry was deregulated, or at least the pipeline, or gas transmission, segment of the business. PURPA provided the impetus to build large gas-fired power stations, and the electric utilities were obligated to buy the power. Continued environmental pressures caused the electric industry to forsake coal for new plant construction. Nuclear power was still completely stuck in the public perception swamp created by the Three Mile Island accident and, in 1986, the catastrophe at the Chernobyl nuclear power plant in Ukraine (then part of the Soviet Union).

The unintended consequence of the FUA was that natural gas prices were driven artificially low, because demand had been choked off, and therefore supply was bursting at the walls of the tank. The industry calls this the *natural gas bubble* and it took 15 years to deplete it.

Enron, and its imitators and brethren in and around Smith Street in Houston, had what could only be called, in retrospect, a vacant lot on which to build a towering figurative skyscraper of a new industry.

There is a technology piece to this chapter of history, too. Just as the electric generation industry shifted from hydroelectric to steam electric in the early part of the last century, a technology called the gas turbine/generator began to challenge the steam electric plant in the 1990s. Derived from aircraft engine technology, gas turbines could be made far more efficient than steam-driven plants when arranged in what is called a combined-cycle plant. Modern gas turbines need a clean fuel like natural gas. When they burn gas, not only are they more efficient than coal plants, they release significantly lower emissions, use less water for cooling, and can be made smaller and therefore less obtrusive to the landscape.

In 1992, the deregulation of the electricity industry continued (Figure 3.3) with the passage of the National Energy Policy Act (NEPA).

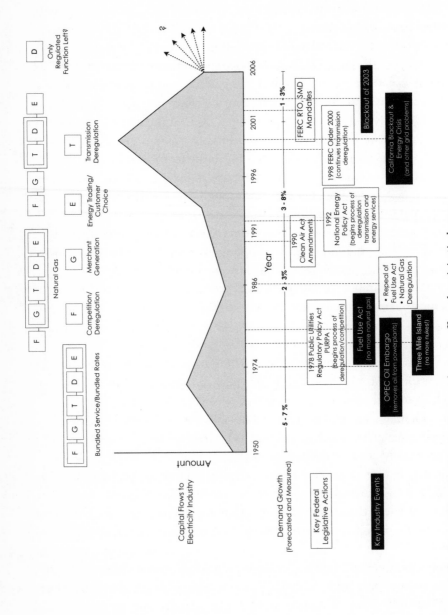

Figure 3.3 More federal policy decisions and events affect electricity industry.

If PURPA was the crack to make the generation segment of the industry competitive, then NEPA did the same thing for the transmission side of the business. PURPA forced utilities to buy power from qualifying facilities. NEPA obligated utilities to "wheel" or transmit power through their systems for others.

That is, if I wanted to sell electricity to you, NEPA required that the utility provide the transmission service (for a price). Unlike the past, the utility could no longer simply say no. What's more, I, as the producer and seller of that electricity, could avoid being regulated as an electric utility.

The alphabet soup of PURPA, FUA, and NEPA caused a convergence between the electricity and natural gas businesses. By 1997, the gas-fired power stations being offered by the new class of independent power producers and merchant generators became just about the only type of power station you could build in this country. Between 1997 and 2001, more than 350,000 megawatts (MW) of such power plants were under construction, on order, or planned. This was close to half of the total electricity generating capacity of the entire country!

The boys and girls on Smith Street, and Enron's neighborhood in general, ruled the energy world—for a few years anyway.

Downing Street: The Seeds of Privatization Are Sown

It was inevitable that the companies of Smith Street would go global. The United States wasn't the only country practicing deregulation. The 1990s were a time of liberalized economic ideologies. A new class of global power company, mostly headquartered in the United Kingdom and Europe, was marching around the world, developing power projects, buying foreign electricity industry assets and even utility companies outright. They were creating new empires. A new word entered the lexicon, the "footprint." Like Godzilla or King Kong, these global behemoths collected infrastructure assets around the world. Many from the United States were unregulated subsidiaries of electric utilities. They owe a debt of gratitude to the United Kingdom and Downing Street.

The United Kingdom may not have been the first country to begin deregulating its electricity business, but it took the concept the furthest and, in retrospect, has resisted trying to "put the genie back in the bottle." The Central Electricity Generating Board (CEGB), a fully state-owned enterprise, was broken up by Margaret Thatcher's government in 1989. This break-up was more analogous to the breakup of the American Bell Telephone Company than it was to the U.S. electric utility industry. That's because electricity production and delivery for all of England was a state-owned enterprise.

Around the same time, the production of natural gas from Britain's North Sea was getting into full swing. The "dash for gas" for electricity production in the United Kingdom preceded the one in the United States by at least five years. European and United States utilities were able to buy up United Kingdom utilities. Transmission, however, remained a monopoly.

In keeping with another theme, once again we cannot forget the role of shifting ideology. The Berlin Wall came down in 1989. The Soviet Union was fracturing. The Western business model of free, or at least *freer*, markets seemed to be a natural response following political liberalization. And this unleashed an unprecedented wave of investment from the private sector, best symbolized by Wall Street. Most everyone in the energy business wasted little time going global.

Wall Street: Where Investment Flows

The domestic and global feeding frenzy, just like in the days of Insull and his cronies, itself had to be fed—by private capital. For decades, Wall Street firms sold sleepy, modest returning, but dependable utility stocks and bonds to widows and the like. Utility analysts at these firms were always the fresh meat out of MBA school. It was a relatively easy sector to understand and cut teeth. Now, the brokers, supported by their independent "analysts," could sell glamorous "growth" stocks of energy companies such as AES, Enron, Dynegy, Calpine, Mirant, El Paso, Williams, Aquila, and many others. They could dust off those moldy oldie utility stocks, too. The debt and equity for privately financed power projects could be raised from wealthy private and institutional investors.

The regulators designed the markets and the deregulatory plans state by state and at the federal level, but Wall Street and the investor class was in almost complete control of the game. While the high net worth investors and institutional investors (pension funds, insurance companies) were providing the long-term risk capital to build infrastructure, the stockbrokers were pumping up the stocks of these new energy companies. Meanwhile, the emerging energy and electricity traders, considered necessary to make the markets "efficient," had figured out how to "game the system" in their favor.

Then the California electricity market collapsed. The governor of that state, Gray Davis, was essentially booted out because of the crisis. There were basic flaws in the system, some that were exploited by the traders, but others that likely would have brought it down even if the traders were honest. The attack of September 11, 2001, sealed the fate of the economy and the industry for the next several years.

The Dark Street: When Electricity Does Not Flow

There is one street that no one really likes to talk about or even acknowledge. You can't see the street sign at night because the street lights don't work. It's in a really bad section of our imaginary town. The houses feel haunted.

In 1965, New York City and much of the Northeast went black. The electricity grid failed. Most of the population spent a rare evening without Walter Cronkite's newscast, lights, electric ovens, operating subways, or cold beer. Some spent the evening stuck in elevators. Popular lore has it that nine months later, a population boomlet occurred because there wasn't much else to do in the dark that evening. Popular lore also has it that because this blackout hit New York, the media capital of the world, the world was going to hear about it.

Hear about it we did. The great Northeast Blackout of 1965 proved another inflection point, this one focused on the transmission grid. Reliability became a watchword for operating the grid. Such an event was never to occur again. Although much consternation consumed Washington, the industry actually got on the same page and came up with new guidelines on how to collectively operate the segments of the grid under the auspices of the hundreds of individual utilities, to achieve reliability for all. That worked for almost 40 years. New York City did experience a blackout in 1977, but it did not affect the larger region.

Then it happened again in August 2003. Once more, the Northeast was the epicenter and New York City was deeply affected. And, the evidence is clear that for an outage to penetrate our national psyche, it has to happen in and around New York City or California. People remember the California blackouts of 1998, but they tend to think of them as self-induced (and in many ways, they were). But much of the western United States experienced a severe blackout in 1997; and Chicago experienced a series of summer outages in 1998. The frequency of serious "grid events" was increasing. The street that everyone wants to forget was finally getting serious attention from the industry and government.

Even these outage events pale in significance to our industry compared to the 9/11 attack on the World Trade Center towers. It is said that 9/11 changed everything. Many of those changes are in our face and stark. Regarding the electricity business, the changes are nuanced. I would argue that the attack has caused many to rethink globalism and global economic expansion. 9/11 has also imposed a whole new element in the design and shape of energy infrastructure, that of how to enhance national security and prevent and/or recover from terrorist attacks.

Without the benefit of hindsight, we must make some educated guesses as to where all of this will lead us in the twenty-first century.

Our Town Now

Today, the electricity industry is in a funk. No particular ideology seems to be driving us forward. No new technology is emerging to disrupt the traditional ways of doing things or, at least, not a perceptible technological trend. Utilities and independent electricity firms have spent the last five years recovering from what many in the industry call *Enronitis*. Most of the activity has been in repairing financial balance sheets and returning to the good graces of Wall Street.

Growth in electricity demand continues to be modest, holding at a 1.5–2 percent average per year (Figure 3.4). Commodity prices for

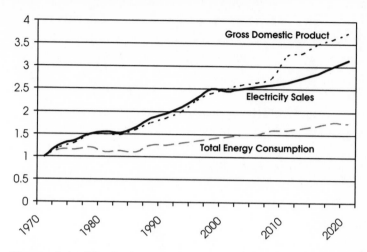

Figure 3.4 Electric demand growth in the U.S.
SOURCE: U.S. Department of Energy Transmission Reliability Multi-year Program Plan.

petroleum and natural gas have skyrocketed over the last three years, putting upward price pressure on all source of energy. The global War on Terror, combined with the rising fuel prices, has renewed calls popular in the 1970s for energy independence. In a variety of ways, the industry resembles what it looked like in the 1970s. Will the industry's version of *That 70s Show* play for long?

Infrastructure building is a boom and bust business. 1997 to 2001 was a boom period in our industry, unlike anything we've seen since the 1960s. 2001 to 2006 has been mostly a bust period, but the prospects for a new boom are percolating. The industry is excited about inching away from "back to basics" to moving forward. You can feel the buzz at all the industry conferences. Energy is on the front page of the newspapers now. The Energy Policy Act of 2005 is fueling a great deal of the buzz.

Before we address the question about how long our 70s show will play, we need to go back to the worst-case scenario. Based on some of the issues we've just raised, and the history of the industry, there are some clear directions and lessons that can be applied.

Chapter 4

Preventing the Worst Case

C ontrary to what you might expect and or have been led to
believe by countless energy experts, armchair policy makers,
and environmentalists advocating their "solutions," preventing
the nightmare scenario does not involve radical change. It *does* involve
reorienting our priorities with respect to regulation, infrastructure, and
consumption. It also involves a great deal more personal responsibility.
Here I intend to outline the elements of a go-forward strategy, all of
which will be amplified in later parts of the book.

You Can't Build Infrastructure with Ideology

First and foremost, we must quit thinking about electricity infrastructure in terms of ideology. The first 50 years of the electricity industry
was a private-sector free-for-all, analogous to the robber barons of the

railroads and the wildcatters of the oil fields. The second 50 years of electricity proved to be far more socialistic in nature, with highly regulated electric utilities and a great deal of government control. The last 20 years saw an attempt to return to a market-based orientation, with much of the industry—even its boldest proponents—now declaring that experience to range from marginally successful to an unmitigated failure. What is clear is this: We must quit thinking about electricity infrastructure in terms of ideology. History has shown that ideology swings the industry to extremes, such as the periods when Samuel Insull and Enron ran amuck due to unfettered competition, or the period when regulation almost choked the life out of the industry from about 1978 to 1986.

In the nascent years of an industry, unfettered capitalists dominate the scene. In the beginning years of the electricity business, as businessmen saw the potential for electricity, investment rushed in, entrepreneurs formed companies, and progress accelerated rapidly without much regard for the consequences. Unfortunately, exuberance and greed tend to best business sense, expectations are not met, and the industry begins to collapse. If this sounds familiar, the same cycle just happened recently with the Internet, the Web, and with the tech-based companies.

Then, as consumers (read: *voters*) rebel and investors demand protection, politicians step onto the playing field with new rulebooks (read: *regulations*). With electricity, government stepped up its activities in the 1930s, not only to rein in the "robber barons," but also to make electricity service more equitable and available to those, usually in rural areas, who could only be served at much higher cost. Profit-minded companies were not interested in those customers.

Whatever good intentions politicians have, their regulations usually tend to go too far. In the case of electricity, instead of protecting ratepayers, regulation caused prices to increase and distorted utility decisions. So, in the 1980s, big business, which had long been subsidizing residential rates, staged a rebellion. Their demands? They wanted a market-based approach to electricity supply.

History teaches us over and over again that ideology, whether it's a belief in pure free markets or in heavy-handed regulation, often leads to disaster. Ideology never goes away, however, and in the case of electricity it extends far beyond public versus private or market forces versus regulation. For example, advocates of a wholesale transition to renew-able energy tend to be allied with the ideological left and are more radical about their environmental priorities, while those who favor coal are linked with the ideological right and, not surprisingly, usually hail from coal-producing states. The left wants a cleaner environment even if it comes at a higher price, while the right talks about job creation and "market forces." However, these days, both sides seem to be converging on energy independence.

Energy independence, by the way, is not going to happen in the United States. It means completely substituting domestic sources of en-ergy (primarily coal and biomass), for foreign-sourced ones, (primarily petroleum and liquefied natural gas). In other words, energy indepen-dence means King Coal would rule again and would be coming to a neighborhood near you. Energy independence is a "feel-good" issue, but it is simply impractical to think this country will ever wean itself off foreign sources of energy. Just get that out of your mind, regardless of your political stripe.

Back to ideology, conservatives tend to focus on the supply side of the infrastructure, liberals on the consumption side of the value chain. This means that Republicans solve energy problems through supply-side, while Democrats prefer to manage through demand management. For example: Republicans generally favor opening the Alaska National Wildlife Reserve (ANWR) to drilling for petroleum. Democrats favor reducing consumption so we don't need that additional energy from ANWR.

It is idealistic, to be sure, to think the electricity business will not be politicized, even polarized. Even those with entrenched interests should at least start with the right priorities. The next section outlines what we should be looking at.

The *Right* Side of the Value Chain

In our prescription, the first thing to do is to focus, not on supply vs. demand (or production versus consumption), but on delivery versus supply. Another way I like to state this is, focus on the right side of the value chain—but don't neglect the left side. The left side (no allusion to politics, by the way) is the creation of the electrons. The right side is the delivery and consumption of these electrons (as shown in Figure 2.1).

Fix Transmission Now

The transmission sector was the neglected stepchild of deregulation. Initially, "the wires" were thought to be a "natural monopoly" even by many of the free marketers. Incumbent utilities, forced to divest of their generating assets, had to figure out how to make money from the distribution business that was left to them. Meanwhile, the generation subsector went hog-wild building deregulated, competitive gas-fired power stations around the country. Some of these generating plants were in fact substitutes for better transmission facilities. As I explain later, generating units can often be located so that they actually facilitate the transmission of electricity. Electricity markets were also created, usually in the states and regions with the highest priced electricity.

Today, there is a dichotomy. Independent system operators, or ISOs, *operate* the transmission system. They are responsible for the movement of the electricity through the grid. However, the *physical* responsibility for the assets themselves—such as who pays for upgrades and expansions—is not often as clear. Some states, Michigan and Wisconsin, for example, went as far as to privatize their transmission systems.

From a regulatory and infrastructure perspective, the transmission grid is like connecting two weighty barbells. It may be difficult to build, own, and operate power stations, but at least it is clear how to do it. There are still utility organizations that are explicitly responsible for "the customer." It is not clear to the industry what to do about transmission. The "bar" between the barbells has to be made stronger, both institutionally and physically. No one will invest in transmission if there is not a clear framework on how to do so and, perhaps more importantly, how to earn a return on investment. This is the first element of worst-case prevention.

Limit Markets to Where They Work

The second element step is to apply market-based economics and choice where it does the most good and keep regulated utility economics where it does the least harm. For the most part, this means more competition and markets for the supply of wholesale electricity, and less competition and markets for supplying retail electricity.

ELCON: Fanning the Flames of Deregulation

Long-term industry observers remember that one of the major instigators and promoters of competition and deregulation in the electricity industry was an influential group of energy-intensive industrial companies that banded together to influence Washington under the Electricity Consumers Council of America, or ELCON. Companies such as Dow Chemical, General Motors, and DuPont were members. For several decades, utility regulatory economics generally resulted in industrial electricity rates subsidizing residential rates. In other words, industrials paid a disproportionate share of the infrastructure and operational costs, so that consumers could pay less. Electricity rates are a significant component of production costs for ELCON members. Therefore, its objective was to reduce these costs by forcing once-monopolistic utilities to compete for their business. Industry experts can argue about how much influence ELCON had, but few can argue that it was a catalyst and deciding force in electric utility deregulation.

For a large oil refinery, electricity rates could be 10 percent of its cost of doing business. For an aluminum smelter, electricity could be more than 50 percent of the costs of producing raw aluminum. For most households, the electric utility bill might amount to less than 5 percent of the average monthly budget. You are better off concentrating on refinancing your mortgage if you want to save money, than thinking that one electricity supplier can supply real savings over another.

Sadly, most deregulation programs tried to convince us that competition would be good for *all* ratepayers. That probably was never going to be true. Like other goods and services, those who buy in volume get discounts and those who buy piecemeal don't. Even worse, states that went for competition big time tried to mask this reality by freezing retail rates to consumers or mandating lower rates for the first several years of competition. Last I checked, artificially freezing prices doesn't jibe well with deregulation and competition. In fact, it is not only contrary to the idea of deregulation, it merely postponed the day of reckoning, *which is here now,* as electricity rates escalate across the country.

So, the second element of worst-case prevention is this: Promote competition for wholesale markets, restrain it for individual consumers. The larger a buyer is, the greater chance of that buyer being sophisticated enough to make competition work. For the small buyer, especially an individual, the chances are near zero.

Add Inventory Control

If there is a radical aspect to our prevention strategy, this next element probably qualifies. *Our electricity infrastructure must have more storage capability.* The technical concept of energy storage translates, from a business perspective, into control over inventory. It requires the addition of infrastructure pieces that are unfamiliar to electric utilities today and it would mean that the grid would have to operate differently.

Electricity from renewable sources is unpredictable and inconsistent. For this reason, it has a low value with respect to grid operations, even though it may have high value with respect to the environment. All that changes if you could store electricity generated from renewable sources and inject it into the grid on a controlled basis. Storage transforms renewable energy from a variable, undependable source of electricity to a consistent flow of electrons directed when and where it is needed the most. It makes renewable energy matter.

The biggest obstacle to establishing functioning electricity markets, whether wholesale or retail, is inventory control—or rather, the lack thereof. Every commodity, indeed even finished goods, are more compatible with markets because they can be stored. Simply, storage balances temporary dislocations in supply and demand.

With a *just-in-time* (JIT) inventory system (i.e., the grid), one of the ad hoc ways we accommodate supply/demand disruptions is by *cycling* large power stations. Cycling simply means that the station is "turned on or off" or up and down in output to meet demand. The problem is that these stations were never intended to operate this way. Any machinery that is turned on and off suffers degradation of performance and equipment—unless it is specifically designed to cycle. Your automobile behaves this way. Power plants behave this way. Even the human body behaves like this. When you bicycle long-distances, for example, your goal (and the intention of your bike's many gears) is to pedal at a constant rate regardless of the terrain. There are significant, hidden costs associated with cycling large power stations that were not designed for this duty. As if to add insult to injury, units that are cycled generally exhibit higher emissions on an energy input basis.

Energy storage devices are expressly designed to cycle up and down in load output and to be dispatched on and off frequently. Storage takes the burden off systems that suffer from cycling and puts it squarely on systems specifically designed to operate this way.

Storage has a critical role to play in enhancing national security, as well. Consider the Strategic Petroleum Reserve (SPR). It really isn't about us lowly consumers, although it has been tapped (for political purposes) in times of rising gasoline prices. The SPR exists as an insurance policy for our military assets and government infrastructure in the event of a national disaster. But wait a minute. Let's consider that national disaster. If there is an extended electricity outage, what would happen to the pumps in the petroleum tanks? Or the massive government computers that would quit grinding data? Or the critical military and civilian communications infrastructure that would shut down without electricity? (I recently heard the developer of a small battery storage technology remark that military experts and soldiers in the field will give up the extra weight of additional body armor in exchange for adequate battery power to ensure extended communications capability.) Yes, I know that we have backup power systems for much of this infrastructure. But they usually are powered by diesel engines, and as so many disaster situations have taught us, those tanks can run dry before the emergency is over. This is what happened during the blackout of 2003; many emergency generators ran out of fuel after a few hours of operation. Do we want to continue to stake our national security on the hopes that we can get the grid back online before the diesel generators run dry?

Large bulk electricity storage assets, strategically placed throughout the country, would help us survive and cut short national emergencies.

Taking it one step further, distributed electricity storage assets such as at offices, small businesses, and homes would help minimize disruptions to electricity service.

Today we try to solve electricity inventory problems by storing fuel or water atop mountains. We need to shift our philosophy from storing electricity as bulk fuel to storing our electricity in ways that can respond almost instantaneously to the needs of the grid.

Empower Consumers, Instead of Making Them Feel Guilty

We've addressed delivery in terms of transmission and storage. The next element of worst-case prevention is controlling supply, demand, and price at each electricity consumption point. What we mean here is not simply telling everyone to conserve, use less electricity, or otherwise make us feel guilty about the electricity we do use. Although that may be a noble objective, it has been demonstrated to be unrealistic. The following statistic tells the story: The average size of the American home has doubled since 1950. Plus, it should be clear by now that the rest of the world desires to live like Americans, and Americans don't want to live like the rest of the world.

Depending on where you are in the world, electricity consumption growth averages between 1.5 percent and 10 percent per year! Nowhere on this planet does it decrease—unless, of course, in the case of massive natural or military disaster or political disruption.

No, what we are talking about here is providing the tools for consumers to better manage their own consumption habits, whatever those habits are, in ways that keep them comfortable and guilt free. These same tools can be used by utilities to better match supply with demand at any given moment. Such tools are available, they are being deployed, and they represent an exciting class of new technology.

One category of this technology is called *automatic meter reading* (AMR), although this is somewhat of a misnomer. The better term is *advanced meters with two-way communication*. The ideas are to: (1) Provide consumers information about the price of electricity at specific times of day, so-called time of use rates, so that they can modify their behavior to either reduce consumption or save money; and (2) allow the utility to more accurately quantify what the real-time demand for electricity is at any given time. Such meters also allow utilities to reward consumers for using less electricity during periods of peak demands.

This technology provides the backbone for a new way of thinking about how you consume electricity. Have you ever seen that scrolling electronic sign that displays a calculation of the national debt in real time? Imagine how you might modify your behavior if you watched your electricity meter count dollars instead of (or in addition to) kilowatt-hours! The fact is, most Americans do not understand their consumption patterns, have no idea how electricity prices may vary throughout the day, and therefore feel powerless to control their utility bill.

Acknowledge the Need for New Supply, Don't Try to Ignore It

I noted earlier that a worst-case prevention strategy should focus on the "right side of the value chain, or delivery, without neglecting the supply or production side." When you add up the vulnerabilities and risk factors—including the threat of global warming, the need for energy infrastructure security and progress toward greater energy independence, the need to maintain reasonable electricity prices to the population, and others—you can't help but conclude that we still need a significant number of new large power stations. Whether you like it or not, these large stations are going to be coal or nuclear, based on forecasted prices for natural gas and cries for energy independence. So let's think about how to deploy them intelligently, rather than fool ourselves into thinking we're going to avoid them.

Just as I like to think in terms of the left and right sides of the electricity value chain, I like to think in terms of an electricity infrastructure "backbone" and an emerging integrated network of smaller distributed power assets. The "backbone" of supply is characterized by large coal-fired and nuclear power plants. These plants are built and operated with a high degree of regulation and even government intervention. Why? They require a 50-year investment and planning horizon, which is far beyond the comparative attention deficit disorder of private capital. They also require significant watchdog functions to ensure that operations are safe, materiel does not end up in the hands of terrorists or criminals, and environmental impact is properly managed.

Favor Nuclear over Coal, and Use All of the Coal

Given its potential for the lowest production costs and the least impact on planetary warming, nuclear units should be favored over coal. There are ways that coal can be used, however—intelligently, safely and cleanly—and given that it is our most abundant domestic energy resource, we must do so. Converting coal to just electricity is an inefficient and planet-damaging idea. Exploiting the total energy and resource value inherent in coal, however, is a great concept, something we address in a later chapter.

As just one of many examples, coal combustion results in large quantities of ash, or noncombustible material. Think of the ash piles at the base of your charcoal grill, or the ash in a wood-burning fireplace. Thankfully, all of the ash from a coal-fired plant can be recycled in many ways, reducing the mining of virgin materials. For example, ash can be recycled directly into cement manufacturing and the solid waste from flue-gas desulfurization systems (used to remove sulfur dioxide) can be converted into the wallboard that is used in home and building construction.

The organic material in coal can also be converted to electricity and a number of other high-value energy products. Plus, if facilities that take advantage of coal's *total* energy value are built right at the mouth of the coal mines, rail and truck transportation are avoided. Industries that use coal byproducts can also use the electricity generated right there at the plant. Mine-mouth industrial complexes would be designed to wring every last bit of energy value from the coal in addition to the transmission of coal "by wire" as electricity to the grid. We can even find some uses for the CO_2 produced from coal combustion, although most of it will have to be sequestered, or stored underground, somewhere.

All of these concepts, with the possible exception of sequestration, are applied today. They involve no technological breakthroughs. They add cost to the system, but they result in hidden savings elsewhere in the ledger. The trick is to harness coal's full potential as a strategic national interest, not just build the same power plants under the same mentality we've been using for 50 years. It is past time for some new ways of thinking about coal.

As for nuclear, the benefit is even greater. Between 1958 and 1978, the electricity industry ordered more than 150 nuclear units, of which 104 were subsequently built and are still licensed to operate, with few exceptions, today. Then Three Mile Island (TMI) occurred, and no reactor has been ordered since 1979 (although a few previously ordered units proceeded through construction programs that extended well into the early 1990s).

The *Energy Policy Act of 2005* (EP 2005) provides incentives for utilities to build the first half a dozen or so new units. Many power plant sites where these units are located were designed to accommodate more reactors than are present today. That means the fundamental infrastructure is there to essentially pick up our nuclear construction program where it left off after TMI (except for transmission, which, as we have already seen, is a separate issue). Decades of safe operation mean that the communities where nuclear plants are located are largely "pro-nuclear" and want the economic benefits.

Yes, a small high-level spent fuel waste stream must be properly managed for hundreds of years or regenerated into more nuclear fuel. But the physics are undeniable: Uranium is the highest density energy source available for generating electricity. The economics are compelling: Uranium is plentiful and additional sources of production can come onstream quickly. The environmental impact is obvious: Nuclear power plants produce no global warming agents, and no other pollutants like sulfur dioxide, nitrogen oxides, and ash.

Regulate Nuclear Power as if It Is a National Interest

Although I'm essentially an advocate of less is more in terms of government intervention, I think government intervention is especially appropriate for nuclear. Why? For all its free-market bluster, the Adam Smith club never really gets government "off our backs." Burden is simply shifted from one place to another. Government should be the provider of essential services that cannot be efficiently provided by the private sector. The federal government builds and maintains a network of interstates as a backbone to our transportation system. The federal government is primarily responsible for building airports and running air traffic control as a backbone to air transportation. Our government backstops the financial system with bonds and the setting of the prime interest rate. Home mortgages are back-stopped by Fannie Mae and Freddie Mac, both of which are quasi-governmental agencies. Oh, and the government built the Internet, too, funded in large part by the *Defense Advanced Research Projects Agency* (DARPA).

It is my contention that the federal government should guarantee and oversight a system of large power stations and a "national" grid (which really doesn't exist today) that ensures a minimum level of economical supply to all classes of customers, maintains security by protecting the flow of electrons throughout the rest of the infrastructure, and minimizes the impact on the environment. The fact that most of the power stations should be nuclear units makes the government's role that much more imperative as the party responsible for the back end of the nuclear fuel cycle. If the solution to global warming is a national (or even global) imperative, then nuclear power should be pursued as if it is in the national interest. France, among other countries, has supported nuclear power successfully as a national imperative. As a result, it has one of the lowest global warming "footprints" of any country in Europe.

Summary

We will never be able to prevent extreme weather events from wreaking havoc with our electricity service, but we can take steps to ensure that service disruptions are not exacerbated by other problems with the supply lines, the infrastructure, and the responsible institutions and organizations that manage them all. To recap, our five key elements for of preventing the worst-case scenario are to:

1. Shore up the transmission grid.
2. Apply market-based concepts appropriate for each customer class.
3. Build an energy storage infrastructure that is compatible with existing production and delivery assets and maximizes the value of renewable resources.

4. Empower consumers with the tools and information they need to manage their consumption.
5. Maintain a highly regulated infrastructure backbone consisting of large, economical nuclear and mine-mouth coal-fired generating plants.

As a reminder, here are the things to avoid:

- Do not pursue an ideologically based energy policy that makes consumers feel guilty about the electricity they use.
- Do not let uneven regulation of different parts of the value chain continue to distort the system.
- Do not ignore the need for new supply.

Part Two

INSECURITIES, VULNERABILITIES, AND AN UNEASY STATE OF THE INDUSTRY

W hy does the United States have a "third-world" grid? Why is the distribution system that delivers electricity to all of us so weak? Why are electric utility rates rising when service seems to be deteriorating? Why is it so difficult to replace the rapidly retiring skilled electricity industry workers? Why have "markets" and competition failed to reduce electricity rates? In sum, why is it that the strongest, most resilient economy in the world is dependent upon a production, transmission and distribution system that is, shall we say, less than robust?

These are legitimate questions. At their core are insecurities, felt not only by consumers but by the industry's top experts. Much of the explanation can be summed up this way: Financial engineering now takes precedence over power system engineering. The old system, the utility compact, in which a monopoly service territory was created in exchange for a regulated rate of return, is gone. Unfortunately, it has not been replaced by anything else remotely resembling a "system." And, in blindly groping toward the future, the industry seems to be futilely grasping at the failed strategies of the past.

Above all, the industry seems to be struggling to define itself after the post-Enron debacle. If you're thinking, "Blame Enron!"—stop. That's only part of the story. It's just the juicy part that the popular media has gravitated to. Blaming the state of the industry on Kenny Boy, Jeff Skilling, Andy Fastow, the accountants at Arthur Andersen, and the rest of the villains from that sordid chapter of the industry's *recent* history is too easy. There's one other factor: It's not accurate. Those guys had plenty of accomplices, legions of imitators, and a cadre of unfettered market admirers who share the blame. I'm not going to revisit what you can reread in the papers. I will, however, in this part of the book, illuminate the consequences that today hover over the industry like a gathering storm.

Some of the issues with our electricity supply, such as the ones I just mentioned, lead to insecurity. Some are inherent vulnerabilities. It's an important distinction.

Insecurities are relatively newcomers on the scene. We didn't worry about our third-world grid a decade ago. National energy security became a national imperative only after 9/11. Five years ago, competitive retail markets in electricity only existed in one state (California) in this country and in only a few other countries (the United Kingdom, for example) worldwide. What is being lamented as the brain drain today was actually a good thing five years ago, at least if you were an industry executive struggling to repair the balance sheet because getting expensive older employees off of the payroll improved the company's financial prospects. Insecurities are, in a relative sense, emergent issues. They could become vulnerabilities in the years ahead if they are not properly managed.

Vulnerabilities are issues that have been kicked around longer. We can't seem to get them off the to-do list. With each passing year, the real and potential consequences grow in magnitude. The way I see it, vulnerabilities share three characteristics: (1) They pose more intractable problems for us, the industry and electricity consumers, to solve; (2) they are very interdependent; and (3) they tend to be global in their impact. They make us vulnerable because they become more complex with each passing day, making it easier for us to throw up our hands, stick our heads in the sand, and move on to something more pleasant. Global climate and other environmental impacts are good examples. Lengthening supply lines for sources of energy is another.

We tackle the insecurities first and then the vulnerabilities.

Chapter 5

Why a First-World Country Has a Third-World Grid

What do we mean when we say we have a third-world transmission grid? The phrase, apparently coined by former Energy Secretary Bill Richardson, now governor of New Mexico, is probably melodramatic. Third-world countries have nowhere near the electricity service we enjoy in the United States The point is that we no longer have a first-world electricity system. It's a catchy, punchy, and very effective sound bite.

What we're really talking about is that our transmission grid is not designed for the way it is now being used, or the way it needs to be operated in the future. After the great Northeast Blackout of 1965, the industry formed the North American Electric Reliability Council (now a corporation) (NERC), and utilities formed partnerships known as regional reliability areas. It was a wonderful voluntary cooperative effort pursued to prevent blackouts. There are around 10 of these "regional reliability" areas today. In fact, transmission between these areas, much less among them, is weakly interconnected. The original idea was to provide enough transmission to move a big chunk of power *during an emergency* from one region to another. Today, we are trying to move big chunks of electricity around to *reduce costs and increase profits* and to make the overall system more financially efficient. Unfortunately, like a frail and grumpy old man, the physics of this old grid doesn't want to cooperate.

The Geeks Try to Communicate

The notion of retail competition in electricity began to get real attention in the late 1980s. Before that, economists talked among each other about how regulated industries could be made competitive to the betterment of all customers. Some utility economists listened very carefully and began to bring the concepts to utility managements, but more importantly, to the federal and state governments. The phrase that took hold was "retail wheeling," which refers to moving power from one area where costs might be lower, to another area, where prices might be higher. Economists and others in the investment community recognized that the gap between lower-cost production and higher-price demand could, conceivably, make someone (perhaps them?) a lot of money.

Meanwhile, power system engineers were holding conferences all over the country telling each other how the electric grid wasn't designed to "wheel" power from one region to another, and certainly not from one "point" to another. The electric grid is a *ginormous* (as my kids would say) and incredibly intricate circuit, and the power flows along the path of least resistance, not the linear path of a farmer's cart to a market. The engineers kept saying that throwing a vast web of market transactions onto this delicately balanced system would not be a wise move, at least not unless the grid is upgraded and redesigned first. As far as circuit design goes, an engineer might point out to an economist that point-to-point wheeling misses the point.

One thing I have learned over the years, as a practicing engineer and as an experienced communicator, is that almost anyone can make a case better than an engineer. So how did the story work out? The free-market economists and the investor class, eagerly salivating at the breakup of the Paleolithic utility industry, won the battle for the hearts and minds of the regulators and their constituencies. And instead of fixing the grid first, then instituting competition and market-based trading, we started with the competition and trading, and then crossed our fingers and hoped the grid would survive.

Now, as we have seen, the grid has survived. It didn't collapse when markets began functioning in California in 1996. And it didn't collapse when markets began operating in New York, Illinois, New England, Pennsylvania, or Texas. But there certainly was a clash on the order of Apatosaurus and T-Rex, between the reliability requirements of the grid and the market movement of electricity. Establishing the markets, in fact, has revealed exactly where the grid's weakest points are. So now we know. The most serious ones are in Northern California, Southern California, Chicago north to Wisconsin, New York City and Long Island, and Southern Connecticut. Now what?

Traders Sound Geeky, But Guess What?

Traders are an active bunch. Remember when I was told in the 1990s that a contract for electricity in the nascent California market would be "traded" up to 30 times before the electricity was actually delivered? It turns out that there was much more trading of electricity contracts than there was actual physical delivery of the electrons. And each of these trades was (and still is) a transaction, from which fees are pulled out by someone. The more transactions, the more fees. It wasn't long before the new electricity traders were accused of gaming the market.

They were only exploiting what was handed to them. The market was made for trading. For example, electricity suppliers could make prices go up in times of high demand simply by withholding supply. I know it sounds like Economics 101, but this was a much regulated, naïve industry. By claiming that power stations had to take a planned outage (usually for scheduled maintenance or repairs), or couldn't return quickly from an outage, suppliers "legitimately" restricted supply. Guess what? Prices skyrocketed.

In California, for instance, there could be ample electricity generation available in one part of the state, but limited transmission to move that power to the load centers, like southern California and the Bay area. Instead of bringing lower-cost electricity from the northern part of the state, utilities had to buy high-priced power from new merchant plants through their traders. There was never a supply or demand crisis in California. It was a purely institutional crisis that emerged from the way in which market demand was designed without regard to the physical limitations of the grid. It was a crisis of our own making.

After the industry meltdown occurred in 2001 and electricity trading was disgraced (for a while anyway), market activity dissipated, but that didn't necessarily spare the grid. Normal growth in electricity demand steadily marches on, averaging 2 to 3 percent per year.

We were fortunate because, under the old regulated system, utilities, rightfully paranoid about reliability lapses, gold-plated the transmission grid in the 1960s and 1970s. A gold-plated system refers, for one thing, to a robust grid with ample spare capacity. This spare capacity may have provided the necessary cushion against shocks from electricity trading and market functionality. However, between normal growth and the resumption of some marketing functions, it is now clear that our precious spare capacity is gone.

Market activity and trading didn't cause a third-world grid. The way deregulation and competition unfolded simply made it much easier to make the big bucks from other parts of the value chain. And who wants to invest in something with a low return when there is opportunity to be had over on the other side of the value chain?

That's probably the most accurate way of explaining why investment in the transmission and delivery (T&D) system has been declining precipitously for 20 years. (See Figure 5.1.)

Six Degrees of Integration

A main premise of this book is that while the transmission sector is a small piece of the overall value chain, it has the largest role in maintaining the security of the electric system. Transmission represents only about 10 percent of the value of the electric system assets and a corresponding

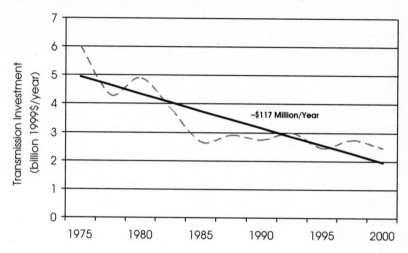

Figure 5.1   Investments in transmission have declined for twenty years.
SOURCE: U.S. Department of Energy National Transmission Grid Study, May 2002.

percentage of your electric bill. Because of the way the transmission system is organized, it is particularly vulnerable to threats and overload from too much market activity. On the other hand, because the market value of transmission itself is low, it is difficult to get people to focus on it.

Four principal "interconnections" make up the national grid, the *Eastern Interconnection*, the *Western Interconnection*, Canada, and Texas. Yes, the state of Texas has its own grid. These four "interconnects" are themselves connected, although weakly. Texas has a DC intertie (tie between the two interconnections) of about 50 MW (megawatts) between the panhandle and Oklahoma.

Second, there are what the industry calls the NERC regions. Over the years, individual utility systems have connected to each other so that they could provide power among each other in emergency situations, and sell power to each other on a wholesale basis.

Substations are located where these systems interconnect. From the standpoint of national security and reliability, they are *critical* substations. Grid system experts know which substations are critical and where they are located. Information is no longer published about these substations—although it wouldn't take a genius to either find the information or figure it out. That's because a coordinated attack on one or more of these substations could cripple the nation's electricity system and, therefore, its entire infrastructure. Although 9/11 has completely changed how we view these critical assets, it was the run-up to the Y2K issues that really motivated the industry to think about grid security before 2000.

Here's the problem: Citizens have been galvanized to support the "war on terror" (in quotes because terror is a tactic, not the enemy, per se) on multiple fronts around the world with greater expenditures to protect our ports and borders. We now tolerate armed security guards and military personnel in our subways and train stations. We're spending millions to harden the security at our nuclear plants. We are doing virtually nothing to protect these substations, except continue to talk quietly about how a coordinated attack on them will take down our nation.

Studies show that airplanes cannot penetrate the reactor containment domes of most nuclear reactors in the United States and yet the possibility of such an attack sends fear into the heart of the American people. Studies also show that these substations are, for the most part, remote, unmanned, protected only with barbed-wire fence, and extremely susceptible to even a very simple attack. Another feature that makes them easy targets for threats is that they are completely automated and remotely controlled. That means that you don't even need to chuck a bomb or drive a truck into them; you can shut them down through clever computer hacking.

I can point to numerous high-level reports that have been issued about the problems with our transmission assets—issuing organizations include the Electric Power Research Institute (EPRI), the Department of Energy (DOE), the General Accounting Office (GAO), and the National Science Academy (NSA). In 2002, DOE even formed the Office of Electric Transmission and Distribution to focus efforts on these issues. Homeland Security has task forces. The president's office has the Critical Infrastructure Protection program. It goes on and on.

Look at Figure 5.2, an expanded version of an illustration we used earlier. Now think about how much of our modern way of life depends on electricity. The flow of that electricity, in turn, increasingly is through an antiquated grid with a handful of critical substations.

Yet, 3 years after the blackout of 2003, 5 years after 9/11, 6 years after Y2K, and 10 years after the California electricity market began

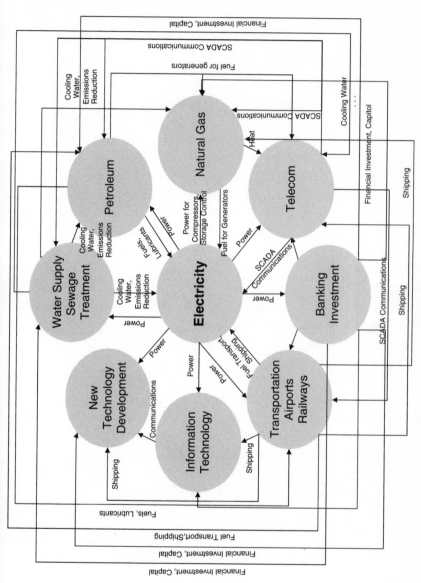

Figure 5.2 Electricity powers modern society; a handful of critical substations support the interconnection of the grid.

83

operating (followed by electricity market development in other regions), the transmission system is virtually unchanged. The Energy Policy Act of 2005 includes incentives for building transmission—but so far at least it has been met with a less than enthusiastic response, and there are few reports of investors lining up to pour money into building out the grid.

What Price Security?

It is hard to see how the present organizational structure can accommodate change. It is true that utilities' expenditures for transmision and distribution (T&D) have been increasing since 2002 after two decades of steady, year-on-year declines. However, this T&D money is mostly being spent only on the utility's service territory for its *captive customer base.* The other category of spending includes transmission lines, substations, and other equipment that strengthens the integration of the system for the betterment of the nation. In theory, this is a classic application of the tragic law of the commons: Everyone benefits from better security and reliability, but calculating the value is almost completely subjective. Therefore, assigning the cost to the appropriate parties is next to impossible politically.

The costs are not trivial either. According to a *New York Times* article, published near the two-year anniversary of the Blackout of 2003, it cost us $1 billion to safeguard federal buildings after the Oklahoma City bombing. The article does not say what that money bought (cement barriers, motion detectors, better access security, deeper profiles on federal workers, metal detectors, etc.), but it does suggest that critical substation protection would cost at least as much and that the cost of a nationwide electricity outage would "dwarf that figure."

Evidence All Around—Except Right in Front of You

We don't need a terrorist attack on critical substations, or a simulated one, to show us how fragile the grid really is. The evidence is all around us.

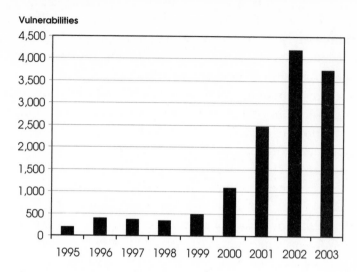

Vulnerabilities

Figure 5.3   Security vulnerabilities are increasing.
SOURCE: GAO analysis based on Carnegie Mellon University's CERT®
Coordination Center data.

Electricity industry analysts have shown that the number of serious or catastrophic "reliability events" has increased over the last 10 years compared to the three decades before that (Figure 5.3). One source (http://www.ece.cmu.edu/cascadingfailures/blackout_frequencies.htm), titled "The Frequency of Large Blackouts in the United States Electrical Transmission System: An Empirical Study," by Paul Hines and other researchers at Carnegie-Mellon University, reveals that, "excluding extreme weather events, and normalizing for demand growth, the average number of blackouts 100 MW or larger between the intervals 1984–1997 and 1998–2004 is 15 and 24, respectively." In the conclusion, the authors state, "The electricity industry is not winning the fight against large blackouts, and there is some evidence that it may be losing."

Actual occurrence of blackouts is damning enough, but there are other forms of evidence for our "third world grid. For example, utilities are obligated to report warnings to the Federal Energy Regulatory Commission (FERC) when lines are maxed out and market congestion is occurring. The number of these warnings has been steadily increasing since 1999. State regulators have shown their concern in surveys about the adequacy of transmission. You can read about the state of the nation's electric transmission simply by visiting the North American Electric Reliability Corporation (NERC) Web site and reading its "Reliability Assessment" reports.

What often cannot be identified with any authority are the causes of blackouts, disturbances, and grid warnings. Opponents of competition and market forces in electricity often point to trading and market activity as a significant factor. Technocrats blame the aging infrastructure and the lack of new technology and replacement components. Utilities usually blame bad weather or rare one-time events.

The answer, of course, is all of the above. But a deeper answer is this: Usually the root cause of a widespread outage is an "act of God," in other words weather-related, or something dumb, like tree branches (which should have been trimmed) falling on power lines. It is the *cascading nature of the original outage* that is of critical concern (Table 5.1). It is the way that first outage affects parts of the system far away from the triggering event, and it has everything to do with (1) the way the system has been designed and built originally; (2) how loaded the system is, and the prevailing direction of the power flows caused by market activity; and (3) the lack of advanced detection, monitoring, and control technology (intelligence) to better manage the dynamics of the system at any point in time.

The blackout of 2003 is a case in point. The "root cause," by official report, was a lack of tree-trimming, and branches that fell on a

Table 5.1 Impact of the August 4, 2003, Blackout

Number of Canadian provinces affected	1
Number of U.S. states affected	8
Deaths	3
Airports closed	12
Cases of looting in Ottawa	23
Number of power plants affected	250 +
MW of power lost	61,800
Number of Cleveland residents without water	1.5 million
Total number of people affected	50 million
Amount of economic activity lost	$4.5–$10 billion

SOURCE: GridWorks: Multi-Year Plan, Office of Electric Transmission and Distribution, United States Department of Energy, March 2005.

heavily loaded line. This has been well-established and widely reported. What wasn't discussed is that the first transmission line affected was very near one of the "critical substations" mentioned earlier. It is a substation that is important for moving electricity from the Midwest and the South to the Northeast. The outage occurred on a hot day in August, although it certainly wasn't a record-breaker. But temperatures played a role because market forces were certainly moving large amounts of low-cost electricity (usually as a result of burning coal) from the Midwest and South to the Northeast (dependent on higher-cost gas-fired generating stations) to run air conditioners.

After events like this, "official" reports are issued and the information is run through the political sanitizer machine. The analysis is usually thorough about what happened, but less satisfying about why. It is difficult to correlate the emergence of electricity markets with declining grid reliability. However, we can state unequivocally that market transactions have increased the independencies among parts of the transmission system, and we can also observe that serious reliability events began to increase around when electricity markets began (1996). This is certainly not an indictment of electricity markets and competition. It is, however, a clarion call to pull our heads out of the sand and recognize their potential contribution to the problem.

A call to action for modernizing the electricity grid made it into the President's 2004 State of the Union address. Incentives to translate that overarching policy into concrete programs are included in the Electricity Title of the Energy Policy Act of 2005. (Refer to earlier chapter.)

From a grid security and reliability perspective, and for the sake of our functioning electricity markets, I propose that perhaps, just maybe, we should be treating these critical substations like they were nuclear plants. Here it is a little more directly: our regional substations are critical assets that are essential to our national interest and should be viewed and protected as such. There you have it. So far, however, all the talk of change has gone nowhere fast.

Travels to Byzantium

Transmission, this under-appreciated 10 percent of the electricity production and delivery value chain, is managed through a set of institutions that can only be described as Byzantine. If you actually wanted to invest to upgrade, reinforce or expand the system, you'd be hard-pressed even to figure out to whom to give your money.

As we learned earlier, the physical assets (the poles, transformers and wires, etc.) are still largely owned by electric utilities. An independent system operator (ISO) or *regional transmission organization* (RTO) is responsible for actually operating the assets consistent with the market structure in place in that particular region. NERC, the industry-led group, manages and reports on the flow of electricity among the interconnected regions for the specific (and sole) goal of ensuring reliability of the nation's system. FERC has new-found powers, resulting from the recent energy legislation, to establish permits and rights-of-way for new "transmission corridors" defined as "in the national interest." In a few places, there are also "merchant" transmission facilities, which only operate when they have a contract to move power from one place to another.

Several utilities have asked FERC to designate new transmission projects as in the national interest. One of these is in Pennsylvania. Merchant transmission companies have been planning to build a new line that would connect Long Island, New York, with Connecticut across the Long Island Sound. Although interest has waned, a group of companies was planning to build a huge DC intertie to link large power stations in Wyoming to the heavily populated California cities.

Most of these projects are moving slowly, if at all. And why should investors be so patient? After all, it took a major Midwest utility 10 years to gain all the approvals necessary to build a 30-mile transmission line in West Virginia. No wonder the smart money invests elsewhere.

Who's in Charge Here?

Power plants may change ownership, but at any given time, at least you know who owns them and is responsible for operating them. It is decidedly less clear for transmission.

We learned earlier that generation and transmission are intimately tied together. You can strategically locate generating stations within the grid and change its operating characteristics, for better or for worse. The RTO or ISO may dispatch each power station according to market-based prices for electricity. For the most part, however, the utility owner ultimately decides when and whether to move the power over its lines to obey its own safety guidelines. (When an RTO or ISO *dispatches* a power station, it simply means that at any particular moment, it selects a power station from which to get power for the grid based on the price the station has offered for that particular time period.) Again, we have seen that utilities have power stations that must run for the effective functioning of the grid. They also own power stations in some markets from which they want to maximize profit. The upshot is that what the RTO or ISO may want to serve the market, what the transmission lines need to keep functioning, and what the utility wants to do to turn a profit are not, in any real sense, synchronized.

The situation in California, often a bellwether for the rest of the country, was summed up in the report, "2005 Integrated Energy Policy Report," issued by the California Energy Commission (report no. CEC-100–2005-007-ES) in November of that year. "However, the state still lacks a well-integrated transmission planning and permitting process that considers both generation and transmission needs, evaluates non-wires alternatives, plans for transmission corridors well in advance of need, and allows access to essential renewable resource areas in the state.

Federal regulators may want national electricity markets and competition. State regulators may want local consumers (native load) to be served before any power is wheeled out of—or into—the state. Utilities accuse energy marketers and independent power plants of overloading their facilities. Marketers and independent power plants, in turn, accuse the utilities of favoring their own assets, using the excuse of reliability that they have to use part of their power to maintain the grid.

You can see how trying to expand or upgrade the physical assets is so difficult. Customers want low-cost electricity. Utilities want a fair return on their investment. Private power companies want to maximize their revenues and profits. Government entities want to ensure reliability, encourage economic growth, and not be blamed when there are problems. Expanding or upgrading the grid in one place might create new "stranded assets" (assets which have been installed and are still being paid off but are no longer needed) for someone else. Additional transmission might expand competition, but at the expense of the existing generators. And we haven't even talked about siting new T&D assets yet!

So we have what is known as congestion. Bottlenecks in the grid, the cause of congestion, raise the price of delivering electricity to some. Remove a bottleneck and the grid characteristics, and the pricing structure of delivery, change. You could build a power plant just past a bottleneck, and theoretically move power to customers at a more favorable price. But then what do you do when the transmission grid is upgraded and others can also move power to the same customers? Those responsible for transmission don't know when and where new power plants will be located, which will affect how transmission flows. Those building new power plants can't determine what to do about transmission.

I remember interviewing for a job once. On the plane home, I realized that the position offered gave me tremendous responsibility and accountability, but none of the authority to actually get the job done. The ISO/RTO has a similar problem: It has much of the responsibility to ensure effective, reliable markets and operations, but it does not own the assets, nor does it have enough budgetary or regulatory authority to act on its own.

Our third-world grid can be summed up this way: Critical assets are being governed by questionable institutional structures, with unclear budgetary pathways toward improvement, upgrade or expansion. It's a sure-fire recipe for disaster. It may not happen all at once, but it certainly could over time.

Chapter 6

Living with a Transaction Economy

I'm not an economist but that doesn't mean I can't have an economic theory. It may not be completely new—and others have approached the same idea coming from different directions. Nevertheless, I've developed my theory by being immersed in the electricity business for two and a half decades. I think the theory can be applied to other industries and sectors.

We live in what I call a "transactions-based economy." It is fueled by the multidecade transformation from a manufacturing-based economy to a services-oriented economy. In simple terms, our economy must have more and more transactions that are larger and larger to satisfy all the workers in the growing service (especially, financial services) industries. The service industry is now, according to most economics analyses, five-sixths of our economy, manufacturing a meager one-sixth. The result, as I alluded to earlier, is that financial engineering takes precedence over physical engineering. With respect to the electricity system, the impact is this: Investors are making more money buying and selling assets than they are investing in those assets for the long term. When you're playing for the big money in this game, short-term return on increased transactions always trumps long-term investment in upgrading—or even maintaining—infrastructure.

More than Monopoly

In the electricity business, the buying and selling of power plants is a good example of transactions. Twenty years ago, an electric utility, or a group of utilities, financed, built, and operated power plants. These assets were intended to be owned and operated by that same utility, or utility consortium, for 40 years or more. Investors purchased utility bonds so utilities could borrow the money to build these plants, and bought utility stocks to support the investment. Electric utilities were stable, modest yielding investments suitable for your grandparents' retirement fund. In other words, they were boring, from the perspective of the financial services industry. Some utilities and their power stations are still like this: boring.

Today, however, around 40 percent of the power generation in this country is not like this at all. These power plants can be classified many ways. I classify them as *nonutility* power plants. Three components make up these plants: (1) plants that utilities, in states pursuing vigorous competition, were required to sell; (2) most of the gas-fired power stations built over the last 10 years; and (3) independent power and cogeneration plants built under a 1980 law known as the Public Utility Regulatory Policies Act (PURPA). Many of these plants have been bought and sold at least once and more likely twice. Most of them will be bought and sold several times over their useful lives. One private equity investor recently made an obscene amount of money buying "distressed assets" in Texas and then selling them back to a publicly traded power company only a year or two later. It all reminds me of playing Monopoly when I was a kid.

Remember how boring home mortgages used to be? Who needed to track interest rates? You got a 30-year fixed interest loan and you paid it off, month after month. If you moved, you got another one, just like the one you had. Today, homeowners refinance their loans multiple times. What's more, those mortgages are bought and sold "behind the scenes" by professional investors, also called mortgage *real estate investment trusts* (REITs). Similarly, the buying and selling of power plant assets has emerged as a way to "restructure" utility balance sheets.

There are numerous examples of transactions running amuck in the electricity business. A decade ago, electricity was *not* a commodity that could be bought and sold like soybeans or platinum. Today, sophisticated Wall Street trading firms such as Morgan Stanley and Goldman Sachs trade electricity contracts, futures, derivatives, and the like the same as any other commodity. The merger and acquisition wave in electric utilities, and then with electric utilities and natural gas companies, is another good example of transactions, perhaps at the highest level.

Hmmm. I wonder if a service as critical as electricity to our nation's security, economic well-being, and down-home creature comforts should remind me so much of Monopoly.

From Smith Street to Wall Street

Late in year 2000, a close colleague in Houston casually relayed to me a disturbing rumor going around Houston, where market-based electricity was converging with other energy forms, particularly natural gas, to create fast-growing, exciting companies like Enron, Dynegy, Williams, Duke Energy North America, El Paso, and others. The scuttlebutt was that the big Wall Street trading firms were not happy that electricity trading had made its home in Houston. Apparently, they thought its proper place was Wall Street.

Don't look now, but five years later, Wall Street firms now control most of the electricity trading operations in this country. I'm not crying conspiracy theory, but a connection of some sort seems obvious.

Then, early in 2001, I was sitting across the table with an executive at one of the biggest energy firms in Houston and in

(continued)

the country. He told me that someone needed to get the story out that all of the Wall Street stock brokerage houses were pressuring energy companies such as his to use the same tactics that Enron was using. He explained that so-called "mark-to-market" accounting, sanctioned by the Financial Accounting Standards Board (FASB), essentially allowed you to create and apply your own model for forecasting your future revenues. Enron was using the most aggressive models, Wall Street liked what it saw, and was encouraging others to "create shareholder value" through what I might politely call customized accounting. My friend knew I had connections in the trade press and almost pleaded with me to "get the story out."

The market didn't need me. A few months later, the story around Enron began to leak out, like air around a rusty nail in a bulging tire. By December of that year, Enron had declared what was then the largest bankruptcy of any U.S. corporation. (Enron listed $63.4 billion in assets when it filed for Chapter 11, but was quickly surpassed by WorldCom with $107 billion.)

These two anecdotes conveyed by my two colleagues in Houston stayed with me while I watched the entire electricity industry proceed through a Chernobyl-like meltdown, and then rehabilitate itself, all within a five-year period. You can extrapolate what you want from these stories. I can tell you this with certainty, however: Enron was the most egregious of the players, but the meltdown was caused by an increasingly aggressive and vicious circle dance among Wall Street firms pushing irrational exuberance in the stock market, the accounting industry rubber-stamping the financial engineering necessary to make the future so much brighter than it was ever going to be, and the energy companies busting out of a 60-year period of regulated utility economics, like prehistoric sauropods suddenly seeing some running room at the edge of the swamp. In the end, the consumer, the small investor, the little guy, got trampled.

Who makes money every time an asset like a power plant is sold or bought, or when two utilities merge? Consultants, lawyers, accountants, financial advisors, and the other growing members of the elite service side of the economy win. Meanwhile, the budgets for the people who operate, maintain, and manage this asset safely and reliably, inevitably shrink.

In fact, assets are not the focal point of a valuable company anymore. The balance sheet is. Today, energy companies are scrambling to add renewable and alternative energy technologies, companies, and divisions to their operations. Twenty years ago, oil companies added solar and wind and other alternative energy activities; within a decade, they either divested them or they went dormant internally. Now we're at it again. Why? The answer is no different than if you bought an emergency home generator to run your critical appliances. You are hedging your bets against a disastrous electricity outage. Energy companies add assets to hedge against the future, a future that might reveal sustained high-energy costs. When the "threat" or risk goes away, so does the asset, which can be a company, a factory, a power plant, land, or just about anything else they can think up.

Twenty years ago, the utility's assets were the focal point of the business. However, it's not fair to say that this was the golden age, unless you were a utility engineer. By and large, an engineer had grown up through the organization to run the business as CEO. Today, few power system engineers run utilities, and even if they do, their MBA and financial acumen have been the focus of their executive training. This is reflected in how the businesses are run. Engineers gold-plated the system by adding layers of cost that were borne by customers, usually the large industrial and commercial accounts. It was a lot to pay, but it was also a reliable system. Today, financial engineering is stripping away that gold-plating and trading it back and forth to keep extracting profits at the margins.

Of course, it would be silly to say that financial engineering has ruined our electricity system (Figure 6.1). It would also be incredibly naïve to think that crucial dollars are not being sucked out of the businesses to pay for services that have nothing to do with the design, operation, or maintenance of our most strategic infrastructure.

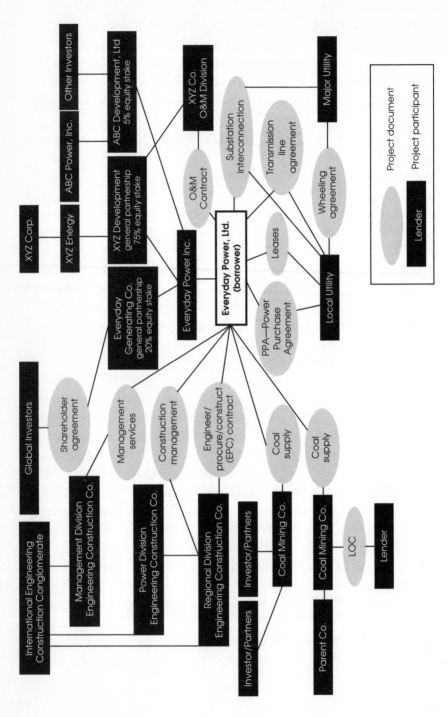

Figure 6.1 The financial engineering of power plant construction.

Securitization: I'll Gladly Pay You Tuesday

According to Leonard Hyman's popular and, frankly, brilliant text, *America's Electric Utilities: Past, Present, and Future* (Public Utilities Reports, 2005), this is how one form of functional engineering securitization, worked for disaggregating generating assets:

> *Regulators pushing competition wanted utilities to divest of their generating plants so they would not control the source of the commodity (electricity). Utilities, on the other hand, had made investments in those assets under a regulated regime. They insisted on recovering those "stranded costs," preferably all at once. To satisfy both sides, the investment banking community came up with securitization.*

To make it work, the utility or the state sets up a special entity. The utility assigns to that entity all future stranded cost recovery revenues that it would collect from all customers as an addition to the utility bill. Then, the special entity sells bonds in an amount equal to the value of that revenue stream. This money is turned over to the utility. The special entity then collects the stranded cost charge, plus interest of course, by means of the special charge.

According to Hyman, "securitization also permitted politicians and regulators to create the appearance of price reductions as an immediate benefit of restructuring. They could structure the collection and payment schedule in such a way that the charge on the consumer is low in the first years, but rises later. That scheme, of course, just adds to the interest payments, in the end, but the people who pay then will not be the people who vote now."

Don't look now, but five years after applying recovery of stranded costs through securitization to generating assets, the financial engineering industry is now pushing to apply securitization to transmission assets. It'll likely be just another way that the investor class works with utility executives to create high-value transactions that have little or no benefit to the rate-paying consumer—or to (dare I repeat it?) the design, operation, or maintenance of our most strategic infrastructure.

Chapter 7

The Brain Drain

At every industry meeting I have attended over the last few years, whether generally about the electric power industry or specifically about nuclear power, coal, or transmission, executives lament the lack of fresh professionals entering the field of electric power. The *brain drain*, as it is called, is felt in all the technical disciplines, from technicians to facility managers. Construction firms can't find enough craft boilermakers, competition is intense for welders, and equipment companies are fighting for mechanical engineers who can design and build pumps and valves.

At one end of the career pipe, experienced workers are leaving at a time of growth and expansion of the infrastructure. At the other end, young professionals with advanced degrees apparently view a career in electricity like a tour of a musty, dank museum. And can you blame them? Here's what an "honest" recruiting ad in our industry might say:

Wanted: Experienced mechanical engineer to serve on design team building power stations pretty much like they've been built for the last

*50 years. Experience with equipment that would probably be recogniz-
able to Thomas Edison is required. Creative thinking is not necessary.
The successful candidate will not be deterred by crushing amounts of
paperwork and regulatory oversight. Salary will look pretty good while
the current labor shortage lasts. Longevity of position is contingent upon
all necessary project permits and approvals being obtained in a timely
manner. Successful candidate must be aware that most project permits
and approvals are not obtained in a timely manner. Most of the valuable
benefits are available after 40 years even though the probability of your
continued employment with the company that long is next to zero.*

Take the nuclear industry. This year, the Nuclear Regulatory Commission (NRC), which is responsible for licensing new reactor designs
and plants, is facing a crushing wave of licensing activities. The agency is
offering nuclear engineers with three to five years of experience salaries
that are 50 percent higher than market rates. In effect, the NRC is
willing to pay for the industry's best and brightest.

At the same time, the nuclear plants themselves are starved for talent.
Because of the age of these plants and the obsolescent equipment, engineers have been pressed into service keeping these plants hung together
with baling wire and spit. It's like taking engineers who thought they'd
spend their careers designing the next generation sports car and putting
them to work changing spark plugs, checking filters and doing state inspections at Mel's Auto Body. Most of what these highly trained nuclear
engineers do anyway is paperwork required to satisfy the regulators.

You can probably see what's going to happen. The best engineers
from the plants are going to leave for the more fulfilling work of being
part of the teams designing and engineering the next generation of
nuclear plants. Plant staffs will then be hurting because there is little
technical talent coming out of the schools. This is a dangerous situation
for plant operators. Because the entire nuclear industry's future is affected
by an accident at one plant, you don't want to be the one rolling the dice.

Nukes Most at Risk

The labor situation is particularly acute for the nuclear sector because
an enormous investment in continuous worker training is necessary.

Workers leaving a nuclear plant leave with more than just their knowledge of the plant. They leave with their knowledge and experience with how to deal with the regulations and with the constant training they have to undergo to certify their capabilities. Much of the industry's knowledge base is walking out that door, since the industry forecasts that *half the nuclear industry workforce is leaving over the next five years.* Think about it. Five years isn't a very long time in the infrastructure business. It's the time it takes more and more students to earn an undergraduate degree today.

I get a little nervous when I listen to nuclear industry executives. You hear things like, "loss of experienced staff is our number one problem" and "we're actually leaner than we should be, we've let some critical skills go." There's no question about it in my mind: The existing fleet of nuclear plants, while turning in stellar operating performances year after year, has been doing so while starved for resources. The plants are getting older (see Figure 7.1) and the older, experienced workers are leaving. How long can you do more with less? Workers at the tail end of their career are willing to stick around under such conditions because they want the full benefit of their retirement package. How do you convince young workers to work this way?

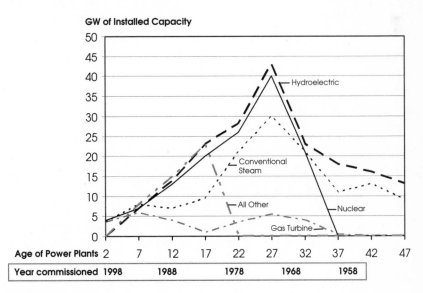

Figure 7.1   Power plants are aging fast.
SOURCE: BD/MI UDI.

Nuclear workers suffer from other characteristics peculiar to this sector. Because the plants operate 24/7 for up to two years, when a planned outage (a period when the plant is deliberately shut down so scheduled maintenance can be done) does occur, everything and the kitchen sink is heaped into the outage's scheduled tasks that must be completed. And, because the units need to get back on line as soon as possible (they are the lowest cost units to run), schedule pressure is relentless. For this reason, huge contingents of workers must be mobilized for short outage periods.

Brother, Can You Spare an Engineer?

The issue may be, in my opinion, most acute for nuclear plants, but the entire industry is affected. The results of a nationwide survey of the coal power business, published in *Power Engineering* in "Aging Workforce: A Challenge to the Industry," in June 2006, show that a large coal plant with 250 employees will lose half its current staff in the next decade. One executive struggles with attracting and retaining electrical engineers who can do transmission planning. One client of mine entered into potential partnership negotiations with the energy division of a large Fortune 10, only to have the big dog steal his best instrumentation and control engineer!

The statistics just keep hammering away. Within five years, half of the nation's electrical line workers will retire. Sixty-two percent of rural-electric-cooperative general managers are 50 or older. Between 20 and 40 percent of all power industry employees in North America will be eligible to retire in the next five years. At the same time, less than 1 percent of engineering graduates select power engineering as a focus or major. These stats are courtesy of *Energybiz* magazine's July/August 2006 edition "Reaching Out: Fresh Answers to Market Exodus." The magazine interviewed specialists in the human resources departments of 15 companies representing 160,000 workers. Every one reported that it "anticipates a serious shortage of workers in the next few years." Skilled tradesmen like line technicians and mechanics are the chief worry, but make no mistake; engineers are in short supply as well.

Now add this tidbit into the mix: Electricity is arguably the largest single industry in the country! Electric utilities alone (and this does not include independents) own assets worth around $600 billion, and annual sales are variously measured at between $250 and $300 billion. It's twice the size of the telecommunications business, and larger than the domestic component of the automobile business. Isn't it ironic that when the heads of the Big Three American car companies travel to meet with the president (as they did towards the end of 2006), the national news cameras follow them? Have you ever seen CNN coverage of the heads of the major electric utilities or even the big guys at the Edison Electric Institute (EEI), the industry's primary lobbying group, meeting with the president? Nah . . .

It's a sobering thought: The largest industry in the country could lose up to half its experienced workers in 5 to 10 years. Our nuclear plants could soon be run by newly minted engineering graduates who don't yet know a pressure relief valve from a pressure cooker. I can poke this kind of fun because I was one of those engineers a long time ago who didn't know which way to turn a valve when I first got to a power plant. The next time the grid in your area goes down, the line workers out in your backyard fixing the equipment may be getting a crash course in English on the plane over from Asia. Remember, only 1 percent of the nation's graduates express any interest at all in working in the country's largest industry.

The electricity industry embodies that Rodney Dangerfield line: "I get no respect around here, no respect at all."

It is clear to some executives that the industry must begin to tap the global engineering talent pool. But that isn't a straightforward process in this day and age of heightened concern about terrorism. Getting visas for foreign workers has become a nightmare. Plus, the places where these workers might originate—Asia, for example—are dealing with their own booms in power industry growth.

The potential impacts of the labor crisis are familiar. Any dislocation in supply and demand raises prices. I remember in the late 1970s, young engineers out of school could change employers every one or two years, and get a handsome increase in salary. In fact, that was seen as the only way to appreciably increase your pay, because the nature of engineering was a few big pay raises in the first few years and cost of living adjustments thereafter, unless you managed to jump to the management track.

It's also important to note that labor rates can significantly impact inflation. Past experience shows that when inflation gets out of hand, the costs to complete projects become less and less predictable.

Thank You for Your Service: Could You Leave Early?

The roots of formation of the labor crisis have two branches. The first, general population statistics, works against everyone. The so-called baby boom generation, those born between 1946 and 1960 comprise 77 million people. Younger workers in their 20s number only 45 million. There's simply a smaller pool to draw from to serve a growing industry.

The other branch is the industry's own doing. After the bust in the merchant and gas-fired power business, beginning in 2001, utilities and independents had to repair their balance sheets. Divesting assets, such as completed plants, projects under construction, electricity trading divisions, and the like, got the headlines nationally. But utilities en masse also instituted layoffs and early retirement programs. Two kinds of people take early retirement packages: Those who really want to retire early, and the motivated who think they can do better as independents.

In fact, the recent wave of reductions is only part of a 20-year trend in the electricity industry. The electric utility workforce has been declining since the mid-1980s. Of course, some of this reduction has simply been a shift in resources from utilities to nonutility segments of the business. Importantly, though, there have been no gains, while electricity demand continues to grow. Between 1998 and 2005, for example, we've added more than 200,000 megawatts of new gas-fired capacity while one estimate shows that the overall reduction in workforce has been around 25 percent.

Once again, my own experience in this regard is instructive. My oldest daughter is college bound. She showed an early interest in and aptitude for science and engineering. Have I encouraged her to seek a career in engineering or, more specifically, in the power industry? Hardly. In fact, I counsel against it. Traditional engineering functions are not valued the same way as the legal, investment, health care, and computer/information technology professions are. In this country, there is no longer any glamour in heavy infrastructure. In fact, my prediction is that we will ultimately import engineering talent from overseas—just like some hire illegal immigrants to tend their gardens.

Another likely scenario is that we will utilize overseas talent remotely. We already have the equivalent of "sweat shops" in Asia that do engineering flow diagrams and process and instrumentation diagrams (P&IDs) for our power stations, as well as basic equipment calculations. This is the only way we're going to keep labor and engineering costs reasonable. In addition, this is where the talent will reside that does not require an investment in training and on-the-job experience. Once again, it is the path of greatest financial efficiency but not necessarily the one of long-term stability of our electricity infrastructure.

My daughter will be better off interpreting the legal frameworks for building power stations, providing investment services, or going into other sectors entirely. What my experience has taught me is that it is better to be associated with the services surrounding the infrastructure, not the physical assets themselves. Is this self-serving? Maybe. Is this the best course for the long-term stability of our electricity infrastructure? Probably not. Is this the best course for my daughter? I think so.

Self-Correction Factors

Thankfully, labor issues have a way of resolving themselves. Most dislocations in supply and demand are temporary, whether in primary energy resources like petroleum and natural gas, or in skilled and professional labor. The problem really isn't one of supply or demand, but of cost. The challenge is to keep labor and engineering costs from skyrocketing.

First, consolidation will reduce the need for some of this highly skilled labor and management. When two utilities merge, part of the motivation is to leverage the existing workforce over a larger number of assets, avoid duplication, and improve productivity. When larger numbers of assets are concentrated under fewer entities, owners enjoy economies of scale. For example, it makes little sense today for a utility to own and operate one nuclear unit. In fact, many of the single-nuke utilities have divested that asset to a utility that has made nuclear power a centerpiece of its asset management and operations strategy.

Second, many people still think that engineering skills have to be located where the work is. Our engineering and construction companies already take advantage of huge pools of engineering talent in India and China. Vast computer systems and software are what really manage the global engineering resources, with huge engineering drawing files shipped or posted via Internet or intranets around the globe.

Third, potential new sources of skilled labor are on the horizon. If we wind down our operations in Iraq, and refrain from getting involved in other conflicts, then the military could become a source of skilled talent. In the 1980s, for example, the Navy's nuclear program was scaled back, releasing hundreds, if not thousands, of highly trained and skilled workers for the nation's nuclear plants. Then, as the nuclear plant construction program ran aground, veterans of the nuclear navy found employment in the cogeneration, independent power, and merchant electricity plants. Military personnel often have the exact skills sought by the power industry, with their vast training and experience—paid for by the taxpayers to boot!

Fourth, dare I whisper that some of these workers are no longer needed? Unquestionably, today's computers, software, automation, telecommunications, and robotics industries have flattened the organizational chart. Power plants that once had their own set of specialists now deploy that expertise from centralized monitoring facilities networked to multiple power plant control rooms. Because the data can be shared and analyzed across a larger collection of workers, mobile unit teams are dispatched to fix things or make recommendations to the operations and maintenance crews on site. In addition, disparate organizations are now tied together through information technology (IT) and telecommunications. Equipment suppliers now routinely remotely monitor their assets in the field, and offer "services" to the owner/operators.

Again, I look to the nuclear business for examples, and if you're wondering why, it's because it is the most labor-intensive sector of the industry. Nuclear plants have hundreds, sometimes even thousands, of people on site because they are based, essentially, on 1950s technology. Unfortunately, the way these plants are regulated prevents them from applying new automation and IT methods to improve productivity and enhance automation, even though there are attendant benefits in worker safety and exposure to radiation. Because of the way it was forced to develop institutionally, the nuclear power sector is, in the context of labor and productivity, living in the dark ages. Just as one example, nuclear plants in Korea and elsewhere are applying state of the art automation based on digital control technology. Meanwhile, in this country, we're still arguing over whether it is even appropriate.

Some organizations with a global asset base, especially natural gas and gas turbine/generators, have centralized monitoring for the entire fleet. As long as you propagate the right data and information to the right people at the right time, IT can substantially reduce the number of infrastructure workers required. It's not a straightforward reduction, however, because a greater number of IT workers are now required to maintain those IT and telecom systems. Also, each data link in a vast information network represents a point of vulnerability from a security perspective.

Make Yourself Appealing

The power industry doesn't just compete within itself but with all other industries. Utility executives admit that their benefits packages are poorly designed for the workforce of the future. The industry's leaders acknowledge that little has been done to enhance the cache of the electricity business. When was the last time you saw utilities running commercials on television telling us (as Verizon, a telecommunications company, does) that "this is a great place to work," "this is a place where you can make a difference."

With respect to how it is perceived by potential recruits, the industry is hamstrung in two ways. First, it is still highly fragmented, despite all the consolidation that has occurred. Second, there are no "brands." I could see why kids today might salivate over working for a company like Apple Computer. Most every one of them I know carries a slick handsomely designed iPod around with them. The Apple brand appeals to people on a gut level. There isn't an electric utility in America that has created a "brand" that appeals to its customers on a gut level. Few utilities in America even acknowledge the importance of a relationship with their customer or the "customer experience."

All Is Not Lost

The industry hasn't been completely sitting on its hands while the crisis gathers. Several utilities have developed partnerships with local universities and community colleges. In New Jersey, the Thomas Edison State College just initiated a program with one of the state's utilities for the "nation's first baccalaureate degree program in energy utility technology." The utility's CEO sees the program as specifically helping to fill positions expected to be vacated through retirements over the next few years. Local utilities have also instituted mentoring programs with nearby high schools. States such as Ohio and Connecticut are funding programs to develop workers for the "energy technologies of the future" like fuel cells.

The Williamson Free School of Mechanical Trades, reported *Power* magazine in June 2006 ("The Future of Workforce Training"), turns out power industry specialists with actual hands-on training: the campus includes a power plant and a minigrid. Bismarck State College in North Dakota is expanding its power industry education and training with technical outreach to schools in other parts of the country. Even our local nuclear plant, 100 miles to the west of where I live, has a partnership with area schools to cultivate replacement workers.

The brain drain isn't a question of resources, but a question of timing, attention, and scale. Continued escalation in labor costs will show up in electricity rates. Acute temporary shortages of skilled personnel could affect our ability to recover quickly from outages. Inexperienced and untrained employees entering the workforce raise the probability of catastrophic events. The big question is whether the industry has waited too long to pay attention to the issue.

And Now for the Good News

Having just depressed any recent graduates thinking about a career in electricity, let me now emphasize that the brain drain issues affect the *left* side of the production and delivery value chain far more than the *right* side. There are some incredibly exciting things going on in the industry:

There is distributed and on-site generation, advanced meters, wind turbine/generators, photovoltaics, power electronics, broadband over power lines (BPL), electricity storage, fuel cells, wireless telecommunications, advanced transmission technologies. Plus there are myriad energy efficiency technologies being developed that have all the hallmarks of design, innovation, and creativity on par with a consumer-products-oriented company. This is the stuff to get excited about. But, these are the electricity industry technologies of tomorrow, not yesteryear or, in most cases, today. These are potentially disruptive technologies that can alter traditional infrastructure investment patterns, as we'll see in later chapters.

Of course, there is always room for true pioneers. Is there a recent graduate or entrepreneur out there who could revolutionize the industry by becoming the first true private "utility" that installs, owns, and operates microgrids (see Chapter 18). Such an entrepreneur could be to our industry its Bill Gates (Microsoft) or Sergey Brin and Larry Page (Google). Instead of trying to adapt an antiquated system designed for the socialized delivery of electricity to the masses (think mainframe computers), how about designing a modern system for 20 customers that meet the needs of the next 40 years?

As the banking industry deregulated, traditional banks set out to become regional, national, and global behemoths. Traditional utilities have embarked on the same strategy. In these cases, the goliaths tend to lose control of the customer experience, creating an opening for local "private" banks or microutilities.

In my opinion, the most successful "brains" will be those that execute a business model for electricity service based on individual customer satisfaction and experience, whether business or household. They will combine customer relationship management with advanced, distributed, infrastructure technologies and architecture. I firmly believe (and have repeated it many times) many of the issues on the left side of the value chain can be resolved with more intelligence on the right side. Right now, I see the potential for a whole lot more innovation on the right side than the left!

In my view, the long-term risk with labor shortages rests not so much in the reliability of our infrastructure but with its potential impact on electricity rates. Short-term, however, some consequences are just plain-old frightening to think about. One serious accident at a nuclear plant, for instance, takes out the entire nuclear sector, not just one plant or one utility. Public acceptance, already tenuous, would plummet. The bottom line is that it is beyond nuts that the nation's largest, and arguably most important, industry should suffer from a shortage of trained personnel.

Chapter 8

Environmental Imperatives

The electricity supply value chain impacts our environment in many ways. Extracting coal, uranium, petroleum, or natural gas from the earth disturbs the natural environment—or ravages it—depending on your viewpoint. Converting fuel into electricity results in huge discharges of emissions to the air, wastes to the ground, and water that is either consumed and released as vapor, or discharged to a receiving body at a temperature different from when it was taken out. Wide paths through woods and forests have to be cut to install the transmission towers and lines that bring electricity to us.

Renewable energy sources also have their impacts: Wind turbines kill birds, often rare birds such as eagles and condors, and bats that are apparently much more important to the food chain than we thought. Wind turbines are also noisy, unsightly, and can even interfere with radar transmission. Solar energy requires covering huge amounts of surface area with solar energy collectors.

Every increment of electricity that we consume is associated with these environmental impacts. The best way to understand these impacts is through this simple statement: What happens at small scale is good; what happens at large scale is bad. What do I mean by this?

At the turn of the last century, the automobile was hailed for, among other things, a solution to the problem of horse manure in the cities. Think about it. We want to remember quaint horse-drawn carriages as a symbol of a simpler time. But the cities were crammed with horses, and the manure was not only a nuisance but a serious health issue as well. The first few cars tooling around town must have seemed like, well, a breath of fresh air. It was impossible to comprehend what tens of thousands of those tailpipes would eventually do to the air. Today, we have almost as many cars on the road as people in the country.

Will a Really Good Solution Please Stand Up?

Solving environmental problems in electricity is a tough business. We all want energy. And it is impossible to go back to the good old days of horse-drawn (manure-producing) carriages or wood-burning (forest-destroying, carbon emitting) fireplaces. There are no good solutions, only less bad ones. What seems like a good idea at small scale often comes back to haunt us at large scale. At some point, supporting the "little guy," like renewables, passes a tipping point and becomes big business. Then, it is a natural target for attack. (See Table 8.1.)

Coal is a case in point. The public, except for voters in coal-producing states, mostly loathes coal. This is not an exaggeration. In fact, maybe "loathes" is too polite. The only other people who like coal believe that free markets take care of everything and it doesn't matter what fuel you choose.

Coal is a big business, responsible for 50 percent of our electricity. It's visible. Its affect on the public is visceral. Like protesters against Wal-Mart, it's a big, convenient target of public wrath.

On the other hand, the public seems to love renewables, like wind. It's small; less than 2 percent of our electricity generation comes from

Table 8.1   Sources of Electricity Generation

	1970	1980	Today
Natural gas	24%	15%	~13%
Petroleum	12%	11%	~3%
Coal	46%	51%	55%
Hydroelectric	16%	12%	9.5%
Nuclear	1.4%	11%	21%
Renewable*			2%

*Renewable energy today comes mostly from wind.

wind. Imagine if 50 percent of our electricity came from wind. We'd see a wind turbine as often as we see a streetlight. We'd also see three times more than most people even imagine because wind can only generate about one-third of the kilowatt-hours as a coal, nuclear, or gas-powered plant. Is it really efficient in the long run to put in three times as much capacity as another option?

Some very vocal environmentalists and electricity experts believe that the best solution is to use less electricity, or use it as efficiently as possible. This is, of course, absolutely true. Electricity not generated and not consumed represents emissions not discharged and an environment not impacted. Conservation is a noble pursuit; it is not just a personal virtue. As the sole focus of an electricity strategy, however, it is impractical. No matter what we've done in this country, electricity demand grows by an average of 2 to 3 percent per year.

Now think about those growing economies in China and India and the rest of Asia, South America, and Africa. Hundreds of millions of people don't even have electricity yet. They haven't experienced what life is like with electricity. There are some who are trying, but I, for one, am not going to go around trying to convince them that they should continue living without it, just so "my climate" will improve. They have every right to reasonably priced electricity as I do. And I'd put good money on the notion that once they experience life with modern conveniences, such as lights and clean running water, they're not likely to want to give it up so North American skies can stay clear and clean.

We could devote a book, and many authors have, to the environmental issues surrounding each electricity supply option. But let's first focus on the biggest of them all.

Tomorrow's Weather Report: Unseasonably Warm

All other environmental issues, as least as currently known, pale compared to the issue of global climate change. It is a looming vulnerability. You read about it in the papers. It makes the front cover of the newsstand magazines. It has even penetrated Hollywood. Al Gore's popular documentary, *An Inconvenient Truth,* made more impression on the media than Lindsey Lohan and Paris Hilton cavorting around half naked. Hollywood films, television shows, and the entertainment media have long been lacing their fare with references to global warming. Mr. Gore took home an Oscar for best documentary.

You can also understand the magnitude of this issue with a simple chemistry lesson. The *essence* of making electricity from fossil fuels is the conversion of carbon into carbon dioxide. That's the purpose, the point, the *raison d'etre,* of a coal-, natural-gas-, or petroleum-fired power station. Global climate change has fundamentally made it wrong to simply discharge the carbon dioxide to the atmosphere. And that is a problem.

Australopithecus' Missing Tooth

You will decide whether global warming is an imminent threat to the planet. You will do so on ideological, political, or scientific grounds. It may be as simple as pointing out the broiling summer that you just experienced or the rash of severe weather events we had in 2005. Or maybe you reject it by thinking that if the damn weather man couldn't predict yesterday's rain that left you soaking wet without an umbrella, how the hell can anyone predict weather 50 years into the future?

For my part, I still have fundamental questions about the computer models used to predict rising global temperatures in the future from limited hard data from the past. I've seen *An Inconvenient Truth* and I acknowledge that Mr. Gore makes an effective and compelling argument, better than his 1992 book, *Earth in the Balance.* But I'm a dyed-in-the-wool skeptic. It's my nature. In the financial world, you are required to live by the statement, "Past performance is no guarantee of future success." Climatologists, apparently, do not have to live by this creed.

I remember taking an introductory anthropology course in college. We learned about the amazing experts who essentially constructed an entire skeleton and "model" of Australopithecus, an ancestor of Homo sapiens, from one tooth. One tooth! This reminds me of how climate forecast models are created. The "tooth" is what I would call "hard data" or direct measurements with a low probability of error around them. There is a limited amount of such data to validate the complex computer models used by climatologists. Therefore, global climate change arguments are built from what a courtroom would label circumstantial evidence. The models don't have any, uh, teeth. Even if global warming does exist, the rate of contribution of human activities versus naturally occurring events (e.g., volcanoes, natural temperature fluctuations) is ambiguous.

I'm treading on thin ice. Oops, another bad joke. I can hear my wife arguing: "How can you discount the informed analyses of hundreds of the world's leading scientists?" (We clearly have a difference of opinion, here.)

Okay, please disregard my poor attempts at humor. I'm really here to tell you that it doesn't matter. My opinion. Your opinion. Even my wife's opinion. Informed or not, they simply don't matter. The science is, at this point, almost beside the point. Public sentiment now overwhelmingly agrees that global warming exists, is a serious problem, and must be dealt with. Opinion has pushed this issue past the "tipping point."

The only person who seems to be unequivocally unconvinced that global warming is real and that it may conceivably pose a threat to life as we know it on this pale blue dot is President Bush and his diminishing cadre of scientific experts frantically trying to stem the tide of public opinion. Even the electric utility executives are, for the most part, finished fighting the issue. That two-decade front in the battle against environmentalists is over. They've moved their resources to another front. All they want to know now is the regulatory framework they're facing so they can conduct their business with some semblance of certainty. Or at least as much certainty as you ever get in this line of work.

The new front in global warming revolves around what tough choices are going to be made by the industry to begin to contain the problem, what sacrifices electricity consumers are going to make, how much all this is going to cost, and how the cost will be split between shareholders and ratepayers.

Why is electricity so vulnerable? It is the largest single industry contributor to rising carbon levels in the atmosphere. The popular proportions are, one third of carbon emissions come from the electricity sector, one third from the automotive sector, and one third from the all of the rest of industry. Electric power generation is the largest consumer of coal, the fossil fuel resulting in the most carbon discharged. In fact, 90 percent of all the coal mined in the United States is consumed by power plants. Carbon constraints are a constraint on all fossil fuels, however. Natural gas firing results in less CO_2, two thirds that of an equivalent coal-fired plant, but the discharges are still substantial.

Since 70 percent of the installed electric capacity is fueled by some fossil fuel, the electricity industry is the principal target for those advocating solutions to global warming. We are the *bull's eye* for the policy arrows.

Leaving Our Wealth . . . and Our Waste

There are plenty of ways to reduce and even eliminate carbon dioxide discharges. Let's try to remain practical about it, though, if the objective is to continue supplying reasonably priced electricity to the world. Recall the distinction I made in an earlier chapter about base-load and peak electricity generation. Base-load plants in most parts of the world are predominantly coal and nuclear. It is safe to assume that the choice is how many of each to build.

When it comes to global warming, both options involve a legacy that we're going to hand down to our children, and our grandchildren, and our great grandchildren. When we take the short-term view that many politicians take (when is that next election?), the legacy you and I will be handing off to our descendants may seem as far into the future as our friend Australopithecus is to the past. We can build more nuclear plants. They will run from 40 to 80 years. The relatively small but potent amount of high-level nuclear waste discharged from these plants will have to be managed for thousands of years, while the radiation decays through the half-life cycle.

Or we can build coal plants. The carbon solution everyone is fixated on for coal-fired plants is called sequestration. That means that instead of discharging CO_2 out the tops of smokestacks and into the atmosphere, we're going to "sequester" the gas underground. No one has actually proven that this can be done without massive leaking at some point in the future, although theoretically it seems pretty straightforward. After all, we store natural gas underground. We store petroleum underground in caverns and abandoned salt mines. Carbon dioxide should be even easier since it is a relatively stable and innocuous compound.

But, and this is a big *but*, mankind hasn't done any of this storage for more than a few decades. What if we screw up? What if there's a massive release of carbon dioxide into the atmosphere? Well, for one thing, people, plants, and animals would die because there would be no oxygen at the point of release.

Do you see the dilemma? Whether it's spent nuclear power plant fuel rods, or huge quantities of carbon dioxide, this "exhaust" has to be properly managed for a long, long time. In the scheme of human business or political planning cycles, you might as well concede that the material has to be managed *forever*. Let's be clear about what I'm saying: For electricity producers and consumers, the solutions to global warming for our generation create intended consequences that must be managed *forever*.

This is a huge vulnerability with multiple dimensions. Here are just two issues to consider: What if we sequester all this gas and it springs a leak and we don't know about it? What if the government does build and operate a long-term repository for nuclear fuel rods, and it becomes the singular focus of terrorists? I can tell you emphatically that I haven't heard anyone in the top ranks of the electricity industry, in think tanks or in the environmental movement discussing the implications of these issues. If they are, they are being strangely quiet about it. It used to be that the legacy we dreamt of leaving to our children consisted of our accumulated wealth and dreams of increased opportunities for the future. Now, we can no longer escape thinking about the less savory aspects of our legacy.

Trade You 20 Methane for One CO_2

Everyone, it seems, has a favorite means of arresting global warming. However, no one seems to recognize basic realities.

Let's take natural gas. During the 1990s, natural gas had become "the cure for what ails ya" in the electricity business. There was plenty of it, so it was inexpensive. It is used in more compact machines, so power plants could be made smaller and less obtrusive, and the electricity generated more efficiently. It is largely free of other pollutants, like sulfur and ash. Best of all, from a global warming perspective, natural gas has a lower carbon density than coal. Just take a look at its chemical formulation: CH_4, also known as methane. That means that it produces only one carbon dioxide molecule for each carbon atom and most of the energy is released from oxidizing the hydrogen into harmless water.

This is all well and good at the power plant. But across the natural gas delivery chain, the story is not so positive. Carbon dioxide isn't the only global warming agent in the sky. It isn't even the most potent. Water vapor, interestingly enough, is worse. And methane is worse still. Methane is approximately twenty times more potent as a warming agent. How much methane do you think is released to the atmosphere between the point at which it is extracted from a well and the point at which it reaches the burner at a power plant, or the burner in your furnace at home? Industry estimates vary, but the range appears to be from 2 to 10 percent. One methane molecule escaping into the atmosphere from the pipeline or the well is the equivalent of 20 carbon dioxide molecules from the power plant. Did you get that? Here it is again: $1 \; CH_4 = 20 \; CO_2$. Although natural gas looks good at the plant, over the entire value chain, it doesn't fare nearly as well. It doesn't take much leakage to liquidate a substantial portion of the advantages ascribed to burning gas, with respect to global warming anyway.

Build Three of These for One of Those

Renewable energy enthusiasts have an answer to global warming. Quit burning fossil fuels. Use renewable energy. The problem is that renewable energy sources are also intermittent energy sources.

One of the basic indices of the effectiveness of a power plant is the capacity factor at which it can operate. Capacity factor (CF) is measured as the number of hours in a given time period (week, month, year) that the power plant operated, times the kilowatt per hour rate, divided by the total number of hours in that time period.

Nuclear plants run at 90–100 percent capacity factors and coal plants at 70–90 percent. Gas plants could also run at high capacity factors but are usually intended to run at lower factors because of the high cost of the fuel. The CFs at renewable energy power stations are more like 20–35 percent. Even the best wind energy plants are only expected to deliver their full electricity output only 40 percent of the time.

You would need to build two or even three times as many wind power stations to equal the output of a coal or nuclear plant. The fuel may be "free" but twice as many assets translates into additional costs. Also, the intermittency of the "free fuel" has to be taken into account in other ways. The electricity grid system operates at a near constant 60 Hertz (50 Hz in other countries). Really bad things happen when it doesn't. (That is why we have to use some of the power generating capacity to maintain the grid itself.) To reach that constant frequency, the turbines at the power stations have to spin at near constant speeds. Wind turbines cannot turn at constant speed because they must follow the strength of the wind at any given moment. The strength of solar energy poses the same constraints as the earth rotates around the sun and cloud cover disrupts the energy flow. Making these devices behave properly when sequenced with the electric grid also adds costs.

I'll Gladly Trade You a Carbon for a Hydrogen

It is no wonder that the serious problems with the carbon part of the fuel molecule have people focusing on the hydrogen part. In fact, an entire new approach to producing and delivering electricity has been conceived, and it's called the hydrogen economy. It's been embraced by a lot of people, including President Bush, and it truly represents a wholesale change to energy life as we know it.

On the face of it, it is a beautiful solution to global warming. The gist of transforming ourselves into a hydrogen-based economy is that burning hydrogen results in, simply, the H_2O—water. That's it. End of story.

But where do we get the hydrogen to burn? Ay, dear reader, there's the rub. The quandary here is producing the hydrogen. Hydrogen, of course, can be extracted from fossil fuels; but this liberates the carbon along the way, so we're back to square one. Hydrogen can also be produced through the electrolysis of water. It seems so elegant. Generate electricity, split the water molecule, oxidize the hydrogen, and what you get is water. There are actually two rubs here. For one thing, no one is thinking about what to do with all that oxygen. For another, as we noted earlier, water is a global warming agent itself. Remember, things at small scale become problems at large scale.

Water vapor and oxygen aside, renewable energy enthusiasts see a future in which the electricity needed for the electrolysis to produce the hydrogen comes from solar and wind. The traditionalists in the industry think that nuclear power is a pretty good way to economically generate all the electricity needed to power the brave new hydrogen world.

The point, and the big challenge, is this: Hydrogen is not something, like coal, petroleum, or natural gas, that *comes* from the earth. It has to be produced. And it takes energy to produce. It's more like gasoline. It is an energy *carrier*, not an energy *resource*. But you can see why some experts arrive at hydrogen as the solution to all things carbon. If you just look at the chemical reaction, the chemical equation, you are tempted to say, "Eureka!" But if you consider the implications of the hydrogen value chain, the economics, the sources of hydrogen, the need to create a hydrogen production and delivery infrastructure, and the safety aspects (like storage tanks), your reaction might be more like, "Yikes!"

I gave a presentation to a group at a local university, in which I called the so-called hydrogen economy "the latest energy seduction." The "hydrogen economy" is one of those phrases that causes members of Congress to cough up a lot of R&D funds, and seems to get many different industrial sectors, such as automotive, transportation, electric utility, petroleum, etc., all hot and bothered all at the same time. It's the kind of thing that academics believe can galvanize and sustain funding, like putting a man on the moon, or fighting the Cold War.

Unfortunately, it doesn't make much practical sense. In my view, there are simply too many new technology pieces that are necessary, such as economical hydrogen storage devices for on-board automotive and refueling stations, fuel cell engines that run on hydrogen, and economical large-scale electrolysis facilities. A hydrogen production, delivery, and consumption infrastructure would have to be built from scratch.

Using our electricity infrastructure to make hydrogen to fuel transportation—well, the middle step just seems like a waste. Why not just generate the electricity and develop electric vehicles or transportation networks. Much of the world already has an electricity production and delivery infrastructure. We know how to make electric vehicles. In fact, many of the vehicles at the turn of the last century were electric. Making them practical simply means evolutionary extensions in battery or electric storage capacity and other devices like power electronics inverters to make charging them from the grid a reality. I think it's easier to think in terms of making efficient electric cars, instead of starting from scratch with hydrogen.

We have most of what we need for an electricity economy; we don't for a hydrogen economy. In my view, the "latest energy seduction" is more come on than put out.

The Rest of the Story

I have deliberately focused on global warming and carbon dioxide in this chapter even though power generation involves a host of other environmental issues. The reason is that most of the other impacts have been addressed by technology or are being actively addressed by legislation and technology. Still, they bear mentioning.

Power stations emit huge quantities of sulfur dioxide, nitrogen oxides, and fly ash. However, almost all new large coal-fired power stations worldwide will be built with emissions control devices to handle these pollutants. Many of the existing ones have been, or will soon be, retrofitted with such devices. Smaller coal-fired plants will be phased out of operation, or will switch to less polluting types of coal. An emerging slate of retrofits will handle mercury emissions, another pollutant for which controls are now being mandated. The solid waste discharges from power stations are being adequately managed. Much of the ash can be beneficially recycled into other industries or put back into the mines where the coal came from originally.

Environmentalists, regulators, and industry insiders still fight over these emissions and the costs of control. If these issues are "holes" in the fabric of the industry, at least they are not gaping, expanding holes. Or they are holes that are progressively being sewn up, unlike carbon discharges. In another way of explaining it, how we deal with these emissions will not change the complexion of the industry, the costs or characteristics of our electricity service, or the very nature of the planet on which we live.

Chapter 9

Houston, We Have
a Problem

I n the last chapter, I stated that public sentiment (and clearly an overwhelming majority of the scientific community) believes that global warming is a problem and must be addressed. Once you accept this premise, you next have to extend the line of thought to the consequences of global warming and their impact on the electricity business. Two categories of impacts that need to be addressed are: (1) incremental changes to the environment; and (2) catastrophic weather events.

I have no doubt that, over the next 10 years, the emphasis in the scientific and meteorological communities will be in strengthening the correlation between global warming and extreme weather events. The rise in global carbon levels in the atmosphere was never in doubt; the controversy has always been whether mankind's activities were a principal culprit or whether the rise was mostly due to natural causes that are not within our control. Similarly, no one seems to doubt that the last

10 years has seen a noticeable increase in extreme weather events. The issue is whether global warming is partially or mostly responsible.

You can summarize the recent obsession with this question in one word: Katrina. The brutalization of New Orleans and the sustained imagery of that catastrophe transmitted to the entire world have made thinking people pause. Global warming is thought to have reinforced the conditions that lead to hurricanes in the Atlantic and Gulf coast regions and contributed to warming ocean temperatures and rising sea levels. According to an article in August 2006 *National Geographic* ("Super Storms: No End in Sight" by Thomas Hayden), one prominent scientist now concludes that "during the past three decades, the storms have grown almost twice as destructive." This sentiment has been echoed by others. This period of ever-increasing destructive power of hurricanes, of course, overlaps with a period of relatively rapid rise in carbon concentration in the atmosphere. Whether a scientific correlation is certifiable and whether it points to cause and effect is another matter.

The National Academies' National Research Council and the Committee on Abrupt Climate Change put it this way in a brief based on a 2004 report: "Greenhouse gases such as carbon dioxide are accumulating in the Earth's atmosphere and causing surface air temperatures and subsurface ocean temperatures to rise. These gradual changes, along with other human alterations of the climate system (e.g., land use changes) are producing conditions in the Earth's climate that are outside the range of recent historical experience." The brief stops short of any definitive correlation between global warming and hurricanes, but the implications of one are there.

Again, I don't profess to be a meteorologist, a climatologist, or an oceanographic expert. Many references are available for you to determine on your own whether you think hurricanes in the Gulf, and extreme weather events in general, are on the rise, both in number and power. What I do want people to understand is how this impacts our present and future electricity infrastructure.

Hurricanes and Houston: Imperfect Together

Katrina seriously disrupted the nation's supply of oil and natural gas from the drilling rigs in the Gulf of Mexico. A significant percentage of our domestic natural gas supply comes from the Gulf Coast. Fortunately, the impact on electricity production was minimal. The recent rise in natural gas prices had already made most gas-fired generating capacity too expensive. Unavailability wasn't the issue. The lack of supply from the Gulf was made up for by supply from other areas, like Canada and the western Rockies region.

The broader problem is this: Houston and the Gulf Coast serve as the de facto capital of energy for the United States and the current and proposed energy infrastructure located there is threatened by any rise in extreme weather activity. If plans on the drawing board today come to fruition, the current crop of oil/gas rigs may be the least of our worries.

In other chapters, I have discussed the forecast for massive increases in imports of liquefied natural gas (LNG). Huge new receiving terminals, at my last count more than 40, are being planned up and down the East Coast, the California coast, and along the Gulf Coast. Most are facing protracted permitting delays. Many will not be built because of intense public opposition. However, the one area that is most receptive to these terminals is the Gulf Coast.

This is a logical place to site such terminals if for no other reason than many of the gas pipelines that will be required to move this fuel inland already originate in this area. But the receptivity to this development goes deeper. From the wildcatting days of the Texas oil men, to the natural-gas producing wells of today, there are entrenched beneficiaries of energy development in Texas, Louisiana, and the Gulf region. The region already exhibits a profound concentration of petrochemical processing facilities; LNG receiving, processing, and pipelining is simply a natural extension.

Few readers will likely understand why I am now going to bring wind energy into this volatile mixture of rising extreme weather events and energy infrastructure concentration. But, it fits and here's why: Texas just surpassed California as the state with the highest amount of wind-generated electricity. Most of this capacity is currently located in the arid region of west Texas. However, wind-generated electricity has an increasingly exciting future in Texas and many regard the next frontier as, you guessed it, offshore in the Gulf of Mexico.

If you extrapolate out 20 years, it becomes apparent that the Gulf Coast could be home to a significant fraction of the nation's petroleum-based products (e.g., gasoline, diesel fuel, jet fuel, etc.), natural gas supply, and wind-generated electricity. Meanwhile, if the relationship between global warming and hurricanes that ravage the Gulf Coast is established unambiguously, then our energy future is in even greater jeopardy. Now, when you're talking wind energy, you certainly prefer to site your turbines in the highest wind areas. Most developers, however, are interested in wind speeds of about 40 to 60 mph, not 175 mph. (As a Category 5 storm, Katrina reached sustained wind speeds of 175 mph as she approached the Gulf Coast.)

Talk about a vicious cycle! Electricity demand leads to high carbon levels in the atmosphere leads to rising temperatures leads to more numerous hurricanes leads to the unavailability of those electricity generating options that limit carbon discharges (wind and to a much lesser extent, gas-fired power). Plus, when the electricity from power plants equipped with emissions control devices isn't available, everyone not willing to hunker down and wait it out runs to The Home Depot to get their hands on a backup generator. So those who can crank up a diesel or gas-fired generator, which generate uncontrolled emissions, just aggravate the problem.

To add insult to injury, most electricity service outages are caused by, you guessed it, violent storms that pass through and destroy transmission lines and distribution feeders. It seems reasonable to assume that if extreme weather events are going to be more frequent, then electricity service disruptions will be, too.

Yes, Houston, we do have a problem!

Or do we? Maybe global warming creates new and stronger wind patterns that could be exploited with new technologies to increase the production of electricity. If we had to struggle through more frequent blackouts, would we learn to live with it and simply consume less electricity? Higher frequency of hurricanes could be just the thing to force this country to install more electricity storage assets, which would go a long way toward keeping the lights on during extreme weather events.

The August 2006 *National Geographic* article quoted earlier has a figure that blew me away. An average hurricane apparently contains the energy equivalent in its winds of half the world's entire electrical generating capacity. We need to get some robust spinning turbine/generators in those winds, capture the energy, and store it as electricity! Well, that's clearly a pipe dream, but you get the point. There are effects from these extreme weather events that we haven't even begun thinking about.

How we manage extreme weather events could define our electricity needs for decades to come. But it's like that admonition about the stock market: Past performance is no guarantee of future success. Everyone seems to agree that the period from 1995 to today brought a serious uptick in hurricane activity and subsequent destruction, death, and disaster. But as scientist Gary Bell of the National Oceanographic and Atmospheric Administration (NOAA) is quoted in the *National Geographic* article, "We're 11 years into the cycle of high activity and landfall, but I can't tell you if it will last another 10 or 30."

Other Industries Are Bringing Their Umbrellas

Whether the science is definitive or not, the insurance industry, and by extension the financial services industry, is taking global warming-induced extreme weather events more seriously than the electricity industry, based on what I've read. One new twist in the whole discussion of global warming is the arrival of a corps of sharp-penciled financiers. Bankers, insurers, and institutional investors have begun to tally the trillions of dollars in financial risks that climate change poses."

One thing I do know for sure: When Wall Street talks, Main Street electric utilities listen! What Wall Street is saying right now is, in fact, "Houston, we have a problem and New York no longer is going to sit back while you ignore it."

Insurance firms certainly agree on one thing: Insured losses from catastrophic weather events have already increased 15-fold in the past 30 years. Many of them apparently also believe that more is needed to explain the phenomenon than surging development along coastlines and other vulnerable areas. The article goes on to say that the investment community is actively pushing energy companies, and energy intensive industries, to think about greenhouse gases as a material risk, much like other financial risks that threaten future earnings. Maybe there's a direct cause and effect correlation between recognition of the financial risk of global warming and the looming lack of insurance companies willing to underwrite policies on the beach houses in the Hamptons owned by Manhattan-based financiers.

Let's face it. Electric utilities and multinational corporations have gotten on the global warming bandwagon because of two basic issues:

Investors and other stakeholders see it as a serious financial risk, and the companies see that addressing the issue can either reduce costs or increase revenues. It's become a bottom-line issue, and when something affects both sides of the ledger, management ends to get more serious. And it makes for good PR to boot.

Change by a Thousand Blips

Extreme weather events are one thing. Incremental perturbations, whose effects accumulate over time, are another. The most (and probably the only) reliable predictor of electricity consumption day to day and season to season is the weather. Of course, a real wag would comment, "well, no one can predict the weather, so no one can forecast electricity demand." Still, if we know the planet is gradually getting warmer (regardless of how or why); this alone has grave consequences for electricity infrastructure.

First of all, it might be logical to assume that air-conditioning-related electricity demand will rise. Correspondingly, so-called daily peak demand (explained in other chapter) increases, which is normally met with natural-gas-fired power plant assets. Increasing natural gas consumption further pressures the infrastructure in Houston. Houston's problem is aggravated.

Second, water supply and rainfall patterns are expected to change. Most of today's power stations are huge consumers of water, primarily used for condensing steam at the end of the power generation cycle (so the cycle can begin again). The overall water balance doesn't change because most of the cooling water is discharged back to the body of water it was taken from. Some of the water is discharged as moisture to the atmosphere through a cooling tower. Power plants don't consume water, but displace water between the land and the air. If water supply patterns changed abruptly, some power stations would be limited in their electricity output, or may have to shut down completely.

Hydroelectric power is the oldest form of electricity generation in the modern age. In this country, close to 10 percent of our electricity still comes from flowing water. In Brazil, hydroelectricity accounts for up to 90 percent of electricity production. Would our percentage of hydroelectric generation increase or decrease with global warming?

I don't have an answer, but wherever it decreases, presumably it would have to be replaced by another form of generation.

But Can We Make Money from It?

A principal reason why business doesn't mind listening to the investor class on global warming is that financial incentives are being introduced that make the lecture more palatable. Europe has already instituted an elaborate system of carbon credits, which are traded like any other fungible commodity. This mechanism sets a value on a ton of carbon dioxide equivalent, a value that the "marketplace" updates continuously through trading, like stocks and bonds. Such a carbon trading system is emerging in this country as well, although without federal intervention it will probably not be fully realized.

So far, the system is proceeding on a state and regional basis. In the Northeast, for example, *the Regional Greenhouse Gas Initiative* (RGGI) is implementing what is known as a "cap and trade" program. The carbon emissions of power plants, electric utilities, and other industrial sites are set at a limit, and each source is allotted a certain number of "credits." Then, these sources can opt to reduce carbon discharges, creating additional credits, which can then be bought, sold, or retained. Companies can conduct financial evaluations and determine whether it is better to buy credits to cover carbon emissions or reduce carbon discharges and retain or sell the resulting credits.

Successful emissions cap and trade programs have been put in place for other emissions, notably sulfur dioxide and oxides of nitrogen. There's every reason to believe that the same concepts can work for carbon.

If It's a Problem Now, Wait Until Asia Is Fully Cranked Up

If you've seen the computer simulations of what might happen to New York City under a business-as-usual global warming scenario, it may come as little surprise that Wall Street is pounding the gavel, with or without the financial lubricant of carbon credits. Much of Wall Street could be submerged in a few decades, making it the Venice of the United States. Unfortunately, Wall Street has less influence over Asia, because that's where the global warming problems really need to be addressed.

While the United States is considering a renewed love affair with coal, Asia has found its bride for economic prosperity. According to the International Energy Agency (IEA), in an article published in *Natural History* "Cooking the Climate with Coal," by Jeff Goodell, May 2006, the world is planning to build 1,350 GW (each gigawatt is 1,000 megawatts) of new coal-fired power stations by year 2030. Around 40 percent of these power plants will be in China and 10 percent in India. China, by some accounts, is installing a major new coal-fired power generating unit every week! For perspective, 1,350 GW is approximately the sum total of *all* the electricity generating capacity in the United States *and China* at present.

If the planet's atmosphere has been getting rich in carbon over the last 30 years, it ain't seen nothin' yet.

In the computer models, the flooding of Wall Street starts to occur when the total warming of the planet reaches or exceeds 3.5 degrees Fahrenheit. The *Natural History* article argues that we're two-thirds of the way there. Compared to preindustrial levels, the atmosphere has already warmed 1 degree Fahrenheit and another degree of warming is stored in the oceans. The article doesn't go to the logical conclusion, but it seems safe to assume that if we add the amount of coal-fired power planned, then the atmosphere will likely pick up the extra degrees Fahrenheit it needs to exert major damage to our present way of life. What the article does say is the additional 1,350 GW of coal will add as much CO_2 to the atmosphere "as was released by all the coal burned by everyone for every purpose during the past 250 years."

Keep in mind that the issue isn't that we're building all these nasty coal plants. The issue is that we're building all these plants with complete disregard for the carbon discharges. There are potential solutions that we review in later chapters.

Chapter 10

The Impact of Lengthening Supply Lines

How Elastic Are They?

Sixty percent of this country's petroleum is imported. Very little petroleum is consumed at power stations. Only 2 percent of our electricity generation is fueled by oil. Therefore, global petroleum markets have little or no impact on electricity production, right?

Wrong.

In other countries, both natural gas and petroleum are used for power generation, and they compete fiercely in industries such as chemicals and petrochemicals. Thus, there tends to be price correlation between the two energy sources: When petroleum prices rise, natural gas prices (both can be used as feedstocks to a variety of industrial processes) tend to rise as well, which puts pressure on pricing for all energy sources. Most rail lines that ship coal are powered by diesel engines, so increases in petroleum prices increase the costs for coal. When imported fuel costs rise, prices of less desirable fuels like coal also begin to rise, because people believe coal can act as a substitute source of energy (which it can't, at least not very easily).

The vulnerability of our lengthening supply lines really takes shape when you consider that this country is expected to be importing up to 25 percent of its natural gas, in the form of liquefied natural gas (LNG), by the year 2020. This, according to seasoned energy experts, is an astonishing figure at a time when politicians of all stripes are rallying around the cry for "energy independence."

It would be convenient politically, perhaps, if the issue of lengthening supply lines affected only energy imports. Unfortunately, we're shipping coal inside the country greater and greater distances, too. As we learned earlier in this book, much of the coal burned at United States power stations originates in the huge Powder River Basin reserves in Wyoming, destined for plants as far away as Georgia and New York.

In some cases, the lengthening supply line is actually a transmission line. If we want to achieve an oft-stated goal of having 20 percent of the country's electricity met by renewable energy within the next two decades, then we'll have to build vast wind farms in remote parts of the country, where wind energy is strongest, and ship the power to population centers.

Lengthening supply lines affects nuclear power as well. The fuel for nuclear plants is derived from naturally occurring uranium sources primarily in Canada and Australia, but a significant fraction of it originates in Russia (nuclear supply lines are reviewed in Chapter 15).

Recall our production and delivery value chain illustration in Figure 2.2 in Chapter 2. The energy measured at the electric meter on the back of your home probably originates thousands of miles away. It may have crossed the country by railroad or pipeline. It may soon cross the ocean by LNG tanker. It may have buzzed down a long transmission line, or crossed through multiple electricity market jurisdictions.

The questions all of us have to ask are these: How elastic are these supply lines? How strong are they? As they stretch, do they behave like a rubber band? If so, where is the snapping point? Given a "global war on terror," how safe are the supply lines, especially those like the international shipping lanes needed for LNG? How well are they protected and at what cost? How reliable is the freight rail network in this country? The rest of this chapter tries to provide some answers.

LNG—As in, Let's Not Go (There)

I'll be blunt about what I think of LNG supply lines. I think we're nuts to allow a repeat of our experience with petroleum imports, especially since it is unnecessary. If we need natural gas to that degree, we have it right here it at home. We can exploit our naturally occurring gas reserves, of which we have a great deal, or we can find other ways to generate electricity.

The relative quantities of each energy source we'll need for electricity generation is dynamic. Currently, LNG imports make up a small but growing fraction of our natural gas demand (see Figure 10.1). As recently as five years ago, it amounted to only around 2 percent of the total. Today, it is more like 4 to 5 percent. The Energy Information Administration

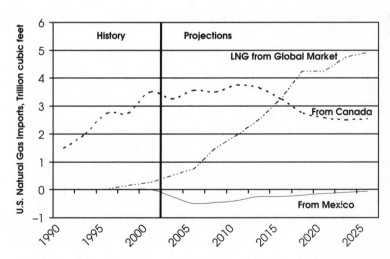

Figure 10.1 LNG imports are expected to escalate over the next two decades.
SOURCE: Energy Information Administration, Annual Energy Outlook 2004, Reference Case.

(EIA), an independent government clearinghouse of energy statistics and forecasts, estimates that the United States could be importing 25 percent of its gas supply as LNG within two decades. More than half of this will likely be used to produce electricity.

The implications of LNG imports for our electricity infrastructure are profound. Natural gas-fired power generation makes up almost 35 percent of our electric generation capability. However, because natural gas prices have been so high for the last few years, gas-fired generation makes up only around 15 percent of the actual power generated (in other words, the gas-fired plants do not run very often).

To import these vast quantities of LNG, the industry is planning to build dozens of facilities along the coasts that convert the lique-fied fuel back into a gas, then shove it into a pipeline for shipment to power stations and other users (Figure 10.2). Most of these facilities will be concentrated around Houston and the Gulf Coast. Only a few of these terminals are under construction because permitting is difficult and protests by local communities are often vociferous.

From geopolitical and national security perspectives, massive LNG imports are ironic in a tragicomic sort of way. Remember the headlines when a British subsidiary of a Dubai-owned company was about to "take control" of several U.S. container ports? Most of our LNG imports originate from similar locations.

Let's face it, the two countries reported to have the largest natural gas holdings (and therefore the greatest potential to export) are Iran and Russia. The former is as close to a sworn enemy of the United States as can be, and the latter, well, we've been trying to figure out how to deal with that country in a post–Cold War way since the Berlin Wall fell in 1989. It's true that countries friendly to us also have significant quantities of natural gas to export: Qatar, Trinidad, and Tobago are examples. Given the percentages forecasted, however, it is likely that we'll have to expand our dealings with hostile or unfriendly suppliers of a key fuel for electricity generation. Although Russia is the undisputed king when it comes to natural gas reserves, 75 percent of the world's proven reserves are said to be located in the Middle East.

If geopolitical aspects are unsettling, then safety considerations are ominous. LNG tankers are often described as floating bombs. LNG is explosive and flammable. As long as the material stays a liquid and is

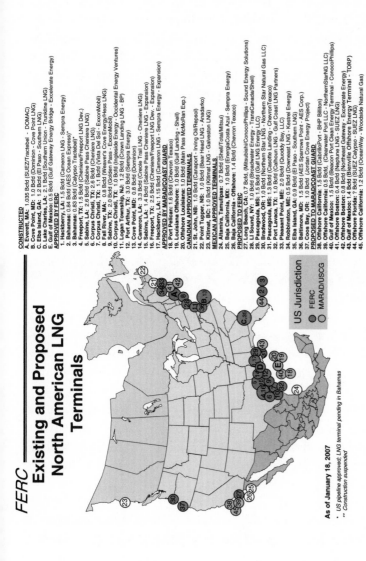

FERC
Existing and Proposed North American LNG Terminals

As of January 18, 2007

* US pipeline approved; LNG terminal pending in Bahamas
** Construction suspended

US Jurisdiction
- FERC
- MARAD/USCG

CONSTRUCTED
A. Everett, MA: 1.035 Bcfd (SUEZ/Tractebel - DOMAC)
B. Cove Point, MD: 1.0 Bcfd (Dominion - Cove Point LNG)
C. Elba Island, GA: 1.2 Bcfd (El Paso - Southern LNG)
D. Lake Charles, LA: 2.1 Bcfd (Southern Union - Trunkline LNG)
E. Gulf of Mexico: 0.5 Bcfd (Gulf Gateway Energy Bridge - Excelerate Energy)

APPROVED BY FERC
1. Hackberry, LA: 1.5 Bcfd (Cameron LNG - Sempra Energy)
2. Bahamas: 0.84 Bcfd (AES Ocean Express)*
3. Bahamas: 0.83 Bcfd (Calypso Tractebel)*
4. Freeport, TX: 1.5 Bcfd (Cheniere/Freeport LNG Dev.)
5. Sabine, LA: 2.6 Bcfd (Sabine Pass Cheniere LNG)
6. Corpus Christi, TX: 2.6 Bcfd (Cheniere LNG)
7. Corpus Christi, TX: 1.1 Bcfd (Vista Del Sol - ExxonMobil)
8. Fall River, MA: 0.8 Bcfd (Weaver's Cove Energy/Hess LNG)
9. Sabine, TX: 2.0 Bcfd (Golden Pass - ExxonMobil)
10. Corpus Christi, TX: 1.0 Bcfd (Ingleside Energy - Occidental Energy Ventures)
11. Logan Township, NJ: 1.2 Bcfd (Crown Landing LNG - BP)
12. Port Arthur, TX: 3.0 Bcfd (Sempra Energy)
13. Cove Point, MD: 0.8 Bcfd (Dominion)
14. Cameron, LA: 3.3 Bcfd (Creole Trail LNG - Cheniere LNG)
15. Sabine, LA: 1.4 Bcfd (Sabine Pass Cheniere LNG - Expansion)
16. Freeport, TX: 2.5 Bcfd (Cheniere/Freeport LNG Dev. - Expansion)
17. Hackberry, LA: 1.15 Bcfd (Cameron LNG - Sempra Energy - Expansion)

APPROVED BY MARAD/COAST GUARD
18. Port Pelican: 1.6 Bcfd (Chevron Texaco)
19. Louisiana Offshore: 1.0 Bcfd (Gulf Landing - Shell)
20. Offshore Louisiana: 1.0 Bcfd (Main Pass McMoRan Exp.)

CANADIAN APPROVED TERMINALS
21. St. John, NB: 1.0 Bcfd (Canaport - Irving Oil/Repsol)
22. Point Tupper, NS: 1.0 Bcfd (Bear Head LNG - Anadarko)
23. Kitimat, BC: 1.0 Bcfd (Kitimat LNG - Galveston LNG)

MEXICAN APPROVED TERMINALS
24. Altamira, Tamulipas: 0.7 Bcfd (Shell/Total/Mitsui)
25. Baja California, MX: 1.0 Bcfd (Energia/Costa Azul - Sempra Energy)
26. Baja California - Offshore: 1.4 Bcfd (Chevron Texaco)

PROPOSED TO FERC
27. Long Beach, CA: 0.7 Bcfd, (Mitsubishi/ConocoPhillips - Sound Energy Solutions)
28. LI Sound, NY: 1.0 Bcfd (Broadwater Energy - TransCanada/Shell)
29. Pascagoula, MS: 1.5 Bcfd (Gulf LNG Energy LLC)
30. Bradwood, OR: 1.0 Bcfd (Northern Star LNG - Northern Star Natural Gas LLC)
31. Pascagoula, MS: 1.3 Bcfd (Casotte Landing - ChevronTexaco)
32. Port Lavaca, TX: 1.0 Bcfd (Calhoun LNG - Gulf Coast LNG Partners)
33. Pleasant Point, ME: 2.0 Bcfd (Quoddy Bay, LLC)
34. Robbinston, ME: 0.5 Bcfd (Downeast LNG - Kestrel Energy)
35. Elba Island, GA: 0.9 Bcfd (El Paso - Southern LNG)
36. Baltimore, MD: 1.5 Bcfd (AES Sparrows Point - AES Corp.)
37. Coos Bay, OR: 1.0 Bcfd (Jordan Cove Energy Project)

PROPOSED TO MARAD/COAST GUARD
38. Offshore California: 1.5 Bcfd (CabrilloPort - BHP Billiton)
39. Offshore California: 0.5 Bcfd, (Clearwater Port LLC - NorthernStarNG LLC)
40. Gulf of Mexico: 1.5 Bcfd (Beacon Port Clean Energy Terminal - ConocoPhillips)
41. Offshore Boston: 0.4 Bcfd (Neptune LNG - SUEZ LNG)
42. Offshore Boston: 0.8 Bcfd (Northeast Gateway - Excelerate Energy)
43. Gulf of Mexico: 1.4 Bcfd (Bienville Offshore Energy Terminal - TORP)
44. Offshore Florida: ? Bcfd (SUEZ Calypso - SUEZ LNG)
45. Offshore California: 1.2 Bcfd (OceanWay - Woodside Natural Gas)

Office of Energy Projects

Figure 10.2 Planned LNG terminals connecting foreign gas supply with the U.S. gas pipeline network.
SOURCE: Federal Energy Regulatory Commission.

contained, it is not flammable. If the storage container or pipes carrying the material are breached, the gas will ignite upon exposure to air. Although the industry has a remarkable safety record, given the dangers of the cargo, the issue now is an intentional terrorist attack, not an accidental mishap from human error or negligence.

The most important question is, perhaps, why take either political or safety risks when natural gas is available domestically? There's probably no better place than *CERA Week*, the premier annual confab of energy industry executives, to get a handle on the prospects for LNG imports. This meeting is sponsored by Massachusetts-based Cambridge Energy Research Associates and held in Houston in February. The CERA Week I attended in 2006 made it clear that there is plenty of natural gas right here in our backyard. More than one expert at the conference noted that the cost for extracting this energy and bringing it to market is similar to the cost for importing LNG. Why subject our electricity infrastructure to unnecessary political risk and additional safety risks? The problem boils down to social and environmental issues. Communities oppose the extraction of raw materials in areas like the Rocky Mountains or Alaska, and they oppose the construction of new pipelines.

At some point, people have to make a choice, in this case between national security and greater energy independence or retaining in a pristine condition the acreage where vast domestic sources of natural gas are located. When you understand the extent to which the supply lines are stretched to produce electricity (Figure 10.3), maybe the choice becomes clearer.

Other LNG-related issues include whether or not the quality of imported gas will meet the specifications of the power stations for which it is destined, and the need to substantially expand the nation's gas pipeline infrastructure to move the fuel from the coastal receiving terminals to inland power plants and other consumers.

The Powder River Basin—It's Not a Ski Resort!

Often, trends in this industry seem to move in see-saw fashion: up and down, up and down, with no apparent progress being made. In the 1980s, for example, a large number of power plants switched from burning oil to

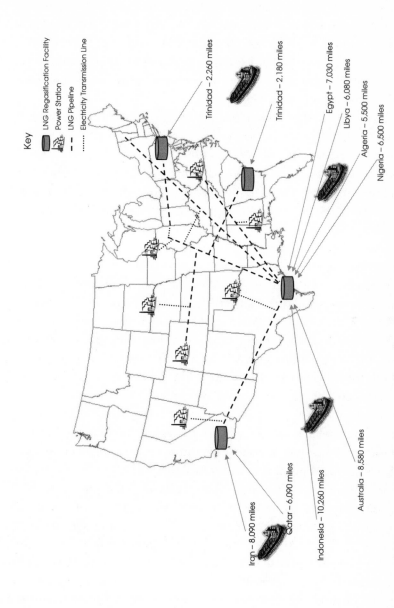

Figure 10.3 Electricity "supply lines" stretch by thousands of miles when LNG is used for fuel.

Key

LNG Regasification Facility
Power Station
LNG Pipeline
Electricity Transmission Line

Trinidad – 2,260 miles
Trinidad – 2,180 miles
Egypt – 7,030 miles
Libya – 6,080 miles
Algeria – 5,500 miles
Nigeria – 6,500 miles
Iran – 8,090 miles
Qatar – 6,090 miles
Indonesia – 10,260 miles
Australia – 8,580 miles

burning coal because the price of oil became too high. Then the plants switched from coal to natural gas because of environmental restrictions.

Over the last 10 years, many coal-fired power stations switched to a low-sulfur coal available from a vast mine and reserve known as the Powder River Basin (PRB) in Wyoming. This is an energy source that is relatively cheap to mine but expensive to transport. In fact, more than two-thirds of the cost of a typical trainload of PRB coal goes to the railroad company, not the coal supplier.

In many ways, this switch has proven to be a Faustian bargain. Plants managed to postpone the cost of expensive pollution controls, but usually this coal has less energy content than the coal it replaced, and more pollutants that were not as tightly regulated at the time. In fact, the reason why the coal has less energy is because it contains more water—roughly 30 percent of the material is water. So, put two and two together. We're paying to transport huge quantities of water that eventually end up as water vapor (also a global warming gas, by the way) discharged through the power plant smokestacks.

The tonnage of the coal—and the water—is impressive. In *Coal: America's Energy Future,* the National Coal Association reports that in 1990 (the year the Clean Air Act Amendments were enacted) shipments of PRB coal were 200 million tons. By 2004, they had more than doubled, to 420 million tons. In 1970, PRB production was a mere 10 million tons. Have you ever waited at a railroad crossing for a coal unit train to go by? That represents around 10,000 tons of coal. Each year, more than 40,000 unit trains carrying PRB coal move around the country. The diesel fuel to power those trains also represents a significant energy impact. Look at it this way: One third of that diesel fuel is moving water because one third of the load is moisture in the coal!

PRB coal supply has not only greatly extended the supply lines for U.S. power stations, it has reduced the efficiency of the plants that burn it and causes them to run in a *derated* condition, meaning that the plant cannot achieve the electricity output it was designed for. It is common knowledge in the industry that the freight rail system is strained trying to accommodate the demand for PRB coal, and some coal-fired plants are having difficulty maintaining adequate inventory of coal at the plant site. Coal shipments now account for more than 40 percent of the nation's railroad freight by tonnage; 58 percent of the coal-fired power stations in the United States are fed only by rail lines, 12 percent by rail and another mode of transportation (truck, barge).

The larger point I am making is that the electricity you enjoy at your home or business is dependent on a vast infrastructure: railroads in the case of coal, pipelines in the case of natural gas, and pipelines and ocean tankers in the case of LNG. All in all, it is apparent that there are key energy and environmental impacts avoided—many of them delineated in Chapter 14—when you closely couple a power station to its source of coal. To me, that means whenever possible, locate a power station adjacent to the mine (Figure 10.4) and shipping the coal "by wire."

The other point I want to stress is that the supply lines for coal were greatly extended for one reason: reduction of sulfur. Better decisions could surely have been made if the other impacts described here had more "value" to utility executives, and the electricity consuming public. Short-term economic gain is often long-term pain in other important areas.

Perhaps there may be a silver lining here. Recent changes to the emissions laws for coal-fired power stations mean that many large coal-fired plants could switch *back* to sources of coal that are located closer to them. Many large coal-fired plants east of the Mississippi are adding highly efficient flue-gas desulfurization units that remove up to 98 percent of the sulfur dioxide. That means they can source coal from eastern mines, once abandoned because the coal's sulfur content was too high.

Shrink Supply Lines and Reduce Environmental Footprint

Lengthening supply lines are not a good thing. Importing LNG contravenes the whole notion of reducing our dependence on global energy sources, and the environmental impacts of this practice. Shipping a low-quality coal thousands of miles involves energy and environmental impacts that could be avoided with a more holistic approach to environmental regulation. Building long transmission lines to carry electricity from wind farms that may only operate one third of the time doesn't make good investment sense.

Key

Mine-mouth coal plant
Transmission line

Figure 10.4 Mine–mouth coal plants shrink supply lines and avoid specialization risks.

At some point, U.S. citizens must acknowledge that if we're going to continue consuming energy the way we do, it might be best to extract the energy as close as possible to where it is consumed. Mine-mouth coal plants are one part of that solution, especially when they are designed with the principles of industrial ecology in mind, which we review in Chapter 14. As a prelude, perhaps the fundamental premise of industrial ecology, at least the way I see it, is that everything we use begins and ends with the earth. As we'll see, a coal-fired power plant can anchor an industrial park—with tenants who can profitably use the material remaining after coal combustion that would otherwise be a waste destined for a landfill.

Another way to shrink supply lines is to promote energy (and especially electricity) intensive manufacturing where the energy is least expensive. In earlier decades, large aluminum production facilities were located in places such as the Pacific Northwest, where very low-cost hydroelectric plants operate. Is it not conceivable that we could similarly locate manufacturing in places like North Dakota, in conjunction with the development of the state's vast wind resources? Good-paying jobs usually attract people.

Close-coupling power plants lowers security risks, reduces our environmental footprint, and allows us more control over our energy destiny.

Part Three

FIGHTING "THE LAST WAR," PLANNING THE NEXT ONE

Hopefully, you are now convinced that our electricity infrastructure is threatened by some combination of insecurities and vulnerabilities. Next, you want to know what the executives of the nation's largest industry are doing to address them. I wish I could report that they are on top of the problem and that everything is under control. But they aren't.

Even as supply lines increase for everything from fuel to labor, the industry seems to be fighting the last war, not the next one. On the precipice of a new construction cycle for coal or nuclear plants, the industry and its regulators have no long-term solutions for high-level nuclear waste or carbon dioxide discharges.

In this part, I'm going to convey the strange sense of déjà vu that I feel. The industry's leaders appear like a collection of retired generals busy reliving the last war. They are planning, permitting, and building a new fleet of coal and nuclear power plants that, with few exceptions, look eerily like the current fleet. They are trying to achieve economies of scale through mergers and acquisitions. Just five years ago, they eschewed assistance from the federal government because the industry was going competitive; today, they ask the government to provide subsidies and financial guarantees. They want to build the infrastructure under the old "regulated rate of return" financial model: We build and buy, you (public utility commission) guarantee our rate of return on invested capital through the electricity rates set for the consumer. Or guarantee us a predictable revenue stream through a long-term purchase agreement with a distribution utility or other user. What has changed? Well, as we saw in the last chapter, not much at all.

That's a shame, because there are numerous elements of a modern electricity system that are being ignored, or not pursued as vigorously as they should be. Technologies that have been developed over decades that could rescue us from the current path sit on the shelves. Some of these are even incentivized through the recent energy bill, but don't have the glamour or the stature of building another large power station.

This part also takes a closer look at what these elements are. In the final chapter, I show how they can be intelligently pieced together in a strategic plan for the "next war."

Chapter 11

It's That '70s Show

L isten to the electricity industry's executives, read the trade journals, or even just pay close attention to articles in the newspapers. You'll witness common refrains:

1. "I feel like we're back in the 1970s."
2. "Prospects haven't been this good since the 1970s."
3. "The last time we talked about new nuclear units was the 1970s."
4. "We haven't planned a base-load generation capacity construction program since the 1970s."

And so on. In fact, you could modify the refrain of that popular song by Prince: "Party like its 1969!" because a wonderful era like the early 1970s is just around the corner.

In fact, this '70s show applies to the energy business as a whole today. The last rapid escalation and sustained high prices for petroleum and natural gas occurred during that decade. In a related way, that decade was the last time the "markets" truly reflected the threat of global energy supply lines being severed because of geopolitical events, primarily focused around the Persian Gulf and Middle East. Actually, those supply lines *were* severed, as a result of embargoes imposed by the *Organization of Petroleum Exporting Countries* (OPEC). For those yearning for the go-go '70s, hearken back to those even-numbered days in 1973 when cars with odd-numbered license plates could just forget about filling the tank, or those lazy days in '79 when some experts estimate Americans wasted about 150,000 barrels of oil each day as car engines idled in gas station lines.

It is worthwhile remembering some other characteristics of that decade. It was indeed a happening time for the energy business. Nixon imposed price controls during the 1973 oil crisis and Carter proposed removing them during the 1979 oil crisis, during which he also argued that the crisis was the "the moral equivalent of war." It was also during this period that the economy hit the skids, at least compared to the prior two decades. It seemed a genuine recession or a recessionary mood, a malaise if you will, engulfed the economy. Persistent inflation was certainly one of the factors at the root of the economic "malaise." Second, by the early part of the decade, the end of the constant reductions in electricity costs, and therefore prices to consumers, became clear. In short, it was a bad decade for consumers and ratepayers, but a decade of extraordinary revenues and profits for energy companies. Kind of like today.

Of course, as you know now, the electricity business has a player that other aspects of the energy business do not: the regulator. Today, even electricity regulators want to party like it's 1969. Across the country, the trend is to recede, retract from competition, and reregulate the industry. Even states that pushed competition and deregulation the farthest appear to be moving backward in time.

Some of the rhetoric is astounding. In Illinois, for example, regulators pursued competition in the late 1990s by imposing rate reductions and freezing them for a full decade. Today, some legislators in that state are calling for an extension of the rate freeze. On November 28, 2006, the *Chicago Tribune* published an editorial by Michael R. Peevey, president of the California Public Utilities Commission, discussing the proposed extension and offering some advice to his friends in Illinois: "Don't do it!"

Indeed, it is economic suicide given that, like most areas of the country, Illinois needs new power stations, new transmission lines, upgraded distribution equipment, and costs for fuel to power those generating plants have escalated substantially. How are electricity companies to make any money under persistent rate freezes?

One thing Illinois and other state politicians might do well to remember: The "regulatory compact" is gone. In the 1970s, and before, the industry's financial structure was based on the fundamental trade-off between a utility's "obligation to serve" and a monopoly franchise within its service territory. Today, electricity generating companies can behave more like insurance companies. If they don't like the way a state regulates the industry, they can leave. When the insurance industry did exactly that some years ago, some states had to institute what was known as the "risk pool." Hard-to-insure drivers, for example, or drivers with no record had to buy insurance at exorbitant sums backed by the state. I know. I was one of the drivers with no record after I moved to Pennsylvania from Manhattan, where I hadn't owned a car for over eight years.

Back to Basics

The electric utilities' response for recovery from the meltdown of 2001, also called *Enronitis* to deflect responsibility, was a program called "back to basics." For the utility executive herd, "back to basics" became the mantra uttered by the C-level gang to show its stock and bond holders that they had a strategy to become profitable once again. The strategy could be described in many ways, but here are a few simplified explanations.

Sell What We Just Bought

First and foremost, the strategy meant rebalancing the split between the electricity company's unregulated and regulated businesses. The latter was to become the utility's core competency, the raison d'etre, the focal point of the business. Unregulated subsidiaries would be sold, and the losses written down or written off. This restructuring could be paraphrased to mean that utilities were no longer growth-oriented. Another euphemism was that the business was going to become "predictable" once again. Utilities were traditionally known for their predictable, dividend-producing financial structures and pledged now to return to that way of life.

Funny, many of these assets and businesses were bought only a few years ago. Remember what I wrote earlier about transactions around the balance sheet. From a balance sheet perspective, the idea was to reduce debt. Debt is good if you are borrowing money to grow. It's bad if you aren't growing as fast you said you could to pay off the debts.

The execution of this strategy simply meant that the utility would sell off all of the divisions and businesses it was encouraged to buy or organically grow in the 1990s. For most of them, these businesses were the international project development, operations, and/or ownership of utility assets in other countries; electricity, natural gas, and energy trading and marketing operations; and natural gas extraction, collection, transmission, and distribution. Gas utilities bought into electric properties; electric utilities bought gas. Then they sold them.

Electric utilities that pursued what was known as the "convergence" strategy in the 1990s, generally regarded as an integration of the electricity and natural gas businesses, have spent the last five years pursuing a "divergence" strategy, selling off the natural gas assets. Instead of "what goes up must come down," the strategy seems to be "what gets bought must get sold." Electric utilities that pursued an international strategy would retreat to a national strategy, those pursuing a national strategy would retreat to a regional strategy, those with a regional strategy would resort to a local one. It's serious contraction action. Well, you get the point.

The operative word in the electricity company lexicon is *footprint*. A footprint can be geographic—or it can represent more diverse activities across the production and delivery value chain. A few utilities were enlarging their distribution footprint by developing and selling distributed power systems in deregulated markets. In some cases, this included even buying up electric service companies that refurbish, repair, and build electric systems on the other side of the utility's meter at a customer site.

So, however it was that electricity industry companies were *expanding* in the late 1990s, for the most part they have *contracted* in the period 2001 to the present. If a utility didn't get carried away and expanded relatively slowly, then it simply stopped expanding. That's what back to basics meant. But back to basics is over.

If We Build It, Wall Street Will Come

Utilities today are going to Wall Street with essentially two strategies: The first is the "if we build it, you will come" strategy. It is reminiscent of an earlier time.

The best example of the "build it" strategy is a Texas company called TXU Corp. This utility wasn't much higher up in the credibility ratings than Enron back in 2001. It had bought utilities in the United Kingdom and had a major growth strategy for Europe. Post-Enron, TXU also had an excess of financial shenanigans it had to explain. Its stock was pummeled by shareholders and regulators alike, but it didn't get thrown into the grave like Enron. Over the last two years, TXU has been an undisputed darling of Wall Street. As this manuscript went to press, two private equity groups had proposed an acquisition of TXU, taking it private.

What happened? It executed its "back to basics" strategy, which might also be termed a "back from the edge of the grave" strategy. But then it was also one of the first electricity companies to sense that the mood had changed on Wall Street, and that it could talk about "growth" again.

In 2005, TXU announced that it would embark on what could only be described as a massive—and fatally flawed—construction program. The company planned to build more than 10,000 MW of new generating capacity, mostly traditional coal-fired plants but also a few nuclear units. Except for additional environmental controls attached to the back, these coal plants are little different from the ones the industry built in the 1970s that have been retrofitted with the same updated environmental controls.

The size of this construction program has to be put in perspective. First of all, at the cost TXU had indicated of $1,100/kW, this is a $10 billion capital campaign over a 10-year period. At the cost other rational experts have pegged for such coal plants, more like $1,500 to 2,000/kW, the total capital campaign could be double what TXU is forecasting.

This is a construction program suited for economic growth in a place like China. Not since the late 1990s has the United States industry witnessed an electricity company so boldly proclaim such capacity additions. Not since the 1970s has the capacity been based on coal.

TXU has a good reason for basing this expansion on coal. It still owns lignite coal reserves in Texas. By announcing that it will build power stations to consume coal, TXU had, with a snap of its fingers, "monetized" the value of those coal reserves.

Most of this capacity was going to be built in Texas. TXU is counting on that state's governor's office to expedite environmental permits as well as necessity and need permits and the like. TXU is also counting on the price of natural gas remaining abnormally high. One reason why Texas appears to need the capacity TXU wants to build is that the natural-gas-fired plants in the state are not economical to run. And, many older oil- and gas-fired units, some once owned by TXU, have been mothballed. If natural gas prices become favorable again and this existing capacity is placed in service, some of TXU's newly announced capacity won't be needed, or at least will be pushed back in schedule.

The company's executives seemed to get bolder with each passing week. At a recent industry meeting, the company reported that it could get coal unit capital costs down to $850/kW by sourcing much of the equipment overseas and by being the "first-mover." Everyone I spoke to about this was skeptical—well, not really, they just flat out didn't believe it. How could TXU build the same plants 30 percent less expensively than anyone else? Lest any of you readers are uncertain where I'm going with this, the ghost of Enron still haunts Texas energy companies. These were the same bold claims Enron executives used to deliver to the same audiences 10 years ago. Many bought it hook, line, and sinker then. And now? Now we just have to wait and see.

That the strategy was fatally flawed was shown literally the day after the private equity groups announced their proposed acquisition: The program to build coal-fired plants the old-fashioned way was scrapped. The buyers apparently recognized, with the help of environmental groups in their camp, what many others have as well. You can't build new coal plants and ignore the CO_2 emissions issue.

If We Merge, Business Will Surge

Almost the antithesis of Enron, TXU, and other electricity companies, Exelon Corp, which is pursuing what I call the *merge to surge* strategy, never fell out of favor during the period between 2001 and 2006. The company is the nation's premier owner and operator of nuclear power stations, primarily located in northern Illinois, eastern Pennsylvania, and the Northeast.

While other utilities were marching across the globe seeking their fortunes, Exelon pursued as contrarian a strategy as there ever was during the 1990s: It bought nuclear plants from utilities in the Northeast forced to divest their generating assets, or simply weary of running nukes where people didn't want them and regulators kept harassing them. At the time, this was even more astonishing because the prevailing wisdom was that at least 30 percent of the nukes would be shut down, because they were uneconomic to run (just like the gas-fired plants are today).

By the time Enron collapsed, and the price of natural gas went through its first miniescalation in year 2000, Exelon's executives suddenly looked like the "smartest guys in the room." They had a collection of attractively acquired nuclear plants with very low operating costs and long-term power sales contracts with their former utility owners, a result of the agreement to take them over.

Nothing lasts long under the "what have you done for me lately" attitude of Wall Street. By 2004, Exelon's intelligent strategy, or at least getting credit for having the right assets at the right time, apparently wasn't enough to keep the stockbrokers whispering its name at the cocktail parties. So the executives decided to grow the asset base through a proposed merger with an adjacent utility in the Northeast, Public Service Electric & Gas Corp (PSEG), operating primarily in New Jersey.

One of the most attractive aspects of PSEG is that it owns and operates two prominent nuclear plants in southern New Jersey. Not only that, they were "troubled" nuclear plants. PSEG was never able to get operations and management at these plants sufficiently under control. Both Oyster Creek and Hope Creek nuclear stations consistently appeared at the bottom of the list with respect to generally accepted industry performance measures. Exelon, on the other hand, has a stellar reputation as a nuke plant operator. Obviously, significant value could be extracted from PSEG's assets. Exelon would also control a significant percentage of the low-cost nuclear capacity in the Northeast.

What appears one way to utility executives often is seen quite differently by regulators. Exelon's merger with PSEG will not go forward. It lacked the approval of regulators in New Jersey. In the end, politicians there did not believe Exelon's story that the merger would ultimately be good for ratepayers.

Both strategies for growth—"if we build it, Wall Street will come" and "if we merge, business will surge"—are giving utilities fits. The problem is that delays, the money wasted on lawyers and consultants, and the general malaise that overtakes an organization under siege, drain time and money from real needs, like modernizing the infrastructure.

The Common Message: Get Bigger!

The common message between the two strategies embodied by Exelon and TXU, and the other electricity companies pursuing variations, is that the only way to grow is to increase the size of the asset base. It boils down to a simple piece of arithmetic: Revenue generated from the asset base divided by the cost of managing that asset base. The popular phrase is *economies of scale*.

The problem here is that the notion of economies of scale in reducing electricity prices to consumers broke down in the 1970s. Maybe it works with other genuinely competitive industries. If we're moving back to a regulated model, perhaps the probability of history repeating itself is too high.

The other issue is framed by a question: "Are these the right kinds of assets to scale up? Given that carbon constraints are inevitable (as we've discussed, even most electric utility executives now believe this), why would you seek to build 10,000 MW of coal capacity with no plan about what to do with the carbon dioxide, and no attention to the cost? Texas lignite, the fuel TXU was planning to use, is not the best coal around, either. From an efficiency and global warming point of view, it is about 30 percent worse than coal available in Illinois, Kentucky, West Virginia, and other states.

How will TXU's new 10,000 MW be moved from supply point (power stations) to customers? It seems reasonable to ask someone who is building 10,000 MW if the capacity to move that power is available in the transmission system. If not, who is building the necessary transmission? Merging a 35,000 MW utility (Exelon) with a 15,000 MW utility (PSEG) doesn't add a single line to the transmission system. And yet, it's TXU that has been Wall Street's current love interest.

From the distribution perspective, substantially increasing the size of the customer base through a merger offers the prospect of leveraging expenses on the distribution side over a large base. Existing and developing programs such as demand side management, application of automatic meter reading, and price-response demand programs (all discussed in later chapters) could benefit. However, I don't hear any of these utilities emphasizing these potential benefits.

True, it is a delicate balancing act to proceed through a merger. As the sponsoring executive, you have to go to Wall Street and tell investors how the merger will generate more cash. Then you have to go to the regulators, politicians, and consumer groups and tell them how the merger will reduce electricity rates. Then you have to prove to the environmentalists that the air, water, and earth will not suffer. You've got to be smoking something to think you can do all three.

Fighting with the Generals You Have

Donald Rumsfeld, George W. Bush's former Secretary of Defense, famously said, "As you know, you go to war with the Army you have. They're not the Army you might want or wish to have at a later time." The same is true for the four-star CEOs leading the electricity industry.

We have to concede that the army of electricity company executives we have is far more comfortable working the supply side of the equation. The investor class sees far more visibility to cash generation with less risk on the supply side of the equation. The regulators merely want to ensure that electricity rates remain "reasonable" and the political party that appointed them remains in power. The politicians are beholden to special interest and lobbying dollars, whether those dollars come from investment firms, utilities, consumer groups, or social and environmental advocacies.

The consumers, let's be honest, don't much care as long as their electricity rates are reasonable relative to the rest of their expenditures and service is not unduly disrupted. The components of electricity costs are generally buried in the monthly rate statement. Buying electricity is not like buying gasoline, where each time you go to the pump, you can experience a visceral reaction to the price.

However, I would submit that the stakeholders we have today behave they way they do because electricity prices have not really begun to escalate. *Real* electricity prices (accounting for inflation) had been declining since the early 1980s. That, dear reader, changed by the late 1990s, as the next chapter proves.

Chapter 12

Sticker Shock (Without the Sticker)

The biggest threat to business as usual in the electricity industry is the relatively rapid escalation in electricity rates. Just in the last year or two, rates have increased from 10 to 60 percent depending on the state or area of the country. Rest assured, they are going to climb even higher.

Don't just take my word for it. Stories have circulated in many of the leading newspapers around the country. At the industry level, the EUCG (formerly the Electric Utility Cost Group) held its annual workshop in the fall of 2006 and concluded that the industry faces its greatest challenges since the 1970s. (It's those '70s again!) Some of the cost factors that are putting inflationary pressures on rates include strengthening T&D networks, refurbishing older power plants with new environmental technologies, volatility in the price of crude oil and its impact on commodity costs, demand for commodities in emerging global markets, and aging infrastructure and workforce. According to the report on the meeting at the *Energy Central* industry news service, EUCG executives see a "1970s-like formula for price uncertainty." Cost issues associated with nuclear power were also foremost in the minds of the EUCG executives.

In some states, the rate increases already instituted amount to sticker shock. In Maryland, for example, rates have increased by more than 70 percent for residents and businesses served by the dominant utility in the state. I've seen this figure reported in several places, and my brother-in-law, a ratepayer in that state, confirmed it. Rates are likely to rise by over 50 percent in Illinois, by up to 50 percent in Connecticut, and by more than 13 percent in New Jersey. I mean, it's one thing to pay a bit more for bread at the grocery store. But what would you think if your grocery bill doubled virtually overnight?

It's Not What You Think

Because these rate increases have coincided with general inflation in energy costs, people naturally associate the two. After all, electricity generation requires fuel, and if fuel costs have increased, well . . .

Yet this is only part of the story, and maybe not even the significant part. Electricity rates in many states have gone up because rate stabilization programs instituted in the late 1990s as part of deregulation programs have ended. Most states seeking competition in electricity supply instituted rate reductions over a multiyear period. This was to protect consumers from any initial shock in the transition to competition. What it did was create a false sense of security and essentially helped quell competition before it could even take root.

On October 15, 2006, in an article titled "Competitive Era Fails to Shrink Electric Bills" by David Cary Johnson, the *New York Times* on October 15, 2006, confirmed the bad news that I suspected for a long time. As many as 40 percent of all electricity ratepayers nationwide were shielded from rate increases as a result of regulatory fiat. The last of those rate protections expires next year. Folks, hang on to your wallet, it's only going to get worse.

The Energy Information Administration (EIA), the best source of historical data on electricity, reported in August 2006 that U.S. residential electricity rates had increased an average of 11 percent nationwide in just the first six months of the year. The year before, the average price escalation to residential bill payers was 5.1 percent.

So Goes Electricity, So Goes the Economy

The impact is going to be felt far beyond the typical household's electric bill. But, in fact, the real danger is with electricity intensive industries, which already face brutal competition from the global market.

Michigan businesses, where the automotive industry is concentrated, are worried: 28 percent, in a recent survey, listed electricity rates the third most difficult cost to manage, topped only by insurance and rising health care premiums. The culprit? The rate freeze, instituted when Michigan went "competitive," ended for the state's industrial customers at the end of 2003, for commercial customers at the end of 2004, and for residential ratepayers at the end of 2005. Michigan gets 55 percent of its electricity from coal, by the way, suggesting that coal does not insulate ratepayers from sticker shock.

Although coal prices have more than doubled over the last two years, and natural gas prices have increased more than fourfold, these costs have yet to be worked into the electricity rate structures, at least on the regulated side. Increases in natural gas prices have affected the cost of electricity in most areas of the country that have functioning electricity markets, although it varies from state to state. Texas, for example, is very dependent on natural gas generation, and is also a deregulated state. That means that ratepayers are deeply affected by the high cost of natural gas (even though much of the nation's gas originates in Texas or the Gulf Coast).

It's Time to Pay the Piper

Fuel represents 80 percent of the cost at a gas-fired power station. For coal plants, it is only 60 percent or so. Generation by itself, as we learned in other chapters, is responsible for only about 50 percent of the price of electricity. If coal doubles in price, then the impact on the cost of electricity should be 30 percent. Coal represents 60 percent of the kilowatt-hours generated in this country. Although gas prices have quadrupled, gas plants don't operate many hours, so the impact on electricity costs is less, on average.

What is scary about these increases is that they are only beginning to reverse the regulated price stabilization of the past and reflect current escalations in fuel costs. What they don't yet account for is the massive infrastructure construction programs that are planned. Over the next 10 years, the industry will be adding an enormous number of new transmission lines, coal and even nuclear base-load power stations, and wind turbine generators as well as upgrading distribution facilities and interfaces with the customer at the meter. At the same time, labor is scarce, driving up labor costs; interest rates are relatively high, adding to the cost of financing new facilities; and environmental control concerns continue to pressure all infrastructure plans.

Inflation Worries Now

What we're looking at here, taking it all in, is massive cost and rate escalation. This cost escalation could have a number of impacts. First, of course, is that it will destroy some demand. When prices rise to consumers, many of them are forced to change their behavior.

Demand destruction then means that many of the large power stations planned by utilities will be rendered unnecessary. If history is any guide, even very recent history like the last few months, public utility commissions will not allow "full" rate recovery, to protect consumers and voters. This affects the shareholders who have bid electric utility stocks up substantially over the last three years. When shareholders scream, utilities will have to reduce costs, because the revenue side won't be growing as fast. One of the only avenues open to them to reduce costs will be consolidation.

Remember Stagflation?

If inflation worries persist, then interest rates set by the Federal Reserve will remain high. The last time this happened, in the late 1970s, we called it *stagflation*. Fighting the last war, then, becomes a reinforcing function. Electricity rates continue to rise, causing inflation in the economy, which in turn causes interest rates to remain high and economic growth to slow. Yup, sounds like the 1970s, all right.

If we continue down this path, the existing infrastructure will be managed by massive, government-like entities. It will be like so many AT&Ts (the 1970s version) operating large swaths of the antiquated grid and keeping it patched up with Scotch tape and twine. The executives fighting the last war are concerned about size, economies of scale, financial efficiency on paper, and providing electricity to the masses within what I believe will be a lower and lower standard of service. In essence, they provide the minimum class of service that will be stipulated by the regulators. Another way of looking at it is that they will own and operate the backbone of the system, but not necessarily the high-value part of the system.

In an ironic twist of fate, the regulated rate freezes and rate reductions imposed to make competitive electricity markets palatable, in order to give competition time to work its magic, are spelling the death knell for competition. And who could blame consumers and regulators for thinking that competition is bad and doesn't lower prices? Prolonged reductions in inflation-adjusted electricity rates occurred from 1983 to 1999. Then competition programs were initiated. What are the perceived results in 2006? Sticker shock on the monthly electricity bill. Competition was supposed to accomplish many great things—like spur innovation, create new energy services, improve the customer relationship, and even create new sensible ways to use electricity—but the one thing competition was absolutely, positively intended to do was lower rates.

Ratings Agencies Are Getting Nervous, Too

Consumers should be worried. Those that rate the debt instruments employed by utilities are already nervous. An article in the February 2006 *Public Utilities Fortnightly*, "Rising Unit Costs & Credit Quality Warning Signals," Ellen Lapson, a managing director at Fitch Rating's North American Power Group concluded this way: "The [utility] sector's credit recovery is now fading, and investors should exercise greater caution regarding the power and gas sector." One thing the article implies, without directly saying it, is that electric utility financial health is threatened by the inability to obtain full cost recovery through the regulated mechanisms, while commodity costs increase, infrastructure expansion goes forward, and electricity demand remains, for most utilities, at or close to historically modest levels (e.g., around 2 percent per year).

Evidence of the inability to recover costs through rates is everywhere. It is also evidence of the backlash by regulators and stakeholders against rising electricity rates. Xcel Energy, a large utility serving Colorado, Minnesota, and Texas, requested $172 million increase in base rates in 2006. The Colorado Public Utilities Commission granted only $107 million, or a mere 62 percent.

If there is any testament that electricity price escalation has U.S. businesses nervous, and that "competition" may in fact be dead, it is that the Electricity Consumers Resource Council (ELCON) pronounced, in a report entitled "Problems in the Organized Markets," that, effectively, competitive electricity markets as currently structured, are not working. ELCON, now composed of close to 30 of the largest electricity intensive manufacturing companies in America, was the one organization that pushed hardest for restructured electricity markets and competition to reduce rates.

Remember the phrase, "the solution to pollution is dilution"? It referred to the way industries built ever taller smokestacks so the emissions would travel farther and be diluted with more and more air. Once it hit the ground, it would be harmless. The same was true for liquids discharged into the water. Well, if the utility's solution to the dilution of profits and the escalation of prices is acquisition (of another utility), it doesn't appear to be working and the regulators aren't buying it. Of the three celebrated potential electric utility mergers moving forward in 2006, only one made it to the finish line. All of the others involved utilities primarily serving states with high relative electricity rates.

Remain Calm! All Is Well!

ELCON, the industrial energy user association referred to earlier, still thinks that the way competition was implemented was the problem.

Implementation was the root of escalating rates, not competition itself. Frankly, I believe that as well. John Q. Public may not be as rational as his monthly bills really start escalating. If electricity rates rise by 10 to 70 percent after five years of competition and electricity markets, then the simple, though erroneous, conclusion is that competition does not work.

Competition hasn't reduced rates. Consolidation and mergers to reduce costs across the enterprise, thereby leading to smaller increases in rates, are in trouble, precisely in those states with high rates. Myriad cost pressures threaten rates in the near term. Sticker shock is likely to find its way to most electricity bills for U.S. ratepayers. It's a Catch 22, or déjà vu all over again. The one thing we can conclude is that "fighting the last war" has only made ratepayers, that is, customers, angrier and more likely to take their wrath out on politicians, and stock and debt holders more anxious about the companies in which they have invested and brought out of the post-Enron bust.

Chapter 13

Electricity Storage

For the longest time, it was thought that, for all practical purposes, electricity could not be stored. That wasn't technically true because tiny amounts of it could be stored in a device called a capacitor, common to many electronic and microprocessor devices. For the purposes of the bulk electricity production and delivery grid, though, it was certainly true enough.

Therefore, electricity has to be stored in another energy form. Batteries store it as chemical energy. Electric energy can be stored in the form of mechanical energy, too. The industry has made much progress in developing large storage systems that are viable for application to the electricity grid. However, it has regressed in the ability to justify storage systems financially and institutionally.

Almost every other business makes use of storage in some way. Some goods can be stored for long periods of time. You can store fabricated steel components for a lifetime, as long as you condition the environment to prevent them from rusting. Factories build inventories of necessary components, which may physically reside at the factory or at the supplier's warehouse. A contract for *future* delivery of material is a form of storage, a contractual form of storage, as opposed to physical storage. *Storage is a tool for managing the supply chain.*

Some goods cannot be stored very long. Perishable agricultural and food products have limited storage capability and often require additional energy inputs, such as air-conditioned storage environments, protection from rodents and microorganisms, and so on. However, storage is still a vital part of the supply.

It's not like we don't have forms of storage in electricity. A 45-day stockpile of coal adjacent to a power plant is a form of electricity storage. A peaking gas turbine generator with a tank of fuel oil next to it, or access to natural gas, is a form of storage. These are not the most flexible forms of storage, though. The industry also has a fleet of large pumped storage hydroelectric plants, which are pretty flexible in the scheme of things. Pumped storage however, for reasons we'll get into later, probably can't be built in this country anymore.

Here's why storing electricity as fuel isn't good enough. Electricity storage has three primary characteristics:

1. Total electricity delivery capacity
2. A charge/discharge rate that is described in units of power per unit of time
3. How fast it can start up and deliver electrons to the system

A 12 MWh storage system could deliver 12 megawatts for one hour or one megawatt for 12 hours, before it has to be charged up again. An important general characteristic to keep in mind about electricity storage systems is that they are purposely built to start and stop, charge and discharge, turn on and off. This is not true of most machines.

Storage has another characteristic that is vital to understanding its value: the roundtrip efficiency. Remember, you are putting energy into the system and getting it back later. No machine is 100 percent efficient. Depending on the storage options, you only get 60 to 75 percent of the energy back. On the face of it, this seems inefficient, until you compare it to other options. The important aspect is not so much how efficient it is, but the value of the stored energy with respect to time. This is critical to understanding the value of storage.

It Worked Wonders for the Natural Gas Business

Perhaps the best way to understand the value of storage is to see how it has transformed similar energy industries. Take natural gas. Many of us burn natural gas in the furnaces in our homes. A variety of industries consume large quantities of natural gas as a raw material, the fertilizer production industry being a good example. Finally, the electricity industry itself has become in recent years a large consumer of natural gas.

What people do not recognize is that storage plays a huge role in making sure natural gas demand is adequately met with supply. You may have noticed large (really large in the scheme of tank design) tanks in urban areas, where you can actually see the roof of the tank at different locations. These are floating roof tanks and they mostly store natural gas. They are owned and operated by what we call the *local distribution company* or LDC. These tanks are charged and discharged from the gas transmission system to meet the consumption patterns of the LDC's customers.

Even larger gas storage assets serve the pipeline companies. Around the country, natural gas is stored underground in large caverns that may exist naturally or may have been carved from salt domes in a process called solution mining. Gas is also stored in underground aquifers, physically protected areas where water sits in and around rock formations. In these underground sites, natural gas is stored to meet *seasonal* demand. Much more natural gas is used in the winter than in the summer because of home heating. Therefore, these massive storage sites are charged between April and October so that gas is available for the heating season.

Pipeline equipment that moves natural gas is no different from other machines. For the most part, the equipment lasts longer and is more reliable if it operates over consistent conditions, or at least within the range of conditions for which it is designed. Thus, the gas transmission system can operate closer to a base-load condition, because the storage assets take the swings in load. Storage is always working behind the scenes to make sure that supply and demand are matched.

As we discussed earlier, the Strategic Petroleum Reserve (SPR) is another example of widespread storage in energy. The government maintains a vast reserve of petroleum, enough for the country to operate for weeks and probably to limp along for months. It is part and parcel of our military preparedness and is an essential part of protecting our petroleum "supply lines."

Numerous Value Buckets

You can probably understand generally how the natural gas and petroleum supply chain and how it could be vastly improved with more and better forms of storage. However, when you go through *all* of what I call the *value buckets* for electricity storage, you will see that electricity is an even greater beneficiary of storage techniques (Figure 13.1).

The first value bucket is national energy security. Our electricity system is vulnerable to threats and attacks as described in earlier chapters. Strategically placed and well-protected storage assets should be considered vital to this country's ability to survive and recover from terrorist attacks or reliability events. Remember Figure 1.1, which showed how electricity is the juice that feeds the rest of the energy, water, communications, and transportation infrastructure. It is nothing short of embarrassing that we maintain such fleet preparedness for our military arsenal but do almost nothing to protect the electricity assets.

The second value bucket is renewable energy. We already know that it is an intermittent resource, but it can be worse than that. Take the case of wind energy, the one renewable energy resource that we are finally capitalizing on in a big way in this country and around the world. The largest contiguous areas with the best wind resources are usually the farthest from where electricity needs are the greatest. We're talking North and South Dakota and, as mentioned before, west Texas. Plus, the daily wind energy profiles run counter to the daily electricity load demands in many parts of the country. Wind speeds tend to be at their highest at night, when everyone is asleep and air conditioners, lights, and businesses aren't running, and at their lowest in the middle of the day, when we really could use the energy. Storage, therefore, provides a key means of *managing* renewable energy supply, of increasing its value. As we've seen, predictability has a huge value in electricity infrastructure planning and operations.

Optimizing the existing infrastructure is a third value bucket. As we reviewed earlier, coal and nuclear plants are designed to run base-load

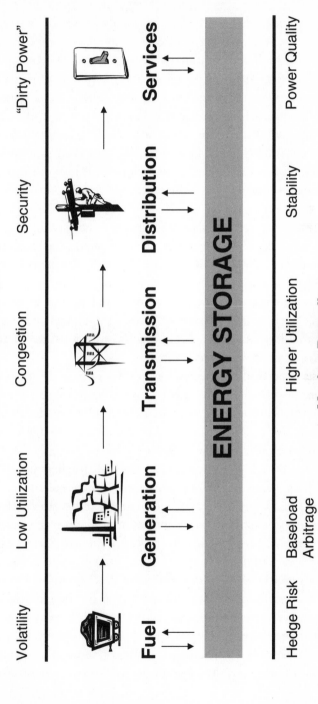

Figure 13.1 Energy Storage enhances the entire value chain.

167

or continuously as much as possible. However, many utilities start up and shut down older coal-fired plants on a daily or weekly basis to meet their load demand curves. This is clearly a suboptimal approach. These are high-energy, high-temperature processes, and the thermal gradients lead to fatigue degradation and raise the risk of equipment failures. There's a reason why auto mechanics tell you that short commutes in your car are so much more damaging than long drives to the country. And that gunning the engine when it is "cold" can be devastating. Metal-laden machines don't like sudden changes! You can stretch this analogy to environmental issues. The noxious emissions out the tailpipe always tend to be worse when the engine is starting up from a cold condition.

In the same way, experts have documented that cycling large coal-fired plants imposes significant costs on the system. The peaking gas-turbine generators usually are not required to be equipped with emission controls. All of us pay for these "hidden costs" in our electricity bill. Some people get electricity bills with a "fuel surcharge." Can you imagine getting a "cycling" surcharge or a "we're running this plant stupidly" surcharge? You'll never see the "cold turbine emissions" surcharge that is paid by the environment, but it's there.

Even top experts in the electricity industry don't recognize that, on average, transmission lines may only be loaded up to 60 percent of their rated capability, just like most power stations (nukes are the exception) run at between 10 to 90 percent of their capability. Storage provides a means of increasing these capacity factors.

Finally, the fourth value bucket comes with intelligent grid management. The grid, as we saw earlier, requires injections of capacity to move the power, maintain voltage, and supply reactive power. (Essential for grid efficiency, reactive power is the amount of power flow attributed to stored energy that cycles back to the energy source.) In many cases, the faster this injection can be made, the better it is for the grid. We keep generating assets in "spinning reserve" mode, and some turbine generators on "turning gear" so that they are ready to answer the call for grid management. Again, this approach is often suboptimal, resulting in hidden costs that we ultimately pay.

On the other side of the meter, storage has an even greater role to play, which we review in Chapter 17 as the concept of *distributed generation* (DG). DG can also be considered a component of intelligent grid management.

Storage offers an array of benefits for fighting the next electricity war and enhances the value of the existing assets and their role in every future strategy envisioned so far. I'm sure you think that the industry is hell-bent on developing and applying storage. Think again.

Value Is Spread Too Thin

Storage is a paradox. The same reasons why storage assets have such value are the same reasons they are being largely ignored. In fact, better storage capability was pursued in a more concerted fashion when the industry was vertically integrated. Today, in its disaggregated state, the values for energy storage are similarly broken apart. Each value by itself is not enough to justify the expenditures for a project. The question becomes, who pays?

The government and the people are the main beneficiaries of storage as an element of infrastructure protection and homeland security. But how easy do you think it is to convince politicians and voters to add this to the list of other pressures for tax dollars—including national defense, road construction, social security and health insurance, mortgage financing, pensions, and so on? Renewable energy is a strong beneficiary from storage; yet the financial viability of renewable energy, even with the great direct subsidies, is tenuous at best. Although adding storage to the renewable energy equation makes the long-term economics look a lot more promising, renewable proponents don't want to burden their systems with additional short-term costs. Owner/operators of older coal-fired plants are beneficiaries, too, but they don't want to recognize that those costs even exist, much less justify participation in an energy storage facility based on mitigating those costs.

Perhaps the best way to understand how electricity storage rates in the pecking order of energy options is to know how it fared in the last energy bill—namely, the Energy Policy Act of 2005 (EP 2005). Let's just say it didn't get star billing! In the bill, there are continuing incentives for renewable energy, mandates for using new electricity meters, government guarantees for building the initial slate of new nuclear reactors, financial incentives for new coal plant designs, but only oblique references to storage as a way to improve transmission grids. I know all this because I was the executive director of a public policy organization called the Energy Storage Council that was advocating on behalf of energy storage in Washington while EP 2005 was debated, drafted, written, and passed. Because storage has so much to offer, everybody wants someone else to take care of it.

Options Abound

So what are the storage options out there? There are many. Several can be considered fully commercial, some are just emerging as viable options, and a few still have some years of R&D ahead of them.

We've discussed pumped storage hydroelectric, essentially pumping water to an upper reservoir, and releasing it back downhill to drive turbine generators when the power is needed. The really impressive thing about this option is that the motor-driven pumps and the turbine-driven generator are the same machine! Essentially, the process is reversed—the motor acts as a generator and the pump acts as a turbine—depending on whether the reservoir is being charged or discharged. Our electricity system includes about 20,000 MW of these facilities.

Unfortunately, their ecological footprint is huge, and they are almost impossible to permit today.

The best alternative to pumped storage is a similar concept called compressed air energy storage (CAES). In this case, pressurized air is the storage medium. Large motor-driven compressors fed with electricity pump air at high pressure into underground storage caverns, the same caverns that are used to store natural gas and petroleum. When electricity is needed, the process works in reverse: the pressurized air is expanded through the turbine (also the compressor) which drives the generator (also the motor). CAES makes use of traditional machines and operates in ways identical to other forms of generating power. However, only two large CAES facilities operate in the world, one in Alabama and one in Germany. It is a technology and an option poised for commercial exploitation.

For more modest storage requirements, there are advanced, large-scale batteries, flywheels, and even ultra-capacitors. Alaska is home to the largest battery power plant in the world, a 27.6 megawatt (MW) asset based on nickel-cadmium (NiCad) battery technology. It is an immensely scaled-up version of the rechargeable batteries used in many consumer electronic devices. The Puerto Rico Electric Power Authority (PREPA) operates a large 15 MW battery facility based on the same technology used in automobiles, lead-acid batteries. A rather unique battery technology, specifically formulated for electricity applications, is called the *sodium-sulfur battery*. A large electric utility in Ohio is demonstrating this technology at a size that is significant to electricity applications. Japan is where the technology was developed and it has been applied commercially in that country.

Flywheels, reverse-flow fuel cells, and advanced batteries are storage technologies that can be used for smaller increments of power. Flywheels are similar to electric motors; mechanical energy is stored in a device that spins on a rotor. Fuel cells are similar to batteries because they convert chemical energy into electricity.

The good thing about most storage technologies is that they are modular. It's not like building a large power plant. Rather, you simply connect up dozens, even hundreds, of small batteries, flywheels, or even reverse-flow fuel cells, to make systems of larger capacity. The benefit here is that it is often less risky to scale up a modular technology than to build a larger unit, such as a larger steam turbine or a large wind turbine.

Chapter 14

Coal

Extracting Its Full Value

C oal—it's the fossil fuel we love to hate. There's no love lost between Americans and petroleum either, but we tend to focus our hate on the overseas suppliers of oil, not the resource itself. When oil is plentiful, cheap, and meeting our insatiable demands for gasoline, it recedes into the background of our lives. That is not the case for coal.

For coal, it doesn't matter. The stuff has been cheap as dirt for decades. Although it has experienced a substantial rise in price over the last few years, that's only because the price of all commodity fuels tend to rise in lockstep with each other. When markets "believe" that petroleum and natural supplies are or will be constrained, they also believe that coal will have to make up the difference. Price therefore goes up with demand, as Economics 101 would suggest. The fundamental reason it remains relatively cheap is that the United States alone has an estimated several hundred years (at present consumption rates) of the stuff still sitting in the ground. It is quite simply a vast energy reserve unlike any other on the planet. Wind and solar energy resources are vast too, but they aren't sitting ready to be harnessed at our discretion. Renewable resources have to be used at the discretion of Mother Nature.

We're not the only ones blessed (or cursed, as the case may be) with vast reserves of coal. Australia, China, India, Indonesia, South Africa, Germany, Russia, and Colombia are other countries with substantial reserves. All of these countries are either going to continue burning this stuff at home to make electricity—or export it to someone who wants to. Hate coal all you want. It is still going to be the main event in electricity generation for a long, long time.

I like to tell my friends if you dislike coal so much, then just cut your electricity consumption in half. Therein lies the problem. We hate the raw material but can't seem to do without more of the product that we enjoy: low-cost electricity. It's the same with gasoline, by the way. If you don't like fighting wars over petroleum supply lines, then quit driving so much. Life is simple, isn't it?

It is difficult to use coal intelligently. But it is not impossible.

Beauty and the Beholder

In the United States, 90 percent of all the coal mined is converted into electricity. Although coal-fired power plants only represent about 40 percent of our installed generating capacity, they are responsible for generating more than 50 percent of the nation's electricity in consumption any given year. Like petroleum and gasoline, we love the relatively low-cost electricity that we get from coal, but we hate the raw material.

Plus, of all the fossil fuels, it is the most difficult to deal with at a power station. It is heterogeneous, meaning that it consists of many different chemical compounds and elemental material. Each lump of coal comes with a handful of impurities embedded deep in its structure. Coal is also a solid material, unlike petroleum and natural gas. As you know from your home furnace, oil and natural gas can be piped straight into the burner in your boiler or furnace. To burn coal efficiently, you have to store it, convey it, crush it, pulverize it, size it, and then blow it into the furnace with air. Finally, coal is inconsistent. Shipments from the same mine or area can exhibit significant variability with respect to its energy value and impurities—and with respect to the emissions it will eventually generate.

On a convenience scale of 1 to 10, natural gas might get a 10, oil an 8. Coal brings up the rear in this beauty contest with a 2 or a 3. Heterogeneous, inconsistent, solid, and loaded with impurities—coal is not your best qualities for a fuel. But, hey, it's a cheap date.

How we use coal at the power station isn't much prettier. After it is prepped, we throw it into the power plant's boiler, which produces the steam that drives the turbine generator. (To make that steam also requires a tremendous amount of water.) Out of the stack come gaseous pollutants and fly ash that can impact human health and the environment. From the bottom of the boiler comes the stuff that doesn't burn or have any energy value. Coal results in electricity (good), warm water discharge (mostly bad), emissions (bad), and ash (bad). Over the last 50 years, the industry has progressively collected much of the emissions and reduced the pollution. Essentially, we've treated it like dirt with some energy worth converting into electricity.

Fortunately, all of that "dirt" is also the key to using the stuff more intelligently. So let's channel all our energy hating coal into a more productive thought process. The coal and electricity industries want you to think in terms of "clean coal." I prefer that you think in terms of *intelligent coal*.

Industrial Ecology

Coal = electricity, emissions, ash, and dirty water. We need to turn that equation around. We need to treat coal as a national resource and extract every bit of value from it that we can. We can do so by applying the same principles found in ecosystems to the coal production and conversion value chain.

If you know anything about a petroleum refinery, you know that petroleum comes in one end, and a variety of "refined products" come out the other, including gasoline, jet airplane fuel, tar (for paving roads), No. 2 and No. 6 diesel fuel, lubricants, and others. If you've ever visited a pulp-and-paper mill, you've seen how every piece of the tree is used in

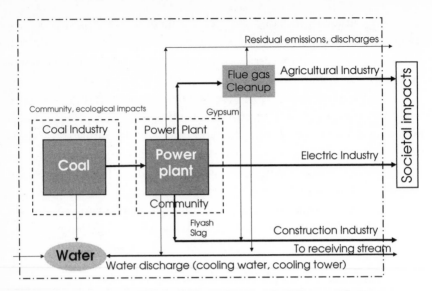

Figure 14.1 E–Equity™ and industrial ecology enable more intelligent use of coal.

some way, with whatever is left used to fuel the mill's boilers. Petroleum and paper are competitive industries, so facilities are motivated to extract as much value from the resource as economically possible.

Likewise, coal needs to be processed in a coal refinery, which includes a power plant. And we need to put the principles of industrial ecology to work at these refineries. Industrial ecology is an academic way of saying that wastes from one industry can be raw material inputs to another. Or, even more simply, one industry's poison is another's raw meat. In my consulting practice, I apply a methodology called E–Equity™ to help industry leaders and ordinary citizens understand how to extract the full value of coal, as shown in Figure 14.1.

First, let's start with the transportation of coal. We've discussed supply lines earlier. The supply lines for coal in this country have lengthened. Two decades ago, it was typical for coal to be trucked to power plants from local mines, or shipped a few hundred miles by rail. Today, at least 50 percent of coal used in the United States is railroaded 1,000–1,500 miles or further. Although the railroads don't like to hear this (coal is more than 50 percent of their freight), the smarter way to utilize coal as a national resource is to build the power plant adjacent to or right near the mine.

Obviously, this avoids shipping costs, a significant fraction of the price of coal. You probably are not aware that more than half of the cost of a ton of coal from the huge Powder River Basin (PRB) in Wyoming to power plants east of the Mississippi is transportation. What's more, much of what we're shipping is water. That's right. Remember when I said coal is heterogeneous? Powder River Basin coal, which is now responsible for more than 50 percent of our electricity production in this country, is 30 percent water. The reason utilities burn it is because of its low-sulfur content and so avoids the sulfur-dioxide emissions that cause, for example, acid rain. Ironically, our relatively low-energy costs in the country allow us to ship coal long distances, even though one-third of what we are shipping has absolutely zero energy value for electricity production. This might be economically viable but it isn't very smart.

Building and operating coal-fired power plants at the mine also avoids the generation and consumption of the energy necessary to power the trains. Anytime you avoid converting energy into power or motion, you reduce pollution.

These are the economic values. There are societal values as well for avoiding the shipment of coal long distances. For one thing, it has been documented that railroads kill between 250 to 400 people each year. If coal represents 50 percent of the tonnage shipped, then perhaps we could assume that coal transportation is responsible for half of these deaths. In conducting safety studies, the airline industry imposes a value on a human life. That value is $3 million annually. Avoiding deaths has a societal benefit that, for purposes of evaluating electricity options, can be quantified. Now, I'm not out to get the railroad industry. I'm simply out to examine *all* the costs of energy production and how we can eliminate waste and wring out every last ounce of value from that process.

Second, let's work with the energy value of coal. The electric power industry has spent the last two decades, and quite a bit of your tax dollars, tweaking a technology called coal gasification. This coal conversion process has been around since at least the 1930s. In its modern reincarnation, it has been paired with a power plant configuration called the gas turbine combined cycle (CC). The objective of coal gasification is to derive a fuel from coal that is similar to natural gas, which can then be burned in a high efficiency power system.

We may be gearing up in the United States to build the nation's first commercial fleet of what's known as the *integrated gasification combined cycle* (IGCC) *plant*. However, almost all of these facilities are intended to produce electricity only.

IGCC plants resemble refineries more than they resemble a traditional coal-fired power plant. So why not extract more high-value products from the coal? Ethanol, hydrogen, even gasoline, can be produced from coal. For that matter, all the energy products of a petroleum refinery can be obtained from a coal refinery. The electric power plant simply becomes part of the refinery. It is one of several high-value energy streams that can result from the raw material. It seems more than short-sighted not to pursue this way of thinking.

Third, let's consider all the impurities. One of the main pollutants in coal is sulfur. When it is burned (or oxidized), it is converted to sulfur dioxide. All new coal-fired plants have to capture most of this sulfur dioxide, and many existing coal plants do as well. However, sulfur is a valuable commodity. It is used in the fertilizer industry as ammonium sulfate. It is used in the construction industry as gypsum, the raw material for making wallboard, which is one of the most prevalent construction industry products. Sulfur dioxide can also be converted into sulfuric acid, a necessary ingredient in many chemical manufacturing processes.

The message: Sulfur, an impurity when discharged up the stack, is a valuable commodity when captured and converted into the right product.

Oxides of nitrogen (NOx) are another pollutant from coal-fired plants. Most power plants today use a process called *selective catalytic reduction* (SCR) to convert the NOx into harmless nitrogen and water vapor. That's not a bad way of getting rid of a pollutant. However, ammonium nitrate is another important component of fertilizer. A variety of power plant emissions control processes have been developed that convert oxides of nitrogen into fertilizer material. Why not put them to widespread use?

The noncombustibles parts of coal end up as either fly ash, which is collected right before it enters the smokestack, or bottom ash or slag, collected at the bottom of the boiler. High-quality fly ash is considered a prime ingredient in cement manufacturing. Slag and bottom ash also have uses in the construction industry. The cement industry has recognized the value of fly ash and, as long as it meets specifications, wants as much of it as power plants can give. Still, we only recycle about 50 percent of our fly ash this way. Why only 50 percent? Why not put the principals of E-Equity™ to work and utilize the rest of it more intelligently as well?

When you substitute recycled materials for virgin materials, you avoid the environmental impact of extracting and using the virgin materials. For example, it has been documented that one ton of fly ash recycled into cement-making avoids close to one ton of carbon that would be discharged to the atmosphere if a mined material had to be processed instead. Using what is known as synthetic gypsum (gypsum produced from a flue-gas desulfurization unit which removes sulfur from the stack) avoids all the energy costs and environmental impacts needed to mine, extract, and transport raw gypsum.

Credit Where Credit Is Due

Part of the E-Equity™ methodology is making sure an option gets credit for things done right and penalized for things not done right. This is nothing more than what you might do to raise your kids: reward good behavior, punish bad behavior. In some cases, like the recycle of fly ash into cement manufacture, the credit is visible. It is the price a cement company will pay for the fly ash.

However, the economics of recycling waste materials are not necessarily straightforward. Here's why: The cement guy knows that if he does not buy the fly ash from the power plant lady, then she will have to pay to put it in a landfill. Even though the cement guy knows it is worth a "price," he may insist that the power plant lady *pay him* to take it off her hands. He might say, "Look, lady. I'm doing you a favor. I'll come get it and truck it to my place for less than you'd have to pay to haul the stuff to the landfill." The economics of the deal are distorted. One reason is that the cement guy is unwilling to give the power plant lady "credit" for the societal value of avoiding the mining of raw material.

With coal, there are many examples of credit not being available where credit is due. Here's a big one: How often do you hear that the United States is the Saudi Arabia of coal and that we should exploit this vast reserve to ensure our independence from foreign sources of energy? Well, rhetoric isn't economics. One of the fastest ways to improve the value of coal is to quantify its national security value and make it "visible." We need to put a price tag on the "societal" value of exploiting an abundant resource sitting in our back yard instead of importing petroleum and natural gas from countries thousands of miles away that are unfriendly at best and that hate us at worst. Put another way, the investment in building and operating coal refineries that also produce electricity can be more quickly recovered if this value is calculated into the economic equation.

Penalties for Bad Behavior

The use of energy and consumer products impose costs on society that are not paid for, not paid for directly, or are not associated with the product. Academics call these costs *externalities.*

You pay for household trash to be collected and either recycled or land-filled. Who ultimately pays the cost of the impact of that landfill on the environment? Well, you might argue, we all do. But the trash equation is not in your monthly bills and it's not in mine. It's an externality, in this case, a cost that is not paid for.

The price of imported petroleum or liquefied natural gas (LNG) does not include a surcharge for our military assets around the globe that protect oceanic shipping lanes, or the military bases located around the world maintained, among many other reasons, to respond immediately to threats to our energy interests and ever-lengthening supply lines. We pay for this protection in our defense budget, funded by our tax dollars. I think everyone agrees that the cost exists, but almost no one will agree on what fraction of our global military budget should be attributed to protecting energy supply lines. Nevertheless, this is an externality on the price of petroleum and LNG because the cost is shifted elsewhere. It is a cost that is not *directly* paid for by producers or consumers of LNG or petroleum. But, that doesn't mean it isn't a cost that we ultimately have to pay.

Extracting natural gas halfway around the world and shipping it to a power station in this country results in some percentage that leaks to the atmosphere. That leakage could range from 1 to 10 percent depending on the methods used. As we showed in the chapter on global warming and environmental imperatives, one methane molecule is equivalent to more than 20 carbon dioxide molecules with respect to global warming. Again, this is an externality not included in the price of LNG, or applied against the electricity derived from it, or charged to American consumers. Again, few would argue that this externality exists, but everyone will debate its magnitude, its impact, and its cost.

It may not be easy to quantify this societal penalty, but I believe it is necessary that we do so. When you value externalities such as global defense expenditures and factor them into electricity generating options, the comparisons shift. When you account for environmental externalities, the economic value of different electricity generating options changes. Recycling fly ash from a power plant to a cement plant is characterized by a societal gain. In the E-Equity™ methodology, we refer to societal gains, or credits, as *internalities.* To more fairly evaluate the economics of coal, it is critical these credits and penalties be transparent. Adding externality and internality values can substantially change the way we view coal as a national resource as shown in Figure 14.2.

I have performed first-order E-Equity™ valuations for a few clients. The results can be surprising, and disturbing. They are exceedingly sensitive to initial conditions and assumptions. However, there is no doubt in my mind that the methodology drives thinking in new directions. In fact, entirely new accounting practices could result. And let me be clear: Environmental accounting, sustainability studies, responsible investing, and other fields use analytical tools aimed at valuing aspects of the enterprise that are essential for the future of the planet. E-Equity™ attempts to integrate environmental accounting, social costs, and industrial ecology into a more intelligent framework that can be applied to coal-based electricity generating assets—indeed to all electricity generating assets.

Who Remembers Synfuels?

We've tried to exploit our coal resources for more than electricity production in the past. In fact, President Carter aggressively funded a

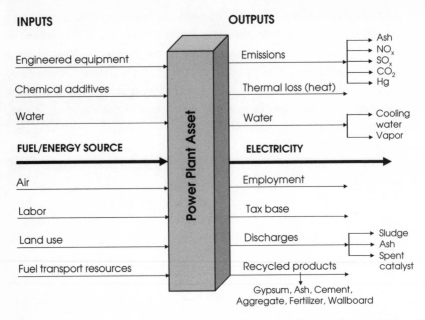

Figure 14.2   E-Equity valuations account for externalities and internalities of coal.

synthetic fuel program called *Synfuels* for this purpose. Its crowning policy initiative was guaranteed price incentives for premium fuels derived from coal. Unfortunately, after the oil embargoes of the 1970s faded from memory and petroleum prices returned to "normal," the Synfuels program was discredited. After President Reagan took office, the program, for the most part, was laughed out of the beltway.

What if we had continued the program for the ensuing two decades? Would the energy "misery index" of the last few years been as severe? Perhaps not. An aggressive synfuels manufacturing base could have maintained a cap on prices in the global market, since the United States is far and away the largest consumer of petroleum.

However, because of the Synfuels program, all the technical resources are available and proven for converting our coal reserves into premium fuels and electricity, and more intelligently using the leftover ash and converted emissions. Coal liquefaction and gasification technologies were proven and demonstrated at full scale. We even have a vast coal-based refinery, called the Great Plains Gasification Complex, in Beulah, North Dakota, that has been operating (even if not economically

so) for many years. The Synfuels program laid the foundation for a domestic energy industry fueled by coal.

Where There's a Will . . .

More than technology and a new economic framework are needed
to capitalize on this nation's vast energy reserves. We need a national
political will and a long-term policy framework. And we need them
now. Electricity infrastructure can only sensibly be built under planning
horizons that are decades in length. If our policy frameworks are not
equally as long, then we are doomed to repeat the cycles of boom and
bust that punish the environment and distort the economics.

That long-term policy must consider subsidies and tax credits as
incentives. Why are we willing to provide tax credits and generous
subsidies for developing renewable energy but unwilling to subsidize
widespread industrial ecology recycling? The United States Department
of Agriculture (USDA) pursues programs to get farmers to put up wind
farms and improve the economic rents from their land. Why shouldn't
the USDA pursue programs that get coal-based utilities and farmers
cooperating to use FGD-derived fertilizer components? Once we start
thinking creatively about the potential synergies available, it's easy to
actually get excited about the possibilities (see Figure 14.3).

There's another more basic reason why we need a national will
translated into a policy framework. I mentioned at the beginning of this
chapter that other industries, such as petroleum and pulp and paper, are
much better at extracting the full value from their primary raw materials.
They are competitive industries. As a general rule, the more competitive
an industry is, the more likely all economic values are being illuminated
and therefore can be exploited. Unfortunately, the electricity industry is
not as competitive. It is still largely regulated. If the market is not allowed
to *illuminate* the credits and penalties, then some form of government
intervention is necessary.

Fly in the Ointment

Okay, there is one fly in the ointment to any progressive scenario involving coal: carbon constraints. No matter how it's cut, a massive program

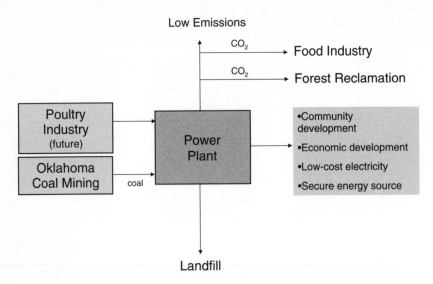

Figure 14.3   An independent power station uses local coal, local wastes as fuel, captures and recycles CO_2, and reclaims old mines with ash.

to develop more coal resources results in a massive quantity of carbon that has to be managed. Small amounts of carbon can be recycled beneficially. Think, for example, of carbonated beverages. Large amounts of carbon dioxide can be used in applications like enhanced oil recovery. As long as the carbon dioxide displaces the oil and stays "down there," carbon injection into oil wells can be a sound way of recycling carbon dioxide.

Even with all the recycling activities currently envisioned, the only real hope for dealing with this pesky "fly" is sequestration. This means putting the carbon dioxide gas underground and keeping it there *forever.* As we talked about in the global warming chapter, forever is a long time. Maybe we need to think in terms of keeping it there until we find something else to do with it. My off-the-cuff suggestion is to bubble it through naturally occurring reserves of calcium oxide, which will stabilize it as calcium carbonate, a compound that is plentiful in the earth, and about as harmless as it gets. Even if we hope we can come up with new technologies to do something different sometime in the future, it means—at least in my mind—approaching the safe management of the storage as a forever proposition.

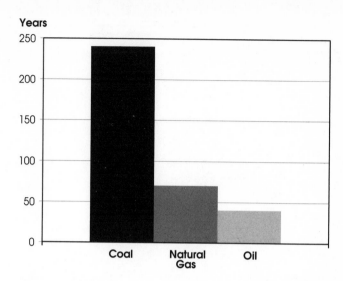

Figure 14.4 Coal dominates the world's fossil energy reserves. SOURCE: PFBC Environmental Energy Technology.

You can look at graphs that show the dramatic increases in carbon dioxide discharges over the last 40 years. Factor in China and India as we've discussed in this book. If you think the amount of this unwanted gas is overwhelming today, just wait 20 years, when it is expected to double!

Yes, there is a fly in the ointment, but let's get back to the practical reality we started with. Coal is going to be harnessed for electricity generation, whether you hate it or not. There's just too much of the stuff at dirt cheap prices not to, especially in economies driven by markets, as shown in Figure 14.4.

The only real questions are: How intelligently do you want to use it? How much are you willing to pay? How radically are you personally willing to throttle back your love affair with the primary consumer product (low-cost electricity) derived from it?

Chapter 15

Exercising the Nuclear Option

There's an immediate solution to global warming that involves no changes to our lifestyle and no changes to how much we pay for electricity—we may even pay less ultimately. It requires no new technology. It is the only solution that can significantly retard the massive increases in carbon discharges expected from world economic growth. The only "political" problem with it is that many of the same social and political leaders who love the idea of solving global warming now happen to hate the only viable, immediate, and ready-to-roll solution available—nuclear power.

In the world of modeling and simulation, we often say that small changes or inaccuracies in initial conditions greatly sway the results. We applied this truism in assessing the reliability of climate projections. A variation of this truism is that the results of a poll can be dramatically altered through subtle phrasing variations in the questions. In other words, how you ask the question makes a big difference in how people answer it. Small changes in perception make huge differences in outcomes.

I am convinced that nowhere in the electricity business is this truer than with nuclear power. When I was very young, I remember the saying, "Close doesn't count except in horseshoes, grenades, and atomic bombs." If society had not associated such language as *atomic bombs*, *atomic weapons*, and *atomic arsenal* in the popular imagination with *nuclear power*, our planet would be suffering far less from carbon dioxide buildup, electricity would be much less expensive, and we would be exploiting the highest-density, naturally occurring energy source available to us courtesy of planet Earth.

Nuclear power is perceived by many to be the equivalent of nuclear bombs. Let's face it, you can make lethal explosives from materials commonly used for fertilizer, but few associate Old MacDonald's Farm with terrorism.

Fears of nuclear power remind me of what pilots often say as the airplane pulls up to the gate: "We remind you that the safest part of your journey has just been completed." What they mean is that when you get in your car to go home, you really are risking life and limb statistically. Of course, we've all seen the statistics that flying is safer than driving. Yet surveys show that most people feel safer driving than flying. I don't know too many people who are as afraid of pulling out of the driveway as they are of taking off from the runway. Fear is often irrational to me, and that includes the fear of nuclear power. As a society, we need to grow up, frankly. We need to put this collective fear behind us once and for all. Fortunately, there are many signs that this is happening.

Atoms for Peace . . .

The short history of nuclear power in the United States is well known. It starts with the government's *Atoms for Peace* program in the 1950s. Once we learned to harness nuclear energy for peaceful purposes, generating electricity, electric utilities were quick to understand the value. By the late 1960s, commercial-scale nuclear power stations were being built at an impressive clip, and this continued until 1979, when the accident at Three Mile Island (TMI) unit 1 occurred.

Nuclear power captivated utilities for many reasons. If you think the word "captivated" is too strong, then realize that many nuclear power stations were given names of the utility executive advocating its support. One of the biggest reasons for this support is that nuclear power could provide base-load electricity generation—remember, this is a plant that essentially runs 24/7 at or close to its full output—as a substitute for coal plants already handling that job at a higher cost.

Earlier I mentioned that, with the emergence of EPA and strong emissions control laws in the late 1960s, utility executives could see the writing on the wall for coal or, at least, the added costs for pollution control on the balance sheet. Their plan was for a new fleet of nuclear units to replace coal-fired ones for the base-load generating duties. Then the existing coal-fired plants would then be relegated to intermediate, or cycling, duty. To those executives, Atoms for Peace also meant peace of mind when it came to dealing with emissions from coal-fired plants.

... Then Falling to Pieces

The government provided significant support to the nuclear industry. For government officials, there's nothing like civilian applications of defense technologies to justify the expenditures. However, there was one key issue that was not well thought out. Actually, it would be more accurate to say that the government made a promise decades ago that it still hasn't kept. The key issue, and the unkept promise, involve long-term management of spent nuclear fuel.

Nuclear waste management proved to be the missing piece from the nuclear power program. And when the nuclear industry fell to pieces after the TMI accident, it proved next to impossible to get anyone to even think about putting the pieces back together again.

TMI proved to be another one of those inflection points that I am fond of pointing out. Because there was such demand for nuclear reactors in the early 1970s, the industry, as is it happens in times of boom, began to get out of control. Prices were escalating, competing designs were available, and each utility wanted a specially designed reactor.

What do I mean by a specially designed reactor? There are only two broad categories of prevalent nuclear power plant reactors: *pressurized water reactors* (PWR) and *boiling water reactors* (BWR). Only four companies supplied virtually all of these reactors to U.S. utilities. When I mention a "specially designed reactor," what I mean is that each utility could only order vanilla or chocolate, but could then heap on M&Ms, sprinkles, nuts, extra syrup, caramel, and a host of other goodies. These "bells and whistles" were deemed necessary so that the design, the operation, the "look and feel" of the control room, and other characteristics were compatible with that utility's current practices.

That was fine when there was little industry oversight. But that became a huge problem after regulators were compelled to get more involved.

After TMI, the Nuclear Regulatory Commission (NRC) was charged with making sure that the existing reactors and the ones still being built would be designed and operated safely. New codes and standards kept being introduced (and kept being introduced and kept being introduced), designers and builders had to continually modify the equipment to meet those codes and standards, and costs began to spiral out of control. Those bells and whistles proved to be sticking points that required NRC's understanding and approval.

The consequences of TMI and the resulting regulatory burden quickly became enormous and are still being felt today. That TMI also occurred during the period of the second OPEC oil embargo of the United States didn't help matters. Since 1979, U.S. electric utilities have not ordered another new nuclear unit, a fact that is still true today (although at the time of this writing, at least one company has preordered equipment for a proposed nuclear unit, and more than 30 new reactor projects are lined up in the preapproval queue). Many of the units under construction in the early post-TMI period experienced cost-overruns of between 2 times and 10 times. You read that right. Some units that were supposed to cost half a billion dollars ended up costing $4.5 billion.

These astronomical cost overruns then led to something that the utility industry desperately wants to forget—which, we'll read later, may come back to haunt them—the prudency review. Public Utility Commissions (PUC), also called Public Service Commissions, instituted hearings to determine whether costs incurred to complete these nuclear units were prudent, that is, in the public interest. Many of the decisions went against the utilities and therefore, they were not granted rate increases and the stockholders ended up sharing the suffering for the sins of pronuclear managements.

That's not to say the ratepayers didn't suffer, too. Electric rates sky-rocketed in areas like Illinois, the Northeast, Florida, California, and much of the East Coast. Dozens upon dozens of planned units were cancelled, after billions upon billions were already spent. The regulatory dynamic reinforced itself: Recovery of the money spent for post-TMI regulatory compliance imposed at the federal level was denied at the state level through prudency reviews. The nuclear power business collapsed.

Then things went from the ridiculous to the sublime. Notorious plants, like Seabrook in New Hampshire, Washington Public Power Supply System (WPPSS) in Washington State, Shoreham on Long Island, Fort St. Vrain in Colorado, Browns Ferry in Tennessee, and Zimmer in Ohio became albatrosses around their respective utility's economic necks. The plants that did begin operating experienced poor performance. Scores of other plants on the drawing boards were simply cancelled.

Then came Chernobyl. The catastrophe in the Ukraine (when it was part of the Soviet Union) seemingly put the final nail in the coffin of the industry, even though the Russian-designed reactors were completely different and far less safe than ours. All of this culminated in what I consider to be one of the most illogical acts ever perpetrated in the annals of U.S. electricity: The Shoreham nuclear power plant on Long Island, New York, with 99.99 percent of its construction complete, became so politically, well, *radioactive,* that it was eventually dismantled. Yes, sold for scrap. The utility owner/operator was denied an operating license. Long Island's electricity rates were then (and still are) among the highest in the nation!

And yet out of this scrap heap a new, vibrant U.S. nuclear power industry is rising. Perceptions of nuclear have changed. The nation may soon begin construction on a new fleet of reactors. Part of this reversal of fortune came from overseas, where nuclear power grew less tumul-tuously.

Other Countries "Deal with It"

As the U.S. nuclear power industry was pummeled into submission, many other countries marched onward and upward with their nuclear power programs utilizing reactors and technologies, ironically, developed here.

France embarked on a nuclear power construction program that culminated in 78 percent of that country's electricity being supplied by such plants today. Whenever you see those charts that show contributions to global warming, France glows, precisely because of its nuclear program. Germany also continued its construction program and today that country gets about 30 percent of its electricity from nuclear power. Other countries that surpass the United States in nuclear-generated electricity (based on a percentage of installed capacity and delivered kilowatt-hours) are Japan, Korea, Sweden, Switzerland, Belgium, and Finland. You might recognize these countries as either global economic engines or countries with very stable domestic economies. That's not to say that these countries didn't have to overcome vocal opposition to nuclear power. It wasn't a "free ride" for nuclear, but neither did the industry descend from the ridiculous to the sublime.

Conditions leading to nuclear power in these countries were different. The nuclear programs in France and Korea grew up on centrally planned economies. In both countries, there is one electric utility (Electricité de France and Korea Electric Power Company). Therefore, planning and operation were centralized, not fragmented, and both countries took advantage of a high degree of standardization to reduce costs, manage the technology, keep regulation sane, and maintain confidence in the option. Neither country, by the way, has suffered a major nuclear plant accident of the scale of TMI or Chernobyl. Japan has few indigenous energy resources, and very strict environmental laws. Therefore, nuclear power proved to be a low-cost option.

One of the most important reasons nuclear power marched forward outside the United States has to be attributed to this fact as well: The rest of the "first-world" countries take global warming far more seriously than we do, at least at the national political level. Perhaps the best evidence of this is that almost every other developed (and undeveloped) country became a signatory to the Kyoto treaty, proposed in December 1997. This treaty essentially commits its signatories to reduce greenhouse gases over a period of time from established baseline levels. A focus on global warming in other parts of the world forced governments to acknowledge that nuclear power was one of the best ways to minimize the carbon footprint.

Getting Our Act Together

Meanwhile, back in the good old U.S. of A., an important positive trend started in the late 1980s, but it was virtually invisible to the public, who only heard about the reactor order cancellations, prudency hearings, cost overruns, and skyrocketing rates. The operations side of the industry began to get its act together. The nuclear industry came to understand its fate in the same way as the airline industry. That is, one airline crash affects the entire flying public. No one cares if Delta is "safer" than Frontier. The flying public is riddled with fear no matter whose name is painted on the tail. Likewise, the nuclear industry realized that even a minor accident at one plant gives a black eye to the entire fleet. As with airlines, the fear may be irrational, but the perception becomes the reality.

It may have been too late to "standardize" the design of the reactors, but it wasn't too late to standardize policies, procedures, best practices, and safety programs and apply them across the board. In essence, nuclear power became an industry within an industry.

Today, performance at each plant isn't judged by who owns it and operates it; each plant is judged against the entire fleet through a process called benchmarking. An organization called the Institute of Nuclear Power Operations (INPO) came into being shortly after TMI (the nuclear industry's 9/11), to create order and stability out of chaos. The industry began to hire the best and the brightest from the nuclear Navy.

Think about having a nuclear-powered engine on a ship or a submarine. You absolutely, positively cannot lose that engine, especially if your "adversaries" are not even supposed to know where you are. Nuclear Navy specialists are especially adept at maintaining the reliability and the availability of the equipment, and when it came to nuclear power, they truly represented the best and the brightest. Their operating practices were transferred to the nuclear power industry.

Not Too Cheap to Meter, But . . .

Economics also began to work in the industry's favor after working against it for so long. Utility executives realized that while these plants had enormous capital costs and loans to pay off, their incremental operating costs were the lowest of any plant in their portfolios. Improving performance at nuclear plants became a means of improving the electric utility's financial health. In 1990, the aggregate capability factor at U.S. nuclear plants was less than 70 percent. This could only be described as pathetic for a power plant that is supposed to operate 24/7, except for planned shutdowns to refuel and repair equipment. By year 2000, average capability factor had surpassed 90 percent and some plants do better than 100 percent some years.

Most recently, the utilities with the most experience in nuclear power operations realized something critical: A "core competency" in nuclear plant operations could be profitably leveraged by acquiring other nuclear units or merging utilities that both have several nuclear plants. As a result, the nuclear power "industry within an industry" consolidated, for the betterment of all in my opinion. Today, two owner/operators, Entergy Corp and Exelon Corp, account for approximately 30 percent of the nuclear capacity in the United States.

It is costly to replace the electric power available from a nuke. At a coal plant, an event like a fire—fairly common, but rarely debilitating—is dealt with quickly and efficiently. Nuclear industry executives recognized that an event like a fire at a nuclear plant meant shutting down the whole plant, reporting the event to the public and the NRC, investigating the incident, developing new policies and procedures to ensure that it doesn't happen again, and so on and so on. Thus, the industry learned how to "prevent" accidents and mishaps. It learned how to apply "preventive maintenance" techniques so a component failure would not bring the plant (and the financial health of the owner) to its knees. It learned how to apply "predictive maintenance" techniques so that maintenance tasks could be scheduled, rehearsed, planned, and completed efficiently during the next planned outage. Prevention, in other words, was a boatload better than the opposite, recovery.

Planned outages at nuclear plants used to take anywhere from 30 to 100 days. Today, planned and refueling outages are typically 10 to 25 days depending on what tasks have to be done. Only outages where major components like steam generators are replaced, or capacity of the unit is to be expanded, take longer.

Okay, so nuclear power never became "too cheap to meter," the motto often associated with the salad days of the Atoms for Peace program. However, it has become the cheapest option to meter, at least when compared to coal, natural gas, and renewables (with the exception of hydro), and assuming we've learned how to build plants without the costly overruns typical of the fleet built before. Only electricity generated from hydroelectric facilities is usually less expensive, but it is clear that few hydro plants can be permitted in this country anymore. Even if they could, good sites for power generation are few and far between.

Positive Momentum

All of this positive change in nuclear power, by the way, took place while the broader utility industry aggressively applied deregulation and competition, Enron and the merchant power companies were remaking the industry in their own image, and the only new kind of power station you could get permitted in the United States during the 1990s had to burn natural gas.

The nuclear industry's turn-around during this time is nothing short of stunning. In the late 1990s, I listened to planning scenarios and forecasts at industry meetings that predicted that 30 percent of the existing nuclear power capacity would be shut down because it would not be economic, it would be viewed as unsafe, and the like, compared to the new natural-gas-fired plants. Utilities would find it uneconomic, and politically unrewarding, to relicense these facilities (most were built with a 40-year operations license) Since then, many nuclear plants have been relicensed for an additional 20 years of operation (the original permits were good for only two decades) and many of them have been "up-rated" so that output is from 5 to 20 percent greater than with the original design. And with nukes our global warming nemesis, CO_2—widely perceived to be the number one environmental issue we face—is largely a nonissue.

All of this positive momentum has allowed utility executives to once again put the nuclear power option on the table for future generating capacity. The industry is poised to construct a new fleet of nuclear plants that could add anywhere from 20,000 to 40,000 MW of capacity over the next 10 years. In recent years, the utilities with the greatest number of nuclear assets are generally the ones most favored by Wall Street and investors.

The United States has 103 operating nuclear power units (and a smaller number of nuclear power stations, since most have more than one reactor on site), which supply close to 100,000 MW of electricity. On the ground this represents only around 10 percent of the country's installed capacity (megawatts), but in reality it is 22 percent of our generated electricity (megawatt hours) because they essentially run all the time at full load. At least a half a dozen electricity companies are proceeding through the site licensing process to construct as many as thirty new units on existing sites. More than a dozen companies have new nuclear units, mostly in their long-term plans. And if this seems impressive, both India and China have ambitious plans for a nuclear construction program. China is planning to build around 30 nuclear units over the next decade, India at least 10.

It's All about Decarbonization

If you take the electricity industry in the context of its history and as a subset of energy consumption in general, expansion of nuclear power makes perfect sense. Since the Industrial Revolution, humankind has been gradually *decarbonizing* its energy sources. We've progressed from inefficient wood-fueled open fires to progressively more efficient use of fossil fuels, transitioning from coal and oil to natural gas. (Incidentally, I've seen recent articles discussing the growing popularity of wood-fired boilers for home heating. While owners love the cheap fuel and cozy heat, their neighbors are reporting increased problems with dirty air, sooty particulates and respiratory problems.) Getting the most out of nuclear and renewable energy sources is the next step in this long wave of development. Because nuclear fuel (uranium oxide) has such a high energy density, mining it, though it does have its ecological impacts, takes less of a toll overall on the earth than fossil fuels.

The extreme makeover for nuclear power is perhaps best-illustrated by the prominent environmentalists and environmental scientists who now support substantial expansion of nuclear power as a way to mitigate global warming. According to a *New York Times* article, "Updating Prescriptions for Avoiding Worldwide Catastrophe" by Andrew Reffkin, on September 12, 2006, James Lovelock is the latest vociferous convert.

Lovelock is associated with the term, *Gaia*, a "conception of the plant's chemistry, climate, and veneer of life as a self-sustaining entity." Lovelock now believes that the threat of global warming is so overwhelming that all-out nuclear war pales in comparison. In the article, Lovelock goes on to call renewable energy sources "largely gestures," that make people feel good. If prominent thinkers like Lovelock are onboard, then I think nuclear power may have a real chance this time around.

Now What about the Wastes?

Positive momentum aside, all is not Terra Firma for the nuclear power business. Accidents still occur at nuclear plants, although none have been as serious as TMI or Chernobyl. Occasionally, there are even embarrassing discoveries, such as when it was discovered that the top of a reactor vessel in Ohio had almost completely corroded through. This event led the industry to spend a great deal of money on a crash basis to replace the reactor pressure vessel heads at many plants as a preventive measure.

As I like to say, for all its progress over the last 10 years, the industry is still one major accident away from another trip to oblivion. Japan has experienced several significant nuclear plant events with cover-ups by the industry. In a very recent example from Europe, a nuclear plant in Sweden experienced a significant safety "event." These events rarely result in radioactive material release, loss of limb or life, or even property damage. At other power stations, they would go unnoticed except for the owner/operator and plant staff. But because nuclear units are so heavily scrutinized, such events are reported, analyzed, and evaluated so that the likelihood of being repeated is low.

And then there is the lingering, looming issue of spent fuel. You may have heard of this place in Nevada called *Yucca Mountain*. It's not a tourist destination, nor a place where Las Vegas taxi drivers deposit gamblers who have lost all their money and can't pay their fares. This is the place the federal government has been "evaluating" for a long-term repository and nuclear waste containment and management. Without an appropriate plan, the federal government accepted the obligation to "take" spent nuclear fuel rods from nuclear plants more than two decades ago. Yucca Mountain subsequently became the "plan." Unfortunately, the government has squandered enough money to build several nuclear units trying to evaluate and permit the site. It is still at least a decade away from achieving its goal, by its own admission, which means the probable date of completion is more like two decades away, if ever.

From Repository to Reprocessing

Five years ago, while I was working with a client in the nuclear industry, utility executive were loudly lamenting the sluggishness of the government's Yucca Mountain program and insisting that long-term waste management was the number one issue holding back the industry.

Today, executives say that they can get by without Yucca Mountain. What they are really saying is that the prospects for building new plants have raced far ahead of the government's ability to live up to its obligation to "take" those pesky spent nuclear fuel rods. And they're not going to squander the opportunity to get more plants up and running while sitting around waiting for Yucca to go online.

The problem is, however, that an acceptable solution to the problem remains in limbo, and this won't lend confidence to the public once they collectively catch wind of it. Perception is everything in this business. Here's another nagging perception issue that could haunt the industry: nuclear fuel is largely imported. The public understands petroleum to be a foreign, or imported, energy source. The public does not attach that understanding to nuclear fuel. In fact, more than 90 percent of our virgin nuclear fuel is imported, thankfully from countries more likely to be friendly to us over the long-term, Australia and Canada. But, we also get a significant percentage from a little-known and unique agreement with Russia to reprocess weapons-grade nuclear material. Thus, the erroneous perception that nuclear power furthers energy in dependence could haunt the industry down the road.

In the electricity business, as I've explained, you don't get a couple of social "goods" without having to deal with some social "bads." The biggest and baddest of the negative social impacts of nuclear power is the long-term management of highly radioactive waste. Long-term in this case effectively means forever. Yes, forever. And this time, I really do mean forever. Radioactive waste management is the political football, the hot potato, the Achille's heel of nuclear power.

Cleverly worded polls may show that a majority of Americans support the expansion of nuclear power. Vociferous environmentalists may be moving into the pro-nuclear power camp. But what if you asked this question: "Do you support the expansion of nuclear power knowing that the long-term management of spent nuclear reactor fuel has not been resolved?" I am reasonably sure that support for nuclear power would plummet with this recognition, at least among those who fundamentally understand that there is a long-term waste issue.

Here's a prescient quote from *Nuclear Power Development: Prospects in the 1990s* by Stanley M. Nealey (Battelle Press, Columbus, OH: 1989):

> *Concerns about radioactive waste disposal have increased sharply over the past fifteen years. However, this issue appears unlikely to prevent a restart of nuclear power development unless it becomes clear that geological disposal is not viable. There is no question that many people feel intense concern over radioactive waste. For them, this issue is reason enough by itself to reject nuclear power. Continued progress of the waste disposal program will, over time, lessen the importance of this issue as a limitation on nuclear power growth.*

Guess what? Since Nealey's book there has been no material progress on this issue. None, nada, zero. There is no polite way to state this conclusion. *Long-term management of spent nuclear fuel continues to be a public policy failure.*

We're Here to Help

The industry built the first set of nuclear reactors back in the 1960s with the understanding that the government would reprocess the spent fuel in a facility specifically being built for that purpose. It was never built.

For the last 20 years, the industry assumed, for lack of a better solution, that the government would provide a long-term repository for spent nuclear fuel. Yucca Mountain would eventually become that repository.

It now appears that Yucca Mountain will never become such a repository, even though one of the reasons it was selected was because it was the site of bomb-making activities and is already highly contaminated. (That's comforting, isn't it?) For the next several years, Harry Reid, the long-time and powerful Senator from Nevada, and now the Majority Leader, will help ensure that his state never accepts a spent fuel rod from a nuclear plant.

In the meantime, what has been happening with the spent fuel rods from the last 50 years? The quiet little secret here is that half of them have largely been hanging around in what are known as on-site (i.e., at the nuclear plants themselves), short-term storage ponds. Plants put them in shallow pools of water, which absorb the heat and are shielded to prevent release of radiation. The other half are also on site in "dry storage."

Because we don't have a centralized repository or management site, we have dozens of little repositories dotting the country. You can argue whether one centralized facility or many distributed facilities is the safer approach, but that's not my real point. The real issue is that we have no consensus about what to do and no real sense of urgency about coming to consensus.

Fortunately, a solution does exist, albeit a partial one. It is called *reprocessing*, which is explained in this chapter's feature box "How Reprocessing (and Other Techniques) Work."

Recycling—of Sorts

In this country, reprocessing is an even more awkwardly shaped football, a hotter potato politically, than a repository. Reprocessing was even illegal, banned in this country by legislation passed by the Carter administration in 1977. Although President Reagan subsequently repealed that act in 1981, reprocessing is still banned by political fiat. However, I am now convinced that this has to be the solution ultimately agreed upon.

How can I be so bold on this claim? First, other countries with extensive nuclear power operations, notably France, United Kingdom, and Japan, all operate reprocessing facilities to some degree. It's not like we're reinventing the wheel or anything; reprocessing is a form of recycling. I freely acknowledge most people who feel good about recycling their bottles and cans do not feel good about reprocessing nuclear fuel. However, for the most part, they don't realize that we already reprocess significant amounts of nuclear material.

Second, the existing storage ponds usually require a separate permit. Because the industry fully expected a "permanent solution" for their nuclear fuel rods, these storage ponds are permitted for a defined length of time, and have only so much capacity. Time and space are running out. Operation of the existing plants is jeopardized if a permanent solution isn't agreed upon soon. The last thing nuclear utilities want is a drawn out, public hearing about these storage ponds that most people don't even realize exist.

Third, I think the industry has quietly given up on Yucca Mountain. When I attend nuclear power conferences today, the subject is not discussed in the same way it was five years ago. In the past, industry's leaders and policy shapers in Washington would beat the gavel on the desk and say, in effect, "Bring me the head of Harry Reid." They rallied to bully Congress and the president into meeting their obligations. And why not? The federal government made a promise. Well, politicians promise many things and deliver few of them. Today, long-term waste management is a giant lurking in the corner. It looms over the future of the industry, but no one seems willing to confront it, at least not overtly.

The fact is, the industry has no choice but to "close the fuel cycle," at least in my humble opinion. If it becomes increasingly untenable to store onsite temporarily, and a long-term site isn't in the cards, what are we going to do? We can't exactly put it all on a rocket and send out to outer space. (Although people have thought of that!) I mean, we could, but what if a mishap occurs and it falls back to Earth?

So what is reprocessing and why is it so scary? It goes back to that nuclear power–nuclear bomb connection. It's pretty easy to reprocess nuclear fuel rods into bomb material. But the reverse is true as well. And that brings me to an interesting irony.

From Russia with Energy

In the early 1990s, the United States made a deal with the (then) Russian Federation: We would take its nuclear bomb material and convert it to material suitable for nuclear fuel rods. In fact, we've been doing just that. It's called the *Megatons to Megawatts* nuclear nonproliferation program. It is one of the more successful outcomes of the thawing of the Cold War. According to public information available from United States Enrichment Corp. (USEC), the equivalent of 11,500 nuclear warheads have been eliminated by recycling them into nuclear fuel. Bomb-grade uranium compounds are shipped halfway around the world, very carefully I assume, and converted in U.S. facilities into fuel-grade uranium.

Isn't it ironic that we reprocess Russian bombs for electricity production but we can't approve reprocessing the waste from our own electricity production for *more* electricity production? Certainly, there's a social value in converting bombs to peaceful uses that isn't being accounted for, but there's also a social value in converting spent fuel rods sitting in shallow ponds all across the country into electricity to run the computer on which I'm typing this sentence.

A Five-Story Football Field

Here's another thing that has always fascinated me about spent nuclear fuel. On a mass and volume basis, there really isn't that much of it to deal with. According to *Understanding Radioactive Waste,* 3rd ed. by Raymond L. Murray (Columbus, OH: Battelle Press, 1989), the annual spent fuel volume from the 100 or so reactors in the United States would fill a football field to less than a foot deep. Do the math. Assume that those reactors have been running for 50 years (although the U.S. nuclear power program is around 50 years old, the present-day fleet of 100 reactors had only been operating for 20 years or so). Maybe the total volume of waste is a football field 50 feet deep or the height of a five-story building. It's still a small total value.

The low volume of waste is testament to the relatively high energy density of uranium. It is also a comparative lesson in waste management. I think my family alone generates a larger volume of household waste in a year! Think about the massive landfills used to manage consumer and municipal waste, the acres of discarded tires, the mountains of ash and scrubber sludge that emanate from coal-fired plants, the millions of tons of carbon dioxide discharged into the atmosphere. Is it that difficult to manage the waste from the least expensive source of electricity all of us consume?

Granted, managing this stuff isn't for the faint-hearted. This isn't material you work with in a home science lab under a "Caution!" label, or something you present in a science fair with a bright yellow "Hazardous Material!" sticker. Spent nuclear fuel is some of the most dangerous stuff on the planet. How lethal is it? According to the Murray text referenced above, the spent fuel rods immediately exiting the reactor emit a radiation dosage of millions of rems per hour (Rems is the official measurement unit for radiation) at the surface of the fuel rods. The lethal dosage is 400 rems.

Okay, so I think I know why the industry refuses to talk publicly about reprocessing: It absolves the government of its responsibility to manage the problem and live up to its obligations. The other reason mum's the word is that the cost of reprocessing has to be added to the total cost of nuclear-generated electricity. Keeping the spent fuel rods in pools of water isn't free, but it may be cheap compared to shipping them to centralized processing facilities and paying to have them converted into more fuel. Deferring this "cost" may be a short-term palliative but by no means a long-term solution.

Here again, this problem of an "externality" crops up. Mining and processing virgin uranium compounds involves its own environmental impacts. Yet it is less expensive than reprocessing spent fuel rods. As long as the use of naturally occurring resources is less expensive than "recycling," economies will favor the natural stuff. However, if you quantify the impact of the waste material, whether in terms of long-term management, hazards and health, and the impact of mining virgin resources, and add those values to the overall cost, then perhaps the economic balance changes.

How Reprocessing—and Other Techniques—Work
Reprocessing is a well-understood technology. France, the United Kingdom, Germany, Belgium, Russia, and Japan all have reprocessed spent fuel rods. For years, we have reprocessed

(continued)

nuclear material in this country as well, at a facility in Hanford, in Washington state. More recently, United States Enrichment Corp. has been reprocessing nuclear warheads, at a facility in the United States, as the exclusive agent for the Megatons to Megawatts program. The uranium from spent nuclear fuel has a higher concentration of the right isotope of uranium than does naturally occurring uranium. "Spent" fuel still contains almost all of the original uranium (around 96 percent of it), but the good stuff, the fissionable U235, is reduced to around 1 percent. Three percent of the spent fuel is comprised of waste products and the remaining 1 percent is the plutonium that was produced while the uranium was "burned up" in the reactor. In other words, the fissionable uranium becomes plutonium in the reactor.

The spent fuel rods can be cut apart into small pieces, and the uranium, plutonium, and waste materials can be separated from each other. The uranium can then be recycled to the facility where uranium oxide is converted into another form of uranium, and the plutonium can be combined with more enriched uranium to create a new type of fuel called a *mixed oxide* (MOX). MOX can be used directly to form the fuel pellets loaded into fuel rods; the only requirement is that the reactor has to be licensed to operate with a uranium-plutonium mix as opposed to a pure uranium fuel.

Recycling the plutonium and the uranium reduces the amount of virgin uranium-containing material that has to be mined and milled. The other benefit of reprocessing is that the residual waste material has lower and lower radiation activity and lower and lower weight. One estimate shows that the weight of the reprocessed material is one-tenth that of the original spent fuel rods. We should be clear on this point: Reprocessing does not eliminate the spent fuel problem; it does, however, greatly reduce the quantity of waste that must be managed, and the radiation levels of those materials.

It's actually the plutonium that gives reprocessing critics ulcers. Plutonium being transported from one place to another could be diverted or captured by terrorists, rogue nations, or common criminals. This is to say nothing of the dangers to workers who have to handle the material and work in these facilities. The other side of the coin, however, is that the safest place for the plutonium is at its ultimate destination—inside the reactor core getting burned up to generate electricity!

Some of the other ways of managing spent nuclear fuel deserve mention, but mostly for their comic, not their practical value. For example, with tongue firmly planted in cheek, I mentioned in the main text rocketing nuclear waste into space. This option has gotten serious attention in the past. The idea would be to keep the material in casks that orbit the moon, or depositing them on the moon's surface. One schemer even suggested shooting them toward the sun.

Another idea was to bury the casks in the Antarctica polar ice caps. Dig a small hole, place them inside, and the casks would slide down through the release of heat to the ice walls on their own. Eventually, the casks would hit the rock base and remain there forever. Given the rate of suspected polar ice cap melting from global warming, more intense heat at the Earth's poles probably isn't the answer.

Similar concepts have been proposed for disposal of the casks at the floor of the sea hundreds of miles from any sovereign nation's shores. A variation on this theme, geological disposal, is to drop the casks into a hole a mile or more deep. At the bottom, the wastes mix with the rock, which melts from the intense heat generated by the waste. This mass then cools and solidifies. Jules Verne must be rolling in his grave!

Well, you can't blame technocrats for thinking. It just seems like they were thinking of good plots for new James Bond movies or presaging videogames for kids.

A National Imperative

To sum up, nuclear power has clearly been invited back to the table for electricity infrastructure expansion, as well it should. However, it needs to be treated differently than the other options. Like the airlines, nuclear power requires a greater degree of cooperation among owner/operators, especially in the areas of safety, operations, and maintenance. It also requires a high degree of support from the government, especially in the area of insurance, liability protection, and long-term waste management. If global warming is to be considered an immediate threat to the planet, then the expansion of nuclear power should be considered a national imperative, and resolution to the nuclear waste issue a national emergency.

As an industry within an industry, nuclear power should not be subjected to the same competitive strictures that might be applied successfully to other parts of the electricity industry. Its primary social good or "internality" is the avoidance of carbon dioxide emissions and the reduction of the global carbon inventory. Its secondary social good could be a reduction in energy imports from hostile parts of the world, and therefore an integral part of our national energy infrastructure security.

For these reasons, nuclear power needs to have its own regulatory framework, one that is not subjected to the vagaries of the free market. In the last chapter, I outline what this framework should be.

Chapter 16

Savvy Consumption, Empowering Ratepayers

More than once in the preceding chapters, you've undoubtedly noticed that I point to a fundamental flaw in our electricity delivery structure: lack of demand response. It continues to boggle my mind after two and a half decades in the energy business how otherwise well-intentioned people focus on only two of the three pillars of economics without accounting for the third, price, and its impact on the other two. The fact is that most consumers today still cannot alter their consumption of electricity at any given time because they have no idea what the price is at any given time.

When you buy a pair of socks, you see the price tag. Over time, you learn who sells good quality socks at what you consider a fair price. When you buy gasoline, you can't avoid seeing the price. When prices are typically low, you may no longer notice the price per gallon. When they are high, or rising, you notice and at least have the choice of altering your driving habits. With electricity, you get a bill every month. It may show the average price you paid for electricity over the month, or even break it down into its component parts. That doesn't give you much choice in how you ran appliances two weeks ago.

However, everyone benefits if consumers can respond to price signals, and are educated to do so. Utility bills include excess costs incurred to maintain, and have available, infrastructure to meet the highest potential demand at any given time. This is called the *peak demand*. For decades, we've maintained the supply/demand balance by working the supply side. The balance can also be maintained, of course, by reducing demand. Demand response, triggered by price signals, reduces the total amount of money invested in infrastructure. It's not rocket science.

It's apparent why utilities don't really like demand response. They make money earning a rate of return on capital invested in infrastructure and they make money selling electricity. Why should they invest in demand response? We get to the answer later.

Making Meters Smart

Fortunately, an exciting class of technology has emerged to solve this problem. It is variously called the smart meter, the intelligent meter, or the two-way meter. The electricity meter you probably have on your house or office building is a dumb meter. All it does is tell the electric utility how much juice you used since the last time a utility worker read the meter. If you are lucky, the meter is a little more advanced and can be read by the utility remotely, avoiding an appointment to come into the building. Today, there are smart meters and really, really brilliant meters.

A smart electricity meter is designed so that the meter's data can be read remotely. Utilities across the country are installing these devices because they reduce their costs. They can quit paying meter readers, or at least pay fewer of them. A really smart meter can record not only the total amount of electricity used but perhaps also separate out the amount used during some periods from other periods. This is helpful if a utility offers what are known as "time of use" rates. The meter tells the utility that you used x amount of electricity under one rate, usually an off-peak rate, and *y* amount of electricity under another rate, usually a peak rate.

A really, really bright meter provides real-time, two-way communication between your dwelling and the utility or electricity service provider. It might be connected to a read-out in your kitchen or next to your thermostat that displays the price of electricity at that time, or maybe the next hour. This critical piece of information then becomes the basis for automating your home.

In the most futuristic vision, your home automation system could be programmed so that when the price of electricity surpasses a threshold of your choice, your thermostat might automatically raise the temperature and cut back on the amount of air conditioning. It could even trigger a lockout on appliances so when your kids come home from school in the afternoon, they don't run the dishwasher or the electric dryer (as if that would happen). With cell phone and wireless technology becoming ubiquitous, you might even change the settings on the automation system remotely over the Internet or from your cell phone.

Marrying advanced communications with electric systems enables other benefits. Appliances, lighting systems, electric motors, and other equipment, equipped with two-communication, can alert service companies automatically when there are problems, or when routine maintenance needs to be conducted. Wouldn't it be nice if your freezer would warn you it's about to break down before you find pools of water in your basement and some sort of suspicious smell lingering in the air? From a commercial point of view, this will be the key to getting the business model right. People and businesses don't really want to "manage" their electricity demand; they just want the lights to stay on at reasonable, or at least predictable, cost.

Plus, it's not just about better communications; it's about reducing energy consumption. You may work in an office building that has motion detectors, which turn lighting systems on when people are detected to be present through their movement. The next step could be lighting systems equipped with dimmable fluorescent bulbs that the utility or local service provider can dim to reduce lighting and energy consumption by as much as 50 percent.

Here's how the Electric Power Research Institute (EPRI), in a recent article by Brent Baker, titled "Turning on Energy Efficiency" in the

EPRI Journal (Summer 2006), describes where this technology will be taking us:

> *The air conditioning system in your office reads tomorrow's weather forecast—a hot day is coming, and electricity prices are going to be high during the hottest part of the day. The customer has already set acceptable temperature ranges or perhaps a cost limit to drive the air conditioner. The AC has already learned, through automated computer learning, that it can make the office comfortable at a reasonable cost by pre-cooling in the morning when prices are low and reducing load during the peak period when prices are high. All of this is done* automatically.

The broader message here is this: computing, telecommunications, Internet, broadband, and cable networks have yet to be integrated with the electric grid. This is what people refer to as the *smart grid*. It is yet another element of what I call the "right side" of the electricity delivery value chain.

We're talking about more intelligence on every level, too. Remember that every Btu (for British thermal unit, a term used to refer to the heat value of fuels or to describe the power potential of systems) of energy or kilowatt hour (kWh) of electricity leaves an unwanted legacy—for fossil fuels, emissions and solid waste discharges; for nuclear, an increment of high-level nuclear waste that must be managed forever. When energy consumption is reduced, that long-term legacy is correspondingly reduced as well.

Getting Utilities to Buy in

With few exceptions so far, electric utilities only pay lip service to demand response. That is, they will talk about it, participate in pilot programs, or step into it weakly if it becomes a requirement for them to pursue their traditional avenues of making money. In the early to mid-1990s, California and several states in the Northeast pushed demand response pretty hard and even figured out how to reward utilities for the investment.

Today, frankly, it may be a bit tougher. For one thing, advanced meters are not cheap. They can cost from $300 to $1,200 each depending on whether they are just smart or really, really bright. The problem is that the low end of that range is still about 10 times what a typical utility earns in profit on the average residential ratepayer. Once the utility installs a meter, it is likely that electricity consumption by that customer will be reduced. Both of these outcomes go against the grain of the utility business model, as noted above. Still, regulatory commissions have figured out how to reward utilities for building big power stations; surely an incentive program could be devised to reward investment in demand response.

The other issue holding up advanced meters is more insidious and less public. Utilities are developing a technology called *broadband over power lines* or BPL. Essentially, this is a means of transmitting communication signals through the same lines that carry the electricity. Think about it. If the utilities wait to invest in a smart grid when BPL is commercial and demonstrated to work on a large scale, then *they* will control the entire smart grid. They do not have to cede control of the communications portion, the intelligence part, of the system to telecom companies, Internet companies, or cable companies. Not only do they control the smart grid, but they can offer competing services in cable and telecom.

In general, the intelligent grid "vision" is also being held up by the lack of accepted communications protocols and standards. Devices have to "speak" a common language. The options are numerous. BPL, the Internet (or an advanced version that is more secure), cable, fiber optics, and various wireless modes are all options in competition with each other. The industry calls it the "last mile" problem—what option controls the last mile into the home or building?

Price: The Best Motivator

So, back to the question: Why would utilities invest in demand response? A small number of utilities are already set up to do so. They are distribution utilities, which no longer own or control generation or transmission assets. They are best positioned to offer a variety of electricity management services to customers. Frankly, they don't have much of a growth-oriented business model, barring population or industrial growth, if they don't. Several utilities were in fact focused on becoming leading distribution-oriented businesses, until the Enron debacle began to infect the entire industry in the 2001 to 2002 time frame. I believe they will reestablish this activity as a way to earn higher profits.

In a rising electricity price environment, like the one we're in now, commissions will be naturally motivated to reward utilities for demand response programs. At the same time, the opportunity to replace revenue lost from lower electricity sales with incremental revenue earned from offering services, such as appliance and electric system maintenance contracts, will keep them solvent. Virtually every other heavy industrial sector has made a painful transition from offering a one-size-fits-all commodity to offering niche, custom products and services around the primary product. The electric utility industry is one of the last to do so. But, make no mistake, it will happen.

If nothing else, utilities are likely to be forced into it. Persistently high electricity prices to consumers will force public utility commissions to act in the interest of voters. Commissioners will design rate programs that allow utilities to recover their investment. The programs won't be new, but they may be new to some utilities.

Let the Entrepreneurs in

When it comes right down to it, the real forcing function will be entrepreneurial energy services firms who will get in between the utility and its customers. The increasing cost of electricity service, and, more importantly, the business cost of unreliable service, will widen the gap between utilities and ratepayers. These so-called energy management or demand side management firms will make the investment in the smart meters, and the energy efficient lighting, appliances, heaters, air conditioners, and other electric-consuming devices. They will then earn a return on their invested capital through what is known as a shared savings, or performance-based, contract. Once these firms prove the business model, utilities will likely acquire them and continue to dominate their service territories. Those who control the information control the outcome. Once those meters are installed, the race will be to see who best can capitalize on the data and information.

Right now, energy management firms are focused on commercial accounts, like large office buildings in densely populated areas. Soon, they will leverage their experience to the aggregation of residential accounts. They will guarantee something that electric utilities have never really had to respond to: quality of service—customer by customer—rather than "in the aggregate."

What Price Quality?

At this point, I need to make an important distinction on the customer side of the meter. The electric utility has always strived to meet reliability goals. Reliability of service is not the same as quality of service, although one is certainly a refinement of the other. Our digital economy, based on computers, Internet, online banking and shopping, and telecom, demands a far higher quality of electricity than our industrial economic base of decades past. Achieving higher and higher levels of power quality will be another way for energy services firms to distinguish their product and services.

What kind of quality are we talking about? Traditional utilities talk in terms of achieving 99.9 percent reliability of service. In practice, that means that the typical ratepayer would be without service no more than eight hours in a year.

In our service territory, the reliability figure is closer to 97 percent, after two storm outages and some customers without power for 10 days. This is nothing short of abysmal. We're not alone. As I've pointed out in other chapters, many parts of the country have seen some of the worst storms in recent memory, and some of the worst electricity outages on record.

Unfortunately, even the target of 99.9 percent isn't nearly good enough for the digital economy. It is said to require "six nines," or 99.9999 percent reliability, meaning only a few minutes of downtime per year. Server farms, telecommunications stations, chip manufacturing plants, assembly lines controlled by digital automation systems, and data centers serving banks, government, and other sectors, must have power 24/7/365. These facilities are often equipped with elaborate back-up and disaster recovery systems, which include *uninterruptible power systems* (UPS) that switch on automatically when the utility service is lost.

Forward-looking, distribution-oriented utilities and energy services firms will provide these services for critical customers. Before the winners and losers on the right side of the value chain are sorted out, however, we're likely to pass through a clash of cultures.

Brain vs. Brawn

Experts in our business have their way of describing this culture war. One popular phrase is iron versus bits. That is, the iron, steel, and copper needed for the physical assets compete in value with the servers, chips, and computers handling the bits of data.

I prefer to look at it as brains vs. brawn. The information *about* a piece of equipment eventually rivals the value of the equipment itself. Already, cell phone providers practically give phones away; the money is made in the thousands of calls you make over that phone. Personal computers have gotten progressively less expensive. Today, you can buy an "Internet appliance" for only a few hundred dollars, and "rent" most of your applications on line. I know people who have personal digital assistants (combo phone, e-mail, minicomputer) that can carry your PowerPoint presentation to your next meeting and transmit the presentation wirelessly to a projector. You can bet that far fewer business people are going to carry laptop computers with them in the near future. (Forget about the hassles at the airport security line, too.)

In the business textbooks, this phenomenon is known as the *razors-for-razor-blades strategy*. Would you rather sell a razor once in 10 years, or control the sale of 10 razor blades per year for 10 years? What about having a sensor in the razor that indicates when the blade is worn, transmits a signal to the blade supplier, who then delivers a new blade to the customer? Service businesses based on the razor blade model are based on knowledge about how the customer is using the product.

Think of all the other hardware that has been, or is being, "disintermediated" and replaced by hardware that is smarter and more compatible with Internet and networked communications: film-based cameras (digital cameras and processing), stereos (iPods), car radios (satellite radio), network television (cable, satellite TV). The 42-inch television I bought last year cost as much as the 14-inch Trinitron I bought in 1979! All the extra money—and much more I am sure—goes to the cable company in the form of a monthly bill.

It is commonly quoted that more than 20 percent of an automobile's "value" today is embodied by all the "smart" devices, automation, electronics, and diagnostics embedded into the steel and plastic. For today's hybrid cars, the figure is even higher, I have no doubt. According to *The Smart Energy Grid,* a report issued by the Center for Smart Energy, "digital quality power now represents 10 percent of total electrical load in the U.S. and is expected to reach 30 percent by 2020." Power quality is managed through knowledge about how the customer uses electricity.

Okay, you get the point. But the real issue is that the integration of digital and wireless communication with electric service has yet to take place in a big way. Server, software, and chip companies might win big because their wares form the "brain." Utilities might trump cable companies if the promise of BPL proves out. However, I have learned over 25 years, and by studying a century of history, that electric utilities do not die nor do they fade away. They contract, expand, screw up, miss bankruptcy by the skin of their teeth, merge with each other, divest assets, acquire assets, and continue to build infrastructure and serve customers. My bet is that, one way or another, all of the new functions for delivery high quality electricity will eventually reside in a utility-like entity.

A Kilowatt Hour Here . . .

Savvy consumption is accomplished by empowering the ratepayer with the knowledge to make better decisions. In the process, we expect to achieve greater energy efficiency, reduce emissions, and improve the planet without sacrificing our lifestyles. That's a noble goal. I am all for it.

Modern economies have reduced their energy intensities substantially over the last 50 years. Given the situation in other parts of the world, which are just now industrializing, any gains we make are vastly overshadowed by growing energy intensity elsewhere. Most of the gains we've discussed here on the "right side of the value chain" are incremental at best. We need technological breakthroughs to make a quantum leap in progress.

At least a glimmer of such a technology may be at hand. It is part of the vast and exciting area of *nanotechnology*. Called *thermotunneling*, it takes advantage of a phenomenon only recently recognized—electrons can be made to jump from one electrode, excited through heat energy, to another if separated by only a few nanometers. As the electrons jump from one electrode, it is cooled and when they arrive at the other electrode, they can flow to another circuit as electricity or they can be stored in a battery or capacitor for future use. Thermotunneling works in both directions, so it can be used for both heating and cooling.

The implications for this technology in electricity production are profound. Right now, this technique has only been proven in the barest of laboratory experiments. If it can be scaled up to a commercial-size device (work is being done now to prove the concept), then low-temperature heat, available in vast quantities from sources as diverse as incident solar energy to power plant stack exhaust, can be converted directly into electric power. That's right. Directly. As long as you can properly separate the two electrodes, the electrons themselves act as the fluid that moves the heat from one side to the other. If the external device used to send or receive the heat is an electric circuit, there's no need for any intermediate steps such as electric motors driving compressors or steam engines driving generators.

Because the laboratory device that accomplishes thermotunneling is similar to a computer chip, the first applications likely will be in computers and other chip-containing devices to more efficiently manage heat production and release. Getting rid of heat is currently the number one problem facing the computer and server hardware industry. Remember the recent computer battery recalls due to spontaneous combustion from overheating?

Making power supply more efficient is another challenge. Currently, microchip-based devices have to convert AC power from a wall outlet into DC power used by the device. According to one report, existing personal computer (PC) power supplies vary widely in efficiency, between 20 and 90 percent. Such power packs, 2.5-billion in the United States and up to 10-billion worldwide, suck up 2 percent of the nation's electricity. Thermotunneling provides an elegant solution for both heat management and efficient electricity supply to the devices. If proven practical, it's a technology that is only as far away as the funding available to commercialize it.

BTUs to Kilowatt Hours

The amount of electricity available from low-temperature heat sources is staggering. Just to give an example, a power plant is only between 30 and 50 percent efficiency at converting fuel energy into electricity. Most of the ones in our country are near the low end of this range. That's because between 1–10 percent of the electric energy is lost in transmission and distribution. A traditional incandescent light bulb loses 90 percent of the electric energy as heat. From a fuel source to device perspective, the entire process from fuel source to light bulb is only about 3 percent efficient! Thermotunneling and other low-temperature heat recovery devices on a commercial scale offers the possibility of converting much of the waste heat in this processing chain into electricity.

Earlier, we discussed how electric power delivery systems will be integrated with communications. Now, overlay a nanotechnology like thermotunneling and suddenly, it does seem like many of the world's energy problems could be solved. Certainly, integrating communications is an activity for the next 10 to 20 years. Applying thermotunneling commercially is an activity for the next half a century. Remember, though, that the electricity era, at least as a commercial enterprise, started with a device to turn electricity into a lighting device and an aggressive inventor/businessman (Thomas Edison) who needed a way to sell them. Wouldn't it be cool if the next 100 years were defined by another inventor/businessperson with a device to convert low-grade heat into electricity and just needed a way to sell it?

The Return of Electric Cars—Again

It may seem counter-intuitive, but using *more* electricity could also be a pathway to greater energy efficiency overall as well as greater energy independence. Power plants are responsible for approximately one-third of the carbon dioxide emissions. Automobiles are responsible for approximately one-third. The more electricity substituted for gasoline in supplying energy for transportation, the fewer emissions we have to worry about, with an important caveat: The method of generating the electricity has to be much cleaner than the car exhaust. The less gasoline we consumer, the less oil we have to import from hostile or unfriendly countries. And so it goes.

The prospect of a massive transformation from gasoline-powered engines to electric vehicles promises to have the greatest impact on the electricity system as we know it. This represents a new source of demand, unlike anything the industry has seen in the last several decades. It could dramatically change the production cycle, because electric car batteries would likely be charged up overnight—during the off-peak period. Utilities love the idea of electric vehicles not only because of the increased demand, but because they would increase the efficiency and productivity of the infrastructure during that off-peak period.

Taking on the Oil Lobby

The only way to meet such a huge potential demand, without aggravating global warming, is to generate the additional electricity with carbon-free sources of energy. That means nuclear fuel and/or renewable energy coupled to energy storage. In this case, wind energy becomes as interesting an option as nuclear. In many locations with strong wind resources, the wind velocity profile is much stronger at night than it is during the day. Under our current demand and consumption patterns, this isn't very helpful. If millions of electric vehicles are charging up at night, however, it's a different story. (And if you've got a storage system hooked up to that wind farm, then the cars can charge up whenever they want!)

When you make a bet on electric vehicles, however you essentially are pitting the entrenched global petroleum business against the more parochial and fragmented electricity industry companies (i.e., the utilities). The largest supplier of electricity is still a dwarf compared to the global petroleum behemoths. The petroleum industry is far more consolidated into a few huge companies; the electricity supply and delivery business is still very much fragmented. It is a daunting prospect to expect the renewable industry lobby and the electricity lobby to take on the petroleum guys.

Consumers offer no help. History teaches us that when petroleum and gasoline prices fall, fewer people care about electric cars, alternative fuels, and so on. That is, unless consumers understand the other financial stakes. For example, the emerging business of carbon credits and trading means that carbon discharges now can be valued quantitatively. Each increment of carbon emissions carries a price—or a cost. A government-imposed "cap and trade" program provides the mechanism to value the carbon footprint in the financial analyses.

What if you also quantified the value of energy independence, as we discussed in an earlier chapter? Imagine going to a filling station and seeing not only the price per gallon, but the hidden cost per gallon to protect our petroleum supply lines, fight wars in countries with oil and natural gas reserves, and lead global military defense! When you compare electricity to other forms of energy with these values and costs illuminated, you begin to wonder why we're not deploying our military to secure and protect nuclear fuel supplies for the next 50 years and not the petroleum supply of the last 100.

The best way to liquidate the advantage of the oil lobby is to redefine the economics of using petroleum-derived fuels for transportation.

In this way, electric vehicles represent greater electricity use but still savvy consumption. Nothing comes free, however. Suitable battery technology still isn't ready for prime time in electric vehicles. And if horse manure in cities was a reason to switch from horse-drawn carriages to automobiles at the end of the last century, imagine what it will be like to manage discarded electric vehicle batteries once everyone switches to this mode of transportation. Let's hope that the creative inventors figure out a way to use materials that are valuable enough to recycle instead of creating a disposal nightmare.

Redistributing the Power

In this chapter's discussion of consumption, we saw how large power electronics equipment and digital equipment are being applied to make the grid more flexible. When you know the amount of electricity flowing across any segment of the system, where power is being used, and can automatically control the usage of that power, you have a brain that can be attached to less brawn. *You have the power, and the power to manage it.*

In the decades ahead, if we can convert a substantial portion of the waste heat into electricity, and add that to the production side of the value chain, we've truly done a service for coming generations on this planet. Finally, if we convert the vehicular transportation system to electricity, we'll need more brawn, but that won't hurt us if we build the right kind of power plants. Add storage to the mix and it looks like a bright future.

In the next chapter, we look at the emergence of distributed power and intelligent microgrids that augment commodity electric utility service.

Chapter 17

Distributed Power

Five years ago, the ghost of Thomas Edison and his shadowy outline of the electricity system that he envisioned more than a century ago reappeared. As discussed in Chapter 3, his system of small grids based on direct current (DC) lost out to Westinghouse, Tesla, and others who advocated a "centralized" alternating current (AC) approach that led to longer and longer transmission lines and larger and larger power stations. The essence of distributed power is short distances between electricity source and user coupled with smaller electricity generating devices. Many of these devices naturally produce DC because they are not associated with rotating equipment.

Gaps from Tectonic Movement

We've already talked about how the competition and deregulation programs of the 1990s, rightfully called *tectonic movement* in this business, pulled apart the production and delivery value chain. A corresponding movement called *distributed energy* (or power) gained strength as well. While in principle, a *distributed power* (DP) system (see Figure 17.1) borrows directly from Edison's vision, the advocacy was being fed from several different directions. First, the big versus small crowd saw distributed power as a way to champion the little guy, the consumer, the ratepayer, over the big utility on its way, in their minds, to extinction. Second, the natural gas industry understood distributed power to be a way to market and sell more of its product (and you'll see why later in this chapter). Third, some factions of the environmental movement believed that anything has to be better than large dirty central power plants or nuclear plants. Fourth, utilities left with only their distribution function saw distributed power as their salvation, as a way to grow beyond collecting a toll for distributing electricity to customers on behalf of other suppliers.

The mystique of DP was enhanced at the time by analogies to the computer, software, Internet, and telecom revolutions taking place in the late 1990s. DP advocates compared central stations to mainframe computers and landline telephones. DP, on the other hand, was a robust network of intelligent devices communicating with each other, all the while empowering consumers to take responsibility for their energy destiny. Some purveyors of DP devices such as fuel cells, microturbine generators, photovoltaic solar cells, and even Stirling engines that make use of lower temperature heat sources, basked in an aura reserved at that time for dotcoms and telecoms. They were certainly on the dance cards of the investor community.

Seemingly, investors were getting on board with the vision. I remember private equity and energy tech venture capital investment funds being launched specifically focused on this sector. Lenders had devised special programs to make it efficient to lend money to many aggregated, small, distributed power projects, instead of arranging large chunks of debt for fewer larger projects. FERC was smoothing the way, too, with a big initiative called *Standard Interconnection*, which would have made it much easier for DP systems to link up with the utility system, and prevent more traditional utilities from torpedoing projects.

Well, by 2002, "I am DP, hear me roar" turned seemingly overnight into a hushed whimper. With the stock market scandals at the turn of the millennium, dotcom, telecom, and Enron all erupted in flames. The carnage engulfed many of the nascent DP firms as well.

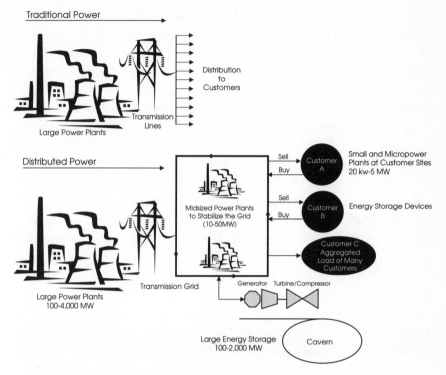

Figure 17.1 Traditional versus distributed power systems.

A change in presidential administrations certainly had much to do with it as well. One of the first things President Bush did after taking office was to convene an Energy Task Force under Vice President Dick Cheney to address the California energy crisis and other serious supply/demand situations in other parts of the country. As I noted earlier, Republicans tend to solve energy crises with a production mindset, while Democrats tend to seek solutions from the demand side. And supply was precisely the tack Cheney's task force took.

Spark Spread Spoils the Party

The biggest cause for the roar to turn into a whimper, however, was more than a fly in the ointment. It was more like a really unhappy gorilla stuck in a fuel oil tank. The DP business model was predicated on low natural gas prices and high electricity prices. With the California electricity market imploding and people nervous about Y2K toward the end of the 1990s, and the economy going gangbusters, electricity prices were indeed on an upward trajectory while gas prices remained relatively low.

In year 2000, this situation began to reverse. The ratio of natural gas prices to electricity prices is called the *spark spread*. It is probably the most important factor in electricity economics, but is especially critical to companies that manage both natural gas and electricity production assets. Essentially, the spark spread tells you when it is more profitable to sell natural gas rather than convert it into electricity and sell that.

The spark spread underlies distributed power, at least as long as natural gas is the fuel of choice for the DP device. A business paying a high electricity bill will consider replacing purchased power with power generated on-site. Depending on the business, it could elect to either pay the capital costs itself, or enter into a third-party energy services agreement and buy electricity from an entity that owns and operates the DP asset on behalf of the customer. Either way, the economics are at the mercy of the spark spread.

When DP was roaring, natural gas prices were around $2.00 to 3.00 per million Btu and wholesale electricity prices were soaring through the roof in many locations, in part because of the trading and marketing shenanigans. Lately, natural gas prices have fluctuated between two and seven times that price and electricity prices returned to stability after much of the trading practices were discredited, and the economy tanked, reducing demand.

This caused the wheels to fall off the DP movement but then the shell of the vehicle started breaking into pieces, too, and the engine coughed and sputtered. FERC ended the Standard Interconnection Initiative. Without this, a utility wanting to keep DP out of its service territory simply has to make the interconnection equipment requirements so onerous that it kills the project with additional capital cost. Another approach was to offer the customer considering a switch a lower rate. This was usually the technique used for important customers with large loads, and it was a technique that usually worked.

Electric utilities, discredited and collapsing from the energy trading scandals and miserable returns on investments overseas, all stampeded to that new business model called "back to basics" that would restore them to the good graces of Wall Street. Remember that part of "back to basics" was to shed *noncore* unregulated businesses—businesses like DP in some cases. DP was a growth strategy that would require investment. Utility investors wanted sanity restored to the balance sheet (i.e., start generating cash, reduce debt). No investment. No DP.

Nothing is static, however. The pendulum is swinging once again, and Edison's vision is likely to have another shot at vindication. Almost everything I've written in this book suggests that electricity rates are going to continue rising for many years. If natural gas prices remain stable or decline, the DP business model, dependent on the spark spread, could again make sense.

DP: As in, Not a Utility

Before we say goodbye (for now) to Edison's ghost, let's pause to answer this question: What exactly is distributed power? Like most phrases from the technical arena that enter the business lexicon, a precise definition is hard to come by. To some, it is any power-generating device that isn't owned by a big, bad electric utility. To others, DP represents electricity that is generated on-site, on the "customer" side of the electric meter, and not on the "utility" side of the meter. Utilities tend to define DP as small generating assets that are interconnected to the grid at voltages typical of the distribution system, not the transmission system. For my two cents, the first time I heard the phrase was in connection with small power generation units installed by the utility to support a substation or a segment of the distribution grid requiring voltage support. It was originally, in fact, a utility-driven concept.

This is how I define DP today: one or more power generating devices interconnected with a grid or in a network and intended to actively interface with that grid or network. My definition of DP does not include a wind turbine/generator that is primarily supplying its output to a utility grid. It also does not include a standby or backup electric generator in the basement of a building that is primarily intended to operate only when utility-supplied power is lost. Finally, it does not include a continuous generating device that substitutes for utility supplied power at a given site, but is not connected into a supply and delivery network.

DP Workhorse: The Recip Engine

Probably the most widely recognized DP device is the oil/gas-fired engine generator, a technology more than 100 years old. Thousands of these old stalwarts are installed in commercial buildings, small municipal and cooperative utility grids, industrial sites, and institutional facilities. They are usually connected to the gas distribution system and natural gas is the main fuel. However, a fuel oil tank often accompanies these installations in the event that the gas feed system is curtailed.

Many buyers and owners of affluent homes are buying the smallest of these devices as emergency generators. You can bet that the Home Depots in our area have sold hundreds of these engines over the last six months. Two week-long storm-related outages in one year, which I recounted in the opening chapter, will do that.

Engine generators can be easily interfaced to a grid, started and stopped frequently with little wear and tear on the equipment, and automated so that they require little attention. However, like your car's engine, they require thoughtful and frequent periodic maintenance, lubricating oil changes, tune-ups, and cleaning.

Most of the advances in this technology of the last 20 years have been in reducing the NOx and carbon monoxide emissions without resorting to downstream emissions control devices, similar to the catalytic converters on your car's exhaust. This points up an important, though little recognized, fallacy with the DP movement: Imagine if that single large 2,000 MW coal-burning power station 50 miles away from the population center was replaced with 10,000 gas-fired engine/generators in a DP network *within* the population center. Which strategy is better for the environment? Personally, I think regulating one utility station to reduce its emissions is more expedient that hammering on the owners of 10,000 engine generator sites. The answer to the question is that the exhausts from those engines have to be almost emissions-free if the citizens of DP town are to stay healthy. For those of you required to get emissions inspections for your car, you know what a pain it is. Imagine everyone in the neighborhood depending on the frequent maintenance and inspection of everyone else's DP generator.

Another scheme DP enthusiasts came up with was to make more productive use of all those standby engines and run them more frequently as part of a network. This poses several problems. First, the emissions problem surfaces again. An engine exhausting into the atmosphere for at most a few hundred hours per year fouls the air only a few hundred hours per year. Second, those engines were designed and purchased as standby engines. You can be certain that the components of that engine were commensurately designed only for the operating mode for which it was purchased. That means that parts meant to operate a few hundred hours per year will break down prematurely if they are operated a few thousand hours. Maintenance expected for a few hundred hours is different from maintenance expected for a few thousand hours.

Engine generator manufacturing is a cutthroat, competitive business. Suppliers don't add one micron of additional strength or durability to the components if they don't have to. A process called *value engineering* ensures that customers only get what they pay for, just barely, and sometimes less.

Turbines and Fuel Cells: Ready for Prime Time?

For these and other reasons, many DP advocates believe that the concept is credible and lasting only if based on new technology. Two options that have been developed over the two decades are fuel cells and microturbine generators.

Microturbines are what the name implies: tiny versions of the gas turbine technology used to power aircraft and anchor the large gas-fired power stations. The basic principle is that a fuel, almost exclusively natural gas, is used to heat air to very high temperature and pressure and then the hot air is expanded in a turbine. This expansion process causes a rotor to rotate, along with the attached generator. Some of the microturbines used in DP are variations of helicopter engines and turbines being deployed in military vehicles. Much DP technology, in fact, comes from defense-related R&D.

Microturbines get a great deal of attention in DP applications because the exhaust can be made much cleaner than engine generators, and they can be packaged in ways that make them appear to be like any other appliance you might buy. They can sit on a concrete pad outside your home, your office building, or your favorite fast-food joint, humming along like an air conditioner. Depending on the model, they can be even smaller than your refrigerator. However, in the scheme of things, they are not very efficient in converting fuel to electricity. A microturbine/generator might exhibit efficiency between 25 to 30 percent, and engine/generator between 30 to 35 percent, an old central utility station between 33 to 35 percent, and a brand new gas-fired combined cycle power plant up to 50 percent.

Microfuel Buyers

There are other flaws in the DP business model. When you combine the efficiencies noted above and remember the importance of the spark spread, it becomes clear that a DP unit has difficulty being more efficient, and therefore a better deal, than utility-supplied power based on efficient gas-fired combined cycles. Not only are utility gas-fired plants efficient, they are efficient buyers of the fuel because they buy so much of it on long-term contracts. Small DP customers cannot hope to buy natural gas at the same attractive prices, all other things being equal.

The microturbine/generator is the greatest victim of spark spread economics because its fuel-to-electricity conversion efficiency is relatively low. It also is a very high-speed machine. An oil/gas engine is directly coupled to its electric generator. A microturbine actually needs a gearbox to reduce its speed from 50,000 to 70,000 rpm to the speed required of electric systems which is 3,600 rpm (3,000 rpm in Europe and other parts of the world on 50 Hz electricity grids). Or it requires a sophisticated power electronics package to regulate the generator's output consistent with the electric system in which it is serving.

From NASA to You: Fuel Cells

If you want to retain the ultra low emissions, substantially improve the fuel conversion efficiency, and keep that appliance-like look of your DP device, you need to upgrade your thinking to a fuel cell. These devices are more like batteries, because they convert the chemical energy in fuel directly into electricity. There is no rotating or reciprocating "engine" per se. Because they are DC machines (like batteries), they also require sophisticated power electronics or conditioning package to make the output compatible with the rest of the AC electric system. The beauty is that the fuel conversion efficiency is more like 55 to 60 percent, or double that of the other DP options. Fuel cell technology has been around for more than 150 years, but it was the space program in the 1950s and 1960s that really brought the technology "down to earth." The big stumbling with fuel cells is cost; after all this time, they are still 5 to 10 times more expensive than engine/generators.

Power in the Collective

The network is the power. The promise of DP lies not in the individual DP assets humming along, doing their thing. It is in harnessing multiple DP assets into what some call a *microgrid*, which is managed by a distributed utility or service provider. The key to understanding a microgrid is to recognize that the flow of information about all of the assets is at least as important as the flow of electricity. This microgrid can be based entirely on DC, and it can be integrated into the larger AC grid through one interface point. Distributed storage devices can—and are—also used to round out the system.

To get the most from these assets, they have to be monitored, operated, and managed just like a large network of utility power stations and T&D circuits, but with far better *real-time information* and corresponding automation. Realistically, it is probably difficult or impossible to imagine such microgrids being retrofitted into existing buildings and structures. However, where new economic growth is taking place, where corporate and industrial parks are built, it is easy to see how a microgrid could better serve everyone's electricity needs.

It might also occur to you that a microgrid serving multiple customers avoids the requirement for electricity supplied from a central station through a T&D infrastructure. This is true. However, one reason why it is a difficult sell for retrofit is that the utility can always make the argument that existing customers wishing to get off the grid must pay their share of the cost originally spent to serve them. When this cost is added to the cost of DP, it makes it less attractive to a potential customer.

Stumbling over Itself

If you apply my golden rule that states what's good at small scale usually is not at large scale, you can probably visualize some of the bugaboos with a DP strategy. The first is that your electricity becomes entirely dependent on natural gas supply. Instead of being dependent on your electric utility, which takes advantage of a diverse range of electricity generating sources, you are dependent for your gas on a *local distribution company* (LDC). Unlike the electric utility, you cannot hedge your production with a diversified portfolio of fuel sources. You are an insignificant purchaser of natural gas and, therefore, will be a victim of retail prices, never enjoying the discounts that come with bulk purchases wholesale. In many ways, DP has been driven by gas LDCs trying to entice new customers away from electric utilities and show revenue growth.

Second, each of these DP options results in carbon dioxide emissions, even the fuel cell. Because that much more natural gas has to be supplied to all these devices, the gains that might be made up in higher efficiency DP devices is lost if you assume that some percentage of this gas is lost to the atmosphere during extraction, transport, storage, and distribution. Remember, methane, the principle component of natural gas, is 20 times more potent as a global warming agent than carbon dioxide. Higher fuel conversion efficiency, such as associated with fuel cells, means that the emissions per unit of heat input or output is lower, but substantial nonetheless.

Institutional barriers are even more significant. Imagine if you are the local electric utility and 10,000 of your customers installed their own DP devices. All of the electricity distribution infrastructure you bought and put in place is now a "stranded asset." The 1,000 MW powerplant down the highway isn't needed anymore. You are saddled with nonproducing assets. Suffice it to say that these big guys would not go down without a fuss.

The Utility We Love to Hate

Probably the greatest fallacy of them all was to think that advocates of an intelligent DP grid could "disintermediate" the electric utility. This term refers to the ability to get in between a traditional supplier and its customers. From the beginning, this was a pipe dream. The notion was borrowed from those other high-flying sectors. Cell phones would render the seven Bells, born of the breakup of Ma Bell, insignificant. The Internet would make shopping at the supermarket obsolete. Amazon.com was going to put traditional bricks and mortar booksellers out of business. DP at the very least was going to make life miserable for the local electric retailers utility.

That's not to say that the traditional service supplier isn't forced to adapt. Booksellers enhanced their business model with leisure and lingering, supported by inside coffee shops, hosting of book and reading clubs, and in general taking the place of a lending library for a quiet place to hang out, look studious, and meet and greet. Intelligent DP players will eventually force utilities to adapt as well.

The fact of the matter is that the vast majority of customers don't want DP. They want electric service they don't have to think about. They don't hate their electric utility, unless they experience an outage. They don't even think about the electric utility unless service is interrupted or their bills are higher, with no good explanation. Customers that do need a higher level of service that DP might provide don't want to spend their scarce capital dollars on a power plant adjacent to their facility.

As the Pendulum Swings...

So how is Edison ever going to be vindicated? The best evidence is that electricity prices are climbing all over the country. As of this writing, natural gas prices had plummeted from the $10 to $15 per million Btu range back to under $5 per million Btu, then settled back around $7 to $8 per million Btu. The periodicity of the spark-spread pendulum is once again becoming favorable to DP. Electric utilities are moving out of the "back to basics" phase of balance sheet repair as Wall Street shows a renewed interest in "growth." There are now bona-fide distribution-focused electric utilities that have to figure out how to grow the business.

Coincidentally, these distribution utilities are mostly located in those areas of the country where electricity prices are rising the most rapidly, places like California, Chicago and northern Illinois, and the Northeast. These are the places where it is most difficult to build central power stations. These are the places where T&D infrastructure is most inadequate. It is perhaps wiser to think of DP not as disintermediating the electric utility, but the physical transmission grid itself. Guess what else? These large population centers, especially the coastal areas, are the most vulnerable to terrorist attacks and infrastructure threats, and most accessible for LNG shipments. Personally, I think a large-scale escalation in LNG imports is a bad idea as explained in an earlier chapter. But a *strategic* escalation near population centers is a way to maintain intrafuel competition, keep fuel prices reasonable over the long term, and feed robust DP networks.

Let's also not forget that the technology of fuel cells, microturbines, and engine generators has had another 10 years to mature.

What was missing before was not reliable or cost-effective DP technology, but an institutional force, a collection of DP utilities, which could make their money by providing a new level of electricity service to those customers that need it and can pay for it. The stage is now being set for just such entities to emerge. In the next chapter, I show what all of us customers, regulators, and other stakeholders need to do to nurture a better outcome this time around.

Chapter 18

Redefining the Grid with Real Intelligence

I have previously referred to the *intelligent grid*. I have also seen it called *smart grid*. I don't like these terms any more than I like "hydrogen economy." These designations are marketing ploys more than they are a vision or a practical plan to get us from point A to point B. Sure, you aren't subjected to commercials on television encouraging you to buy an intelligent grid or a hydrogen economy. The marketing is conducted in the halls of political and corporate power to secure funding for R&D programs, or put investment behind new products.

The "intelligence" refers to the convergence of power electronics, communications, Internet and networks, computers, and digital devices that eventually could automate electricity distribution and manage consumption and demand. I think of this intelligence differently. I think of it as the ability to do things that we can't seem to do on our own. I think of it as the ability to automate certain tasks, which then free us up to do other, hopefully better, things. I fervently believe that the tremendous gains in energy efficiency, reductions in new power stations, lower emissions and environmental impact—all of the social goods afforded by managing demand—will not occur if demand is managed manually. Therefore, I think of intelligence as automation.

My career as well as my personal experience makes me a proponent of this intelligent grid. In my career, I have followed so-called electricity demand management programs, which display a dubious record of success. They are usually driven by electric utilities under the influence of their public utility commissions. The results pattern is a surge in activity and consumer interest, followed by a decline as the incentives and rewards disappear.

In my personal experience, I have tried to instill demand reduction in my household. I try to make my kids turn out the lights, use the appliances wisely, turn off the television when not in use. I try to replace my incandescent bulbs with fluorescents and hope upon hope that they really do last 10 times as long to give me a payback on the much higher price.

Making It a Family Affair

To give you a sense of an intelligent grid, let me first start with how electricity could be managed in my home. The analogy can then be applied to larger swaths of the infrastructure.

We live in the city. We need to keep outside lights on all night as a crime deference measure. My yard lamp has a light sensor that comes on at dusk and shuts off at sunrise. My porch light stays on all night. It's the best place for a compact fluorescent. The backyard needs to be well-illuminated to keep bad people from hopping the fence at the alley. So I've got two floodlights in the back porch fixture. What I really need are lamps connected to reliable motion detectors. That way, our house is consuming energy only when motion is detected, whether it is one of us letting the dogs out for the last trip before bed, a would-be delinquent or a hardened criminal.

That's more intelligent than relying on anyone in my household to turn off the porch lights in the morning.

Inside the house, if we didn't have to rely on wall switches to turn lights on and off, there would be no yelling by mom or dad to turn the lights off when kids left their rooms to go to school for the day. This could truly raise the quality of life in our household! That's displaying intelligence.

One of the biggest energy hogs in our house is the dishwasher. For one thing, the water temperature for the entire house has to be set higher than otherwise necessary to match the temperature required by this appliance. Another problem, more minor, is that the unit has different timed cycles. I never know how to change from the short cycle to the long one depending on what needs to be washed. A booster heater on the dishwasher could avoid the higher temperature for the entire house; a more idiot-friendly control panel on the appliance might make it easier to select the right cycle.

Scientific American, in its September 2006 issue, reveals, in the article "An Efficient Solution" by Eberhard K. Jochem, that a typical refrigerator today uses one-quarter of the energy of a 1974 model. That's great. But someone still needs to come up with a design that prevents teenagers from standing there, just standing there, holding that door open wide while they contemplate the contents. Or how about one that automatically resets the cold-colder-coldest lever for the freezer and the refrigerator depending on how much stuff is in there?

Imagine the Warm Glow of Saving Money

Replacing incandescent bulbs with fluorescent ones is an instant energy-saver. Today's fluorescents use one-fourth to one-fifth the energy of their prehistoric incandescent counterparts and provide as much light, something that wasn't true 10 years ago. Some say the light is softer and more soothing, too. But intelligence to me also means allaying consumer fears. Here's one of mine: Bulbs are fragile. Dropping a regular cheap bulb package means that I'm out a dollar or less. But if I drop a fluorescent, I'm out four or five dollars. And since I happen to have more than my fair share of thumbs, this isn't inconsequential. Packaging for some of these products almost guarantees that someone will drop it between picking it off the shelves at the store and getting it into fixture at home.

The gnawing fact is that two-thirds of all the energy in our original sources (coal, petroleum, uranium, natural gas, and solar) is wasted as it is converted into (1) useful forms of energy (electricity, gasoline, heating oil); and then (2) consumed to do work or provide something. Lighting is one of the worst; the conversion of a unit of fossil fuel to light in your house is less than 5 percent efficient.

In my mind, automation is the key to getting the most out of energy conservation without sacrificing comfort and convenience and without relying on our feeble brains or dubious discipline to constantly berate ourselves to conserve.

Devices that allow the electricity provider to interact with the electricity consumer are another aspect of intelligence. Instead of trying to manage our peak electricity demand by bringing another power generating plant on line, which is incrementally the most expensive electricity available, why not reduce the demand? Devices have been demonstrated and are available, for example, that would automate the shutdown of appliances. The device monitors the power grid in that area for line frequency and trips the appliance off for a few seconds or a few minutes to prevent the line from being overloaded. So-called "grid-friendly" appliances control power oscillations and optimize supply and demand on a local circuit.

Of course, the electricity provider would have to either offer incentives to people willing to have their appliances curtailed or make the program equitable among all ratepayers. The point, though, is that the automation technology, the intelligent devices, are already available; the policies that helps support the purchase and installation of such devices, however, are not.

Now let's take the concept of the intelligent grid to the next level, where in fact it has even higher value.

Farther out on the Network

Consumers can be fickle and often irrational. Businesses, however, have a bottom-line reason for conserving energy. It reduces costs. When entire office buildings begin to apply an intelligent grid concept, real savings accrue.

One way the intelligent network manifests itself for a building or a factory is by managing the interface between its electrical network and the electricity supplier's network. The onsite network can then be powered by a distributed generation device, as described earlier. The Electric Power Research Institute (EPRI), in the article "The Rise of the MicroGrid Power Networks" by Jonathan Lynch, in the February 2006 *Energy & Power Management*, emphasizes that the smart grid of the future enables the integration of DG with traditional central power plants.

It means that the DG system operates in parallel with the utility system. For the most part today, if a building has a power-generating unit, it operates *instead of* the utility as a backup or standby supplier of electricity. Within the intelligent grid, this small power generator operates with the grid, not instead of it. The key enabling technologies for this to occur are: A solid-state power converter that allows power sharing, power flow, and waveform control; and a static isolation switch that allows a "seamless transition between the facility's DG device and the grid connected operation."

Now what about the grid itself? Intelligence still encompasses the same elements: monitoring, automation, and devices that allow the grid to respond to the information. In earlier chapters, I wrote that utilities—although they are loath to admit it—often don't have a good idea of how electricity is flowing in their system any more than you or I know how it's really flowing—line by line and circuit by circuit—in our homes and offices. One key to it all is solid-state power electronics.

High-voltage power electronics devices allow precise and rapid switching of electric power to different transmission lines. That means that instead of simply being fed into a vast circuit following the path of least resistance, it can be "directed" down a specific path. Such technologies can be described as available today, but perhaps not commercially or economically viable. For the most part, these devices offer two things, in terms of intelligence: (1) they react faster to changes in the system; and (2) they are solid-state digital devices, which means they lend themselves to closer monitoring and control.

Examples of Intelligent Microgrids

What has been described as the "first implementation of a microgrid" is taking place in Waitsfield, Vermont (see article reference, p. 237).

A true microgrid can be said to have two primary elements: First, a "cluster of DG devices is interconnected and, through intelligent monitoring and control, integrated together. Second, the cluster is presented to the electricity supplier's grid as one total increment of controllable load. Thus, the microgrid might integrate ten 100-kW power generation units, but the electric utility could also dispatch the total 1 MW of capacity as controllable load during peak demand periods.

The Mad River Park microgrid can connect eight commercial and industrial facilities and up to 14 residences into a power network service area. The DG devices include propane-fueled engines, gas-fired microturbines, a solar photovoltaic array, and even a small wind-turbine generator. All of these units are operated as a system in distinct modes: total isolation from the local utility distribution system during voltage sags, spikes, or transients that cause the utility feed to deviate from defined parameters or several grid-connected modes.

Electricity from the local utility substation will be monitored via a microprocessor-enabled protective relay. This relay detects abnormal power quality events and enables the park's microgrid to "island," that is, separate from the utility network, via a fast solid-state switch. All participants on the microgrid thus enjoy uninterrupted delivery of electricity.

In Detroit, a microgrid being built for the NextEnergy R&D Center includes a diverse fuel infrastructure, including hydrogen, natural gas, and biofuels. Fuel cells are included along with internal and external combustion engines and solar photovoltaic devices. In addition to being electrically integrated, it will recover the thermal energy from the electricity generating devices to replace what would otherwise be an onsite heating system.

A life-cycle analysis of the NextEnergy configuration points out the tradeoffs inherent in microgrids discussed earlier. Compared to the impact of purchasing electricity from the local utility and having a separate heating system, NextEnergy's microgrid has 34 percent lower total life-cycle energy requirements and 65 percent reduction in carbon dioxide and nitrogen oxide emissions. A key component of the analysis is that a microgrid avoids long transmission lines. Line losses for moving power from a large remote power station could be up to 8 percent of the fuel's original energy. On the other hand, the microgrid has a higher upstream energy consumption because the natural gas and hydrogen require energy for extraction and processing.

Strength and Direction

These powerful switching devices and stations provide the muscle for directing the power but not necessarily the intelligence for applying it. That, according to DOE's National Transmission Grid Study issued in 2002, comes from a *wide-area measurement system* (WAMS). The DOE study, by the way, is essentially a technology and policy blueprint for modernizing the nation's electricity transmission system.

Although not stated explicitly in the report, WAMS essentially is a monitoring capability layered on top of the existing monitoring systems. Today, as implied in earlier discussions, an individual utility monitors its T&D system. Regional independent system operators (ISO) also monitor their systems, although the capability to do this is being built up gradually as ISOs gain more control and budgetary authority over the physical assets. A WAMS would be a means of monitoring the nation's interconnected electricity system in its entirety. In other words, it monitors the points at which the smaller regional grids are connected.

Often, the problem isn't one of adding monitoring points but being able to efficiently and effectively analyze the reams of data already coming into T&D control centers. In the case of the 1996 major system disturbance in the western U.S. power grid, a postmortem evaluation of the event showed that evidence of abnormal system behavior was buried in the data being transmitted by the *supervisory control and data acquisition* (SCADA) system. If that data could have been extracted and analyzed in a timely manner, or perhaps automatically through software, operators could have acted in enough time to avoid a grid failure.

Although I feel like a broken record at this point, once again I should point out that grid disturbances can be mitigated either from the supply side or the demand side. When grid operators know how and where load patterns are changing, they can adjust the flow of electricity to avoid problems. The larger the increments of demand capacity that they know about, the better the control of the grid can be, especially during peak periods when the grid is especially vulnerable to upsets.

Perhaps the best way to describe it is that an intelligent network or grid ensures a two-way flow of electricity *and information* between the power plant, every junction in the transmission system (e.g., substations), and the ultimate consumer of the electricity (lighting system, appliance, electric motor, electric-arc furnace, etc.). When you get down to it, the problems with our T&D grid aren't so much associated with the assets themselves but what we know about the condition of the asset at any given point in time.

Chapter 19

The Rest of the World

A t this point, we need to broaden our U.S.-centric perspective and focus on the rest of the world. I am especially fond of the phrase "inflection point" to indicate events that, with the benefit of hindsight, changed the course of the industry. There are two critical inflection points, or mile markers, that I use to introduce our discussion and the timelines: The tearing down of the Berlin Wall in 1989 and the attack and collapse of the World Trade Towers on September 11, 2001.

Both of these seminal events speak volumes about global economics, world trade, globalization, protectionism, and energy supply lines. Few people, even in our industry, understand what I believe are the critical connection of these events to the recent past and future of electricity service. And for good reason: You need to expend some serious time, energy and brain cells to "get it."

Locals Going Global

In 1989, I worked for the industry trade journal *Power*. Later we launched a quarterly international edition of our magazine, *Electric Power International*. Although I had made a few business trips overseas before, I began to travel frequently abroad and pay serious attention to the electricity business in other countries. Around the same time as the fall of the Berlin Wall, the United Kingdom had broken up the government-owned and operated Central Electricity Generating Board, a seminal event in the global electricity business.

At the same time, the European Union gained strength as an umbrella political and economic entity. During the 1980s, the Premier of China, Deng Xiaopeng, promulgated the "open door" policy, and by the turn of the decade, that policy was supporting significant domestic and foreign investment prospects in Chinese power plants. Many countries in Asia recognized that foreign investment in electricity development, which underpins the economy, would accelerate economic growth.

In 1992, the United States passed the National Energy Policy Act (NEPA), further facilitating deregulation of electric utilities, as we reviewed in earlier chapters. By the mid-1990s, it was clear that the once-parochial and largely stated-owned and controlled electricity systems around the world were undergoing privatization. Western-style market-oriented economics was on the march. Socialism, at least as an economic paradigm, had been discredited. The Cold War had dissipated. (It probably isn't fair to say it ended, as no war was ever declared and no peace treaty was ever signed.) At the end of the century, indeed the millennium, only one "superpower" remained standing.

Economic Boots on the Ground

Instead of sending troops and armaments to developing countries, large U.S., U.K., and European electricity companies and suppliers sent teams of engineers, executives, and managers, and financial specialists to negotiate and develop projects as portions of the electricity value chain privatized (usually the electricity generation portion first). These folks were preceded by waves of consultants, economic development and financial engineering specialists (e.g., the World Bank, the International Monetary Fund, etc.) who conducted studies and evaluations showing why and how private investment and development were superior to state-run electricity infrastructure. The Western powers had, you might say, economic and engineering "boots on the ground" in India and China, in the rising tigers of Asia (Korea, Philippines, Taiwan, Thailand, and Malaysia), in South America (Brazil, Argentina, Chile, Colombia, and Venezuela), in Central America and Caribbean (Dominican Republic, Costa Rica, etc.), and in the Eastern and Central European countries (Poland, Hungary, the Czech Republic, etc.) emerging from the shadows of the former Soviet Union.

The fall of the Berlin Wall certainly was more of a symbol than a precipitating event. I remember the speech that President Reagan gave: "Mr. Gorbachev, tear down this wall!" In truth, however, the socialist experiment that was the Soviet Union had been crumbling for years. History nevertheless has given credit to Ronald Reagan for wearing down the Soviet Union and forcing a military defense buildup that it simply could not match.

There is great power in symbols. I personally felt the energy unleashed by removing the boundary between East and West. I had relatives who lived in West Berlin at the time. I visited them several months after the Wall crumbled. They insisted, especially the younger members of this family, on taking me to the where the wall once stood. I even bought a small souvenir bag of rocks and cement that was said to have come from the wall. You could see tears well up in their eyes as they passionately spoke about what that event meant for their country and the rest of Europe.

The globalization of electricity did not start when the Wall fell. I am convinced, however, that the Wall does represent an inflection point, a global recognition of the shift in favor of Western style capitalism as an economic model. Politically, the prevalent trend was to reduce or eliminate socialism or even totalitarianism in favor of democracy. Economically, the shift was from state-run industries and services to privatized structures. Technically, the objective was to transfer advanced technologies, engineering and construction methods, and efficient equipment manufacturing and fabrication quickly and avoid prolonged learning curves. Financially, private investment gradually replaced public money raised through taxes.

This is what I mean by an ideological inflection point. The prevailing thinking shifts on all levels.

By the mid-1990s, EPI had also launched a Spanish edition. Meanwhile, *Power's* Chinese language edition, which started in the mid-1980s, was beginning to get some traction. I, along with other editorial staff, visited huge coal-fired power plant construction projects in countries such as Taiwan, Philippines, Poland, and Indonesia; nuclear plants in Japan, Korea, Mexico, and Sweden; and gas-fired combined cycle projects all over the world. Many of these projects were managed by complex international consortia of companies, mini–United Nations in many respects, and financed using an almost undecipherable calculus involving public and private debt and equity.

Unregulated subsidiaries of U.S. electric utilities, which had heretofore not even ventured outside of their service territories much less their states, developed massive projects, and bought infrastructure assets and even whole utility companies in far-flung corners of the world.

Honey, I Finally Found the Third World

It was an exciting time to be part of this industry. My eyes were opened in many, many ways. Once, I was driven from my hotel in Surabaya, Indonesia's second largest city, to the Paiton power station about three hours away. The first leg of the journey proceeded on a modern but short superhighway toll road built with private investment. Few people used it because few people could afford it. The bulk of the journey, however, was on a secondary highway used by literally everyone else—double-decker buses, doubled-up tractor-trailer trucks, cars, mopeds with families of four riding on them, and groups of school kids walking along the edges of what was supposed to be the shoulder.

The plant was literally carved out of the jungle. While I was visiting with the plant manager, he received a call telling him a worker had been killed. He told me, unfortunate as it was, it happens all the time. Life is cheap here, he noted. We talked about how much these workers get paid. He said about a $1.50 an hour, 10 times more than they could make in the rice fields. At the time, telephone connections were still spotty. While I was out near the plant, I couldn't get through to the States. After several days without my daily check-in call to my wife, she was fairly frantic when I finally got through. "Honey," I said. "I finally found the Third World." Every other country I'd visited to that point seemed much like the United States except for the different language. But this? This was different.

Ugly Americans and Missionaries

During this time, companies such as Enron behaved liked latter-day robber barons. They pushed their weight and their political influence around. Stories circulated constantly about the arrogance with which European and U.S. companies operated in these countries. But for every "ugly American" or arrogant European company, there were also companies run by executives who truly believed that electrification, private investment, and empowered employees could make a difference in the health and well-being of Third World countries. Like most high-growth opportunities, some came for the fast buck; others came to make a difference.

Boom periods rarely can sustain themselves very long. Events in Houston converged with events in India. The era of big-time projects, privatization, and globalization of electricity supply was destined to reverse. The energy companies were beginning to collapse under the weight of the stock market problems of early 2001, precipitated by the fraud that collectively became known as Enron and its partners in white-collar crime. It was also becoming clear that many overseas activities were "me-too" investments, not ones based on sound financial judgment.

9/11 Changes Everything

The seeds of the second inflection point had long been sown, but it was the attacks on the World Trade Towers in New York that sealed the deal. Although there are many instances of globalization still occurring, 9/11 has irreversibly changed the psychology, if not the ideology. Virtually all of the overseas assets of the U.S. natural gas and electricity companies have either been sold off or are up for sale. Except for petroleum companies, U.S. energy companies are, with only a few exceptions, focused on the United States.

To survive and thrive, however, the big suppliers of electricity infrastructure have set their sights on India, China, and other high-growth areas of the world. Competing in these markets means having low-cost manufacturing and supply chains. Thus the supply infrastructure continues to shift away from the manufacturing bases of North America and Europe, to India, China, Brazil, Mexico, and other low-cost countries with a rapidly developing skills base.

The reason is obvious and simple: Electricity demand grows at 2 to 3 percent in the developed Western economies (primarily the United States, Canada, western Europe, and Japan). It is also growing at between 5 to 10 percent in other parts of the world. The scale of the infrastructure buildup in China and India, discussed in the next section, illustrates the challenges posed for the rest of the world, but primarily the United States, as the largest consumer of energy.

The Real Impact of Globalization on Electricity: Good or Bad?

I used the fall of the Berlin Wall and 9/11 as bookends to frame a distinctive period in the electricity business. Now that I can look back at that period, with some dispassion afforded by time, I often wonder; Did we, meaning U.S. and other electricity and energy companies in the West help or hurt the rest of the world after all was said and done? I'm not sure that I have an answer. But two rather unique books, from polar-opposite viewpoints, have helped me in thinking about the question.

The first is *Joy at Work: A Revolutionary Approach to Fun on the Job* by Dennis W. Bakke (Seattle: PVG, 2005)a co-founder and, until 2002, the CEO of AES Corp. AES was a leader in power project development around the world during the 1990s and today is one of the only U.S.-headquartered companies that continues to pursue this activity. Bakke fills most of his pages describing the unique—for the electricity industry—company culture of AES. Only in a few chapters does he directly address some of the overseas projects. Yet his "passion for serving the world with clean, safe, reliable electricity" clearly comes through, almost in a spiritual or religiously zealous way. The list of 23 countries where AES operates electricity infrastructure, especially power stations, includes places most people would agree are difficult to conduct business.

Bakke describes the "primary reason we [AES] existed was to help the world meet its electricity needs." Social responsibility is one of the core values of the company. Today that responsibility is put into the service of supplying electricity to over 100 million people around the world. In many countries, India being one of them, AES has difficulty getting paid. But during the go-go 1990s, AES clearly was the antithesis to Enron. I like to make the analogy that if Enron was the epitome of the "ugly American," AES was best described as the missionary who came to do good—and, let's face it, convert you to its "religion." AES is a different company today, as it has learned that a company with over 40,000 employees can no longer behave like a small business or even a family business. Bakke not only comes across with a religious fervor, he directly ties his religious objectives and values to his business values, especially in the last chapters of his book.

Interestingly, John Perkins, in his *Confessions of an Economic Hit Man* (New York: Plume, 2004), clearly got religion, but apparently sourced from what he confessed are the fraudulent aspects of his work. Perkins describes his career as that of an EHM (economic hit man) because, as he admits, his job was to "encourage world leaders to become part of a vast network that promotes U.S. commercial interests." Perkins's manifestation of this "job description" was to work for what was at the time a

(continued)

leading engineering company in developing rosy projections for electricity demand in third-world countries.

In his words, he was told to "come up with a very optimistic forecast of the economy, and how it will mushroom after all the new power plants and distribution lines are built." Those forecasts allowed the "U.S. Agency for International Development (AID) and the international banks to justify the loans." He writes that he went right ahead and sold his soul to do the company's bidding. The end game apparently was to get countries such as Indonesia, Panama, Iran, Colombia, and others dependent on western funds.

In one chapter, Perkins describes that his team "was commissioned to make a complete survey of the country's [Saudi Arabia] disorganized and outmoded electrical system and to design a new one that would meet standards equivalent to those in the United States." The larger objective was to "assure that a large portion of petrodollars found their way back to the United States."

Perkins's book becomes essentially a polemic against deregulation and privatization and the U.S. "corpotocracy," and in one passage he makes the connection between a U.S.–Saudi money-laundering affair of the 1970s, based on petrodollars, and the funding of Osama Bin Laden and the Mujahadeen in Afghanistan. Most of the EHM activity he acknowledges takes place in the 1970s and 1980s, but obviously it set the stage for the huge wave of privatized power project development that hit the shores of developing countries around the world during the 1990s. This was, at least as he described it, precisely the point.

Perkins's book is, in his own words, a "confession." Bakke's book, distilled, is an optimistic defense of the values and principles he instilled at AES. The truth about what really happened during the 1990s undoubtedly lies somewhere in between. My point, in providing this comparison, is that electricity is so critical to economic growth and the well-being of a nation that it can both serve as the foundation for modernity and as an instrument of geopolitical hegemony.

India and China: Competing for Resources on the World Stage

Sometimes, you can think yourself smart but what you really have on your side isn't intelligence, but numbers. Stockbrokers and investment advisors make this mistake all the time. They think they've "beaten the market" with their portfolio strategies and trades, but all they've done is benefited from an investment period during which almost any moron with money could have done as well.

Simply put, China and India have numbers on their side. Combined, the two countries account for one-third of the planet's population. The United States has less than 5 percent of the world's people but we consume 25 percent of the world's energy resources. China has close to 25 percent of the world's people but consumes only 12–14 percent of the world's energy resources. How long do you think this imbalance will last?

Energy experts don't expect it to last much longer. When we launched *Electric Power International* in 1989, we had just welcomed China into the group of nations (seven), which had more than 100 GW of installed electric power generation capacity. Since then, China has installed close to 300 GW of additional capacity! In 2004 alone, that country installed close to 40,000 MW. For comparison, that one-year total is higher than any one-year total experienced in the United States. Our top figure was 34,000 MW installed in 1973. So, within a few years, China should have approximately one-half the installed power generation as the United States. Sixteen years ago, it was one-eighth.

Whatever we think we're installing in the United States, China will install more. That includes nuclear, wind, hydro, and coal. U.S. utilities are drawing up plans to build 30 new reactors in the next 10 years.

China is building, on average, one coal-fired plant a week. The United States has around 10,000 MW of wind energy capacity operating; China plans to build 18,000 MW of wind energy over the next few years. The list goes on and on. While U.S. coal-fired plants continue to add *flue-gas desulfurization* (FGD) units incrementally to existing power stations, China is planning 40,000 MW of FGD.

Like the United States, only more so, the backbone of China's electricity generation is coal-fired power stations. A whopping 75 percent of China's electricity generation is based on coal. Even though these plants are newer than the ones in the United States, they exhibit similar average efficiencies. You've probably already guessed where this is going: China is on the way to surpassing the United States as the world's number one source of CO_2.

Despite all of this construction and infrastructure, electricity demand still runs way ahead of electricity supply. At the end of 2004, 21 of China's provincial areas still faced power shortages.

What do I mean by numbers on your side? Here's an example: Imagine you are a manufacturer of wind turbines. If the source of greatest demand for your product is also the source of the lowest-cost skilled labor, then you will logically site your manufacturing facilities in that country or that region. It is more insidious than that.

The transfer of manufacturing from the United States and western European countries to Asia began to take place in the 1990s. However, the West still retained the financial, engineering design, and construction skills and technology capability. Today, the Chinese have most of that. And Western companies taught them. In the coming years, very little of the investment in overseas electricity infrastructure will flow back to the United States. U.S. companies that supply the Chinese market will, in effect, be *Chinese* companies or subsidiaries.

The inescapable truth is that China is the world's second largest economy. Therefore, China will have, if it doesn't already, the world's second largest electricity system to sustain economic growth.

To satisfy China's needs, the entire global electricity infrastructure supply chain is being reoriented to cater to China and to a lesser extent India. It becomes obvious why General Electric and other companies are trying to get the U.S. government and power industry to make *integrated coal gasification combined cycle* (IGCC) the new standard for coal-fired generation in this country: Most of revenue and profits from making components for traditional coal-fired plants will flow to other companies and other countries! IGCC is a technology for which U.S. companies retain some semblance of a technological edge and a comparative economic advantage.

Big Dogs Fighting over the Carcass

China wants economic *parity* with the United States. To do so, it has to attract the lion's share of the world's raw energy resources in a way that is remarkably similar and reminiscent of the United States in earlier times. Like the United States, China has vast coal reserves, so it will have no need to import this raw material. However, it is not well-stocked with oil and natural gas, or at least the know-how to extract it. In recent years, the country has been calibrating its political alliances (often with U.S. adversaries) around energy imports. In the coming years, the United States as the current king of consumption will compete with the probable future king of consumption, China, for all things energy.

Let me reiterate that I don't believe this will result in a global shortage of oil or natural gas, although temporary dislocations among supply and demand are always possible. Rather, the presence of another ravenous appetite for premium fuels on the world stage will continue to drive up prices of all raw energy sources and electricity infrastructure equipment, contributing to escalating electricity prices here at home.

That Giant Sucking Sound

When it comes to energy, Ross Perot was right about the giant sucking sound, just wrong about the country. In an article in the March 4, 2005, issue of the *Wall Street Journal*, executives from General Electric Corp estimated that China will be the largest consumer of electricity in the world by 2024. Here's what's even more astounding than the prediction itself: The year in which China is expected to surpass the United States keeps getting moved up. In the early 1990s, I remember sitting in conferences on global electricity trends and hearing things like, "at probable growth rates, China could surpass U.S. electricity demand by 2050." Then, the figure was 2040, then 2030.

It isn't that electricity demand in the United States has stopped. It has averaged 2 to 3 percent per year for at least two decades. What accounts for the difference? Manufacturing and energy-intensive industries. We haven't built a new petroleum refinery in this country in two decades. China is building dozens. We are a services-oriented economy, which is less energy-intensive. Part of that huge manufacturing base in China is dedicated to building all the stuff we need for our electricity system over here. Ironically, our services and digital-based economy needs more and higher quality electricity than it does primary energy, like oil and natural gas.

None of this would be a problem if we had political relationships with China like the ones we traditionally have had with the countries of Western Europe. Unfortunately, we don't. We mostly have an adversarial relationship with China, stemming from our alliance with Taiwan, an inequitable exchange rate, a seemingly irreversible trade deficit, and philosophical differences on issues such as human rights.

But we are intertwined, too. China owns large number of our treasury bills, which, if sold, would cheapen the dollar on world markets. It is, of course, unlikely that China is going to do that any time soon because it is deeply dependent on exporting its manufactured goods back here to American consumers.

American companies cannot even maintain a technological edge against Chinese companies because the two countries have different legal systems and enforcement measures regarding intellectual property, counterfeiting, and corporate theft.

Without spilling over too much into the geopolitical realm, suffice it to say that China may no longer be a state-controlled socialist country, but its economy is still *state-directed*. Most of the financial institutions, energy companies, and infrastructure firms are still early in the transition from state ownership to the form of private ownership that we would recognize in the United States. Yet the United States is intimately and economically dependent on China because of our huge trade deficit.

Can you imagine what could happen to something as basic as our electricity service if a nutcase like Hugo Chavez ever took power in China? And if you think a country such as China that has an "open door" policy can't slam that door shut again, then think real hard about what's going on in Russia right now.

India: Smaller but Growing Rapidly

Although India is quite different politically from China, the scale of its economic growth potential and electricity infrastructure needs is similar. Of the 2 billion or so people who inhabit both countries, 1.2 billion are in China, and 800 million are in India. There's another crucial difference between the two countries: China has restricted population growth and India has not. An article in the September 5, 2005 issue of *Forbes*, "Look to India" by Paul Johnson, estimates that India will have 1.6 billion by 2050, a doubling of the population, surpassing China's expected total population of 1.4 billion. India's recent economic growth rate of 4 to 6 percent per annum does not rival China's 8 to 10 percent, but it is still double that of the United States.

After the fall of the Berlin Wall, India had a total of 50,000 MW of electricity generation. Today, the figure is closer to 120,000 MW, and the country hopes to have more than 200,000 MW by 2011 and more than 250,000 MW by 2015. The share of that generation that comes from coal is even higher than China's, almost 80 percent.

India has plenty of coal, but it's substantially lower in quality than supplies in the United States or China. This means that coal-fired power is less efficient and more polluting, all other things (such as emissions controls) being equal. Because the infrastructure to supply fuel to these plants is less developed, India is currently importing coal from the world market, even though it has plenty of its own.

Banana Republic Utilities

One of the most fascinating aspects of the Indian power sector, something that distinguishes it from most other countries of its size and development, is that electricity theft is endemic and largely tolerated by the authorities. Up to 25 percent of the electricity that is generated is said to be lost through normal transmission and distribution losses, and 15 percent of that is attributed to theft. Talk about a place where there's some low-hanging fruit in terms of minimizing the need for new generating plants. Average total T&D losses in other countries are more like 15 percent.

India was an early adherent to the grand scheme of electricity privatization and globalization that emerged in the 1990s. However, that has probably made the electricity economy more of a basket case than when it was entirely state-controlled. India attempted to deregulate the generation sector, but the distribution companies are still under state control. Independent generation companies do exist. But almost all analysts of the Indian power sector agree that subsidies, cross-subsidies, and transsubsidies (among fuel sources) distort the economics of the sector and make it difficult for foreign investors to have a presence.

The Executive with the Short Skirt

An infamous project of the 1990s illustrates how India's eyes were too big for its stomach, when it came to power project development. The government opened up generation to foreign investment. One of the first companies to make a run at the country was, glory be, Enron, lead developer of the Dhabol project. Stories were rife in the power industry (a notoriously old-boy, male-dominated field) about how Enron's top executive for the project, a woman, would wear fashionably tight outfits to project meetings. At the time, just the sight of a woman executive was enough to make the endeavor a curiosity to many. (Enron paved the way for a lot of shenanigans, but opening the door to the executive suite to women was a good move for the whole industry.)

Dhabol was to be an advanced gas turbine combined cycle plant burning naphtha, a premium fuel that few, if any, power station owner/operators had ever thought about using. Given the state of the Indian power sector at the time, it was almost ludicrous to think that India could afford such a clean and efficient power plant. Eventually, the plant was built, but it was still in litigation at this writing and has hardly operated.

Despite all the construction, the supply of electricity in India is still more than 10 percent below demand. Here demand refers to homes and businesses that are connected to the grid but aren't supplied electricity. This does not include the half of the population that still has no access to electricity at all!

One reason India's electricity needs seem to be more modest than China's is that its economy is more dependent on services and the technology sectors, which are less electricity-intensive than heavy manufacturing. However, India's burgeoning population suggests that residential demand growth will continue to pace the industrial sector.

Numbers Don't Lie

No matter how you parse them, the numbers on electricity growth in China and India are, in a word, scary.

Take global warming. The planet has about 1,000 GW of coal-fired power plants spewing carbon dioxide into the atmosphere. In 2015, if India, China, and the United States add the coal-fired capacity the three countries are planning today, the planet will have at least another 500 GW operating. I am taking into account some reasonable reductions from today's percentages of coal in the generation mix based on historical advances in electricity infrastructures.

If you believe that global warming is an issue today, it will be at least 20 percent more of an issue in 20 years, because coal-fired power plants represent about 40 percent of the emissions thought to be responsible for global warming. What also becomes clear is that any incremental gains in fuel-to-electricity efficiency, which incrementally reduce carbon dioxide emissions, are almost meaningless in the scheme of economic growth in India and China.

Remember, we're not even counting any coal-fired electricity from other countries. Places such as Australia, Indonesia, Japan, Korea, Russia, the countries of Central Europe, and Germany also have significant coal reserves, which could be used for electricity production. Even if you think in terms of sequestering the carbon dioxide discharges forever as a way to retard global warming, you must add that permanent cost to the price of electricity and wonder if there are even enough places to stick the stuff. Remember, we take coal out of the ground as a solid, which takes up minimal volume. With sequestration, we're talking about putting *gas* back into the ground. To reduce the volumes necessary, it has to be put back under high pressure, which impacts long-term stability of the surrounding geologic formations.

Whether you're thinking in terms of carbon buildup in the atmosphere, demand for commodity materials and fabricated components, trade in liquefied natural gas (LNG), or management of waste (and nuclear proliferation) from nuclear power plants, the numbers characterizing growth in electricity supply and demand in India and China have changed the global equation permanently. At the same time, our energy supply lines are stretching around the globe at a time when the U.S. electricity industry has reined in its efforts to go global.

One conclusion I draw, unfortunate as it seems, is that we may resort to defending these supply lines militarily (or at least by projecting even greater defense capabilities around the world), since we no longer are pursuing the business relationships that could be fostering good will and mutually rewarding economic ties. We already do this for petroleum; it would be a shame if our electricity supply lines such as for LNG continue to evolve in the same direction.

Similarly, we may also end up dealing with environmental issues such as global warming unilaterally. Just as one example, the United States and China are curious participants in the Kyoto treaty that addresses global warming. The United States signed the treaty but the Senate never ratified it. China signed it, but is exempt. Both countries are essentially ignoring the treaty. If the two countries continue to compete for the world's energy resources, how likely is it that they would ever agree on how to manage the discharge from that energy consumption?

Chapter 20

A Vision for the Future

Daydream, Nightmare, or a Good Night's Rest?

Personally, I'm a big believer in a good night's rest. But what exactly is the prescription for a good night's rest? At the beginning of this tome, I said that I wanted to accomplish three things:

1. Describe the two-headed beast that is the electricity business.
2. Set out a roadmap for the future.
3. Galvanize you, dear reader, to action.

In order to accomplish these goals, I have to lay out a plan for avoiding the nightmare that could be visited on the next and future generations.

What is that plan? How do we avoid the nightmare of protracted and frequent electricity grid outages? Can we get beyond daydreaming about a planet that is miraculously better off electricity-wise in the future than it is now? Are the lessons from history relevant? *How do we, in good conscious, keep the lights on?*

Well, I do have a plan. It involves all of the elements that I've described in previous chapters. It requires changing our focus from the left side of the value chain to the right side, without sacrificing either. It pleads for avoiding ideological solutions. It accepts certain realities. The plan seeks to account for the myriad trade-offs inherent in electricity production and delivery. It recognizes that there are no good choices for generating electricity, only less bad ones. Sacrifice is part of the plan. There is no such thing as a free lunch, a free kilowatt-hour, or a kilowatt-hour free of long-term impacts.

My plan has six dimensions:

1. Conceptual
2. Technological
3. Regulatory/political
4. Financial
5. Global
6. Social

There is a seventh dimension, the *personal*, which is the subject of the final chapter of this book. My plan is blunt and brief. It is the elevator pitch I would give to the president, my senator, or my congressional representative—if they ever decided to ask me what should be the nation's strategic plan for electricity to carry us through the next century.

Conceptual

Shift Emphasis and Money into the Right Side of the Value Chain, and Away from the Left Side

Don't focus on *reducing* consumption but rather *managing* consumption. By this, Mr. (or Ms.) President, I mean shifting buckets full of government funding at all levels—R&D, policy, tax incentives, and the like—from advanced extraction and production methods to transmission, distribution, and energy services. The left side of the chain—coal R&D, advanced nuclear reactors, oil/gas extraction, even advanced wind

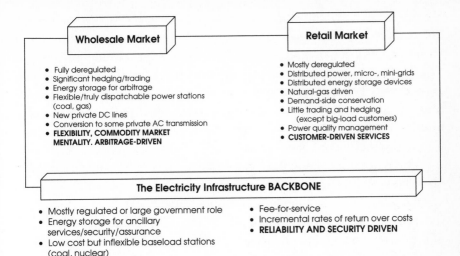

Figure 20.1   Differences in retail, wholesale market should be accommodated; Regulated infrastructure backbone supports the markets.

turbine generators—should be put on a budgetary diet and the right side should be fattened up.

The budgets should reflect what is needed for the next 50 years, not what the entrenched special interests, built up over the last 50 years, can lobby and extract out of Congress.

The initial focus must be on the transmission system. We have two decades of neglect for which to make up. And, because of the way the electricity deregulation and competition programs unfolded, the transmission sector is relatively weak politically. Institutionally, the sector is downright dysfunctional.

We have a federal Interstate highway system, a system of airports managed with great federal oversight, and a health care system that, despite competition, is still federally funded in some way beyond 50 percent of total expenditures. The economic prosperity and national security of our country demands a sophisticated interregional electricity transmission system that forms the backbone for the entire production and delivery value chain. See Figure 20.1. *The urgency for this expansion program must be elevated to national threat level.*

Mr. President, your Department of Energy started on this path around year 2000 with the formation of an Office of Transmission.

However, the initial impetus was to ensure that electricity markets were not hindered by inadequate transmission. Today, this office comes out with some nice-looking reports and alarm-sounding communiqués, but from a practical standpoint, appears to have no political influence. The 2005 Energy Policy Act contains some key incentives for building transmission, and designating transmission corridors that are "in the national interest." Utilities are starting to build new transmission assets, but mostly for serving their own "native load."

This is not nearly enough. We need a national strategy and execution plan for expanding transmission *among* utilities, *between* transmission ISOs and *through* large areas of public and private lands. The policy can include some balance between public and private financing and ownership. Part of the financing could come from a tax on electricity bills analogous to the federal excise tax on cigarettes and liquor. We can build a new mix of AC and DC lines, the former to expand our current electricity-moving capabilities, the latter to move large amounts of power long distances from point A to point B.

Without a serious expansion of transmission, the vast reserves of coal in the Midwest can't be shipped as electricity to the Northeast, or the reserves of Powder River Basin coal shipped as electricity to the Pacific Coast population centers. Power from new nuclear units mostly planned by utilities in the South cannot be shipped to other parts of the country. "North Dakota is to wind energy what Saudi Arabia is to petroleum" is a cute sound bite with no relevance if the generated electricity cannot be moved to population centers. Hardly anybody lives in North Dakota.

Treat the Linchpin with Respect

Transmission has to be viewed as the linchpin in the production and delivery chain, not just something that needs to be refreshed so it facilitates electricity markets or upgraded to prevent blackouts. Electricity markets have exposed the weaknesses in the grid. The Northeast Blackout of 2003 really had little to do with inadequate transmission infrastructure. Transmission is the means by which more of our domestic energy resources—wind, coal, and uranium—are harnessed to serve electricity load. Expanded transmission allows us to generate power from inside the country, and ship it to the population centers along the periphery, rather than import more energy from well beyond our borders.

Mr. President, Tear out this Meter!

The next most important area of focus on the right side of the value chain is the consumer. We need a crash program to capture and convert energy from wasteful industrial processes and consumer activities into electricity. There are some exciting concepts out there for directly converting low-temperature heat into electricity, which can be used right there where it is captured! The infrastructure savings are enormous.

We would avoid an incredible number of new power stations if we managed to convert all the thermal energy emanating from the smokestacks of existing plants into electricity. As a back of the envelope calculation, if we recovered just half of the heat energy lost from today's power stations, the planet could avoid building around one thousand power stations, each one thousand megawatts in size.

Technologies to do this are being developed at the laboratory stage. How could this be accelerated if we took half of the coal R&D budget and shifted it to thermal energy conversion?

Although I don't eschew federal regulation of nuclear power, I do think that the entire process has become Byzantine, grossly inefficient, and wasteful. We have 103 nuclear power reactors in this country. The Nuclear Regulatory Commission (NRC) has around 3,000 employees. Do we really need 30 NRC regulators for every reactor, especially since these reactors only represent two fundamentally different designs? The NRC is screaming for even more people to handle the licensing and permitting of the new plants being planned. What if we shifted some of these funds to better manage how electricity is consumed instead?

Finally, we need more money directed at the regular consumer. Although the low-hanging fruit in energy conservation and efficiency lies with industrial and commercial processes, every consumer represents "leakage" and waste. Every consumer needs to know how much electricity he or she is using at any given time and how much that electricity costs. Armed with the right information, consumers then can alter their behavior. The extent to which this process can be automated and remove the "human element," all the better. *Smart meters at every house, business, and factory in this country provide this information.*

The process of creating a better educated and responsive electricity consumer class could be modeled after our environmental regulations. The EPA sets national policy and the states then implement the policy as they see appropriate. These policies mostly involve reductions in national emissions inventory. There is no reason why an existing federal entity—we want to avoid creating new agencies—couldn't be given responsibility to set policies involving reductions in national electricity usage. (There would be a concurrent reduction in environmental impact, of course.) States would then develop national implementation plans.

Technological (Left Side)

Build Nuclear Plants, Limit Coal to "Intelligent" Coal, Fund a Massive Development Program for Energy Storage, Continue to Commercialize Renewables, and Limit LNG to Strategic Imports for Distributed Power Networks

As I have suggested, on the production side, all dials on our insecurities and vulnerabilities meters point to nuclear as the best option for bulk power generation. It's far from perfect, but it best solves the optimization equations governing the left side of the value chain. We need a policy program that targets nuclear power for up to 50 percent of our electricity, and reduces coal to less than 20 percent. We need to close the nuclear fuel cycle with reprocessing facilities; that way, we reduce the potential amount of uranium that has to be imported and we at least have control over the weapons-grade coproduction threat. We have great experience with nuclear power; we need only evolutionary advances in technology to ramp up the construction program. (We'd really be just continuing the program that was halted in the 1980s from cancelation of orders.)

Concurrent with this, we should reduce the unrelenting oversight and paperwork process surrounding everything that goes on at a nuclear plant. Here's a lesson from history: When we first started building coal-fired boilers, there were serious explosions and catastrophic loss of life and property. The industry publications were full of articles about this dangerous state of affairs. The industry learned to control this danger, design for more safety, and apply codes and standards to operations.

I believe this is where we are with nuclear power. The industry has learned from the earlier accidents. The current generation of reactors has one of the most impressive safety records of any industrial sector. The next generation of reactors was designed with even more and better safety features. Like the early days of the boiler business, the industry can largely police itself now. The economic imperative is there. Downtime at a nuclear plant costs the owner an inordinate amount of money. The industry knows an accident at one reactor, however minor, is an accident at every reactor. Accidents still occur and will occur, but the question is whether the elaborate restrictions and documentation required by the NRC represents energy (and money) properly spent? I think not.

Mr. President, France, Belgium, Switzerland, Korea, and Japan get from 40 percent to 80 percent of their electricity from nuclear plants. They seem like nice places to live with nice people and healthy economies. Why can't we do this here in America as well? We won't be perfect, nor are they, but we have to weigh tradeoffs and respond appropriately. One thing's for sure: The global war on terror and our continuing global defense expenditures has claimed far more lives than accidents at nuclear plants.

The coal industry thinks we should build clean coal plants. That's a good idea, but I have an even better one. If we're going to build coal plants to exploit our most abundant energy resource, let's build *intelligent* coal refineries. Intelligently designed coal plants are located at the mine, so that the emissions and discharges can be put back where they came from and the supply line is minimized. They also would include provisions for extracting other high-value energy products from the coal, and to process recycled materials using principles of industrial ecology. Finally, no coal plant should be built without a well-defined, executable plan for managing carbon dioxide emissions *with transparent costs to do so*. This would be the equivalent of a nuclear plant's emergency-preparedness plan that it develops in cooperation with the local community.

The technological component of the plan also includes a healthy role for electricity storage. Electricity storage is an enabling technology. It "enables" us to have a more secure and reliable grid. It enables renewable energy to have a larger role on the production side of the chain. It enables us to optimize the use of existing generation and transmission assets. It enables distributed generation to become a valuable and continuous electricity production and cogeneration asset, not just a standby or emergency source of power. It facilitates electricity markets, just like storage and inventory control benefits marketers and traders in every other commodity. Every kilowatt hour we get out of an existing asset is one that does not have to come from a new asset.

Right now, the energy storage funding within the Department of Energy is but a pimple on the backside of the federal budget—less than $20 million. This budget should be in the hundreds of millions of dollars. Storage serves as a perfect area of emphasis for the federal government because the benefit of energy storage that accrues to each piece of the broken up value chain is too small for it to be funded by any one sector (transmission, distribution, generation). But because of this, it also has no constituency in Washington or the state houses. Every aspect of the production and delivery value chain benefits if we can commercialize electricity storage options for distributed and bulk applications and drive down the cost. Mr. (or Madam) President, why don't you be the visionary leader who spearheads the new energy storage program?

The Departments of Energy, Homeland Security, Agriculture, and the Environmental Protection Agency, should collaborate with industry to fund a program similar to the Clean Coal Technology Demonstration program focused on electricity storage. This "sixth dimension" of the electricity value chain should be developed in conjunction with new industry players that are focused on storage. After all, this is what happened in the natural gas industry. Once the industry was deregulated in the 1980s, storage became a critical part of the proper functioning of competitive bulk gas transmission.

The nominal goal for bulk electricity storage could be 15 percent of the nation's generation capacity, which is similar to the level of storage available in the natural gas industry.

Finally, just forget about importing large amounts of LNG for bulk electricity generation. It's a bad idea. End of story. I would hope that an outright ban on this practice from government is not necessary, and that the economic proposition will effectively do the job. On the other hand, limited LNG imports to supplement the fuel supply for distributed power and microgrid networks may be helpful. What we absolutely, positively do not want is to be dependent on imported LNG like we are on imported petroleum today and into the foreseeable future. That should be painfully obvious. Threatening LNG imports could be helpful in tempering gas prices, but I wouldn't rely on them for anything else.

Technological (Right Side)

Make Microgrids Effective and Drive the Process from the Consumer's Perspective

The right side of the value chain requires a much greater emphasis on integrating generation, storage, grid interface equipment, and intelligent meters at consumer sites into an intelligent microgrid. These networks need to be managed like large utility networks. Because utilities have lost some of their traditional asset base on the left side of the value chain (divestiture of generating stations, for example, and roll-up of transmission assets into ISOs), they have a marvelous opportunity to make it up through microgrids that more precisely meet the needs of demanding customers.

From a funding perspective, this is an area that can be driven at the state and local level, as it goes hand in hand with economic development. However, tough institutional issues need to be resolved. For example, how do such customers pay for bulk power assets previously built to serve their needs? The question of who pays for such "stranded" assets looms in the development of microgrids, but it is not intractable. This problem was solved through securitization of utility bonds when utilities were forced to divest their power generating assets in some parts of the country. Finally, in some states, distributed power is close to illegal.

To the extent possible, distributed microgrids should be based on renewable power systems—such as roof-mounted solar photovoltaics or small wind turbines on top of tall buildings. However, the reality is that over the near term, such assets will be fueled largely by natural gas, the cleanest fossil fuel. We now have fireplace burners that are "ventless" for our homes that burn natural gas without poisoning anyone. It seems reasonable to think that similar natural gas combustors can be deployed in our urban areas, perhaps aided by catalytic converters and other devices, to ensure that emissions are not a health issue.

Regulatory/Political

The Backbone of the Nation's Electricity Infrastructure Should Be Federalized

Perhaps the best way to characterize regulation of the industry is to say that during the first 50 years, roughly 1885 to 1935, business and the private sector moved way ahead of regulation; during the next 50 years, regulation reined the business in. Then, for 15 years or so, competition and privatization was again unleashed. Today the industry is again being roped and tied.

One mistake we should not make again is to allow the regulatory regime, whichever way the pendulum swings, to get ahead of technology. Of the many reasons competition has failed this industry, an important one is that the consumer has been neglected. Market idealists thought that restraining competition would lead to higher prices, and that unleashing competition would lower prices for most consumers. We now know that instituting competition, mandating rate reductions across the board, and then freezing prices or not providing a way for consumers to respond to higher prices is a prescription for disaster.

Two ingredients are required for competition to work. Consumers need a choice among credible suppliers and adequate price signals. For the most part, today's competitive markets have neither. So, one important aspect of future regulation is to give consumers the tools they need to make competition work. We dwelled at length on advanced electric meters that provide two-way communication between supplier and consumer. We also noted earlier that the 2005 Energy Bill encourages their use.

That's not enough. The regulatory regime should *require* such meters on every home and business as soon as practicable. And not just so the markets can work properly, but so consumers understand how they use electricity, what it costs at what times of day, and in general get smarter, more aware, and more engaged with their energy usage. Consumers can then make decisions about electricity use based on price (electricity rates) and/or on intangibles, such as environmental impact. Major appliances should also be equipped with meters that display electricity consumption. This is doable. This is today's technology.

We also need to face up to the idea that competition in electricity supply may never work at the retail level, at least not for individual ratepayers. However, it appears to have a good chance of working at the wholesale level. This is where it's needed and wanted most anyway. The big electricity-consuming members of the Electricity Consumers Council of America (ELCON) can save big bucks, remain competitive globally, and improve our economy if they can reduce their electricity costs. Therefore, the federal government and more states should continue to push competition aggressively at the wholesale level.

The Wholesale Market
- Fully deregulated
- Significant hedging/trading
- Energy storage for arbitrage
- Flexible/truly dispatchable power stations (coal, gas)
- New private DC lines
- Conversion to some private AC transmission
- Flexibility, commodity market mentality
- Arbitrage driven

The Retail Market
- Mostly deregulated
- Distributed power, micro-, minigrids
- Distributed energy storage devices
- Natural-gas driven
- Demand-side conservation
- Little trading and hedging (except big-load customers)
- Power quality management
- Customer-driven services

I also believe that competition and consolidation will in time force generating costs to decline. I don't think we need 25 utility entities owning and operating 104 nuclear power reactors. A utility that operates one unit or one plant can't possibly hope to compete with a company that focuses on excellence in nuclear power operations throughout the country. Therefore, the regulatory regime should encourage the consolidation of the nation's fleet of nuclear plants into the hands of a "big three" or certainly half a dozen or fewer companies. Nuclear plants are already largely regulated at the federal level so this shouldn't be a big deal.

The same should be true of large coal-fired plants. It can't really be that different to profitably operate a large coal plant in Wyoming than it is in New York, all other things being equal. One of those things should be equivalent regulatory treatment. All of these large coal plants should have to meet certain federal standards for safety, reliability standards for interfacing with the grid, and the like. Beyond that, private enterprise should be unleashed so that the mentality becomes one of performing better tomorrow than you did today—every day the plant staff comes to work.

Therefore, Mr. President, federalize the *regulation* of wholesale electricity generation. Note that I do not say ownership or operation. God forbid, we have another Tennessee Valley Authority (TVA) on our hands for the entire country. Declare eminent domain or something similar and wrench the regulatory reins from the states. Wholesale, base-load electricity generation and transmission should be regarded as "in the national interest." It should be treated like airports and the Interstate highway system. It's absurd, and redundant besides, to have New York state run its own independent (transmission) system operator (ISO). The same is true for Texas.

Make It Rumble When I Crank It Up

On the other hand, *unleash the power of technology and competitive consumer goods marketing at the retail end of the business.* Government doesn't have to impose competition in retail rates. No one "imposed" cellular phone technology on consumers. Yet, in about 10 years, it has completely changed the way we communicate. No one "decreed" that personal computing would make mainframes museum pieces, or that Internet searches would replace trips to the library.

Imagine going to your local electricity store, just like you go to a car dealership, and picking out the model you want custom-built into your new home. What this industry needs more than anything else are entrepreneurial companies that provide home- and business-based electricity systems with the same quality and attention to detail of a home entertainment system. I want to be able to pick from a variety of makes and models. Maybe I want one that makes me feel better because it offers the lowest carbon dioxide emissions. Maybe I just want to be the "baddest" dude in the neighborhood and pick out something that rumbles when I crank it up.

In truth, we had a few companies, subsidiaries of electric utilities, which were gearing up for a consumer revolution in electricity systems. That was when natural gas prices were low and electricity prices were looking high. Today natural gas prices are high and electricity prices are climbing. But electricity can be generated in a variety of other ways—small fuel cells, wind turbine/generators, microturbines, photovoltaic devices, and so on.

Companies that supply these devices at the retail level need to think in terms of providing a service, not a product. They will have to procure fuel, if they are fuel-based, on long-term contract and hedge against price volatility because fuel costs are such a large fraction of electricity costs and because consumers can't be hit with sticker shock. Even better, the devices could be powered by renewable energy, with a storage device deployed to moderate variable renewable energy supply with constant electricity demand. The leaders of this revolution will have to be keen on service. People can't tolerate living without electricity for very long. Or if they can, they should be rewarded by paying lower rates. Repair and maintenance programs would have to be trusted by consumers and geared toward very short response times.

Government policy, through the regulatory regime, should encourage a consumer revolution in electricity systems. Retail competition was first spurred by allowing electricity marketers to compete. However, they supply the same tired, indistinguishable product over the same asset infrastructure, using the same fuel base. Boring! That concept has failed. For the next 50 years, we need to truly allow consumers to make real choices from real options that really compete with the prevailing options of the day. One way government can encourage this revolution is to provide appropriate incentives, such as a subsidy equivalent to the cost of transmission and other grid services that are no longer needed.

When price of the product served up in traditional ways is too high (we're heading down that path), when reliability of the product is suspect (grid outages are increasing with alarming frequency), when the consumer is fed up with the traditional ways of doing things, he or she becomes receptive to alternatives purveyed by upstarts.

This entrepreneurial activity isn't for the faint-hearted or for those with a short-term profit horizon. It can't be driven by companies such as the old Enron, or an antiquated utility trying to act "competitive" in some other utility's neighborhood. Providing responsible, affordable electricity service at the retail level requires meeting performance standards that are much higher than today's model. Why else would anyone challenge the existing system? Different consumers, however, have different objectives. One might be willing to buy interruptible service if the tradeoff is a significantly lower rate. Others might want or need what we've termed earlier *six nines* reliability, which essentially means only a few minutes of outage per year. Another consumer might simply need regular power quality, while another may purchase "premium" or "ultra."

Another way the government can help foster the retail side of the business is to facilitate the transfer of electricity-based defense technology to the private sector. There's no grid on a battlefield, at least not until you capture the enemy's infrastructure. For this reason, the military has developed an incredible array of technologies for such programs as the all-electric ship, high-power density motors and generators for propulsion, small turbines for aircraft, storage devices, lightweight materials, and power electronics that manage DC power or convert AC to DC and vice versa. These technologies, redeployed for consumer service, will ultimately form the backbone of a revolution in retail electricity systems. We have a long way to go, but the changes in regulatory regimes outlined here will make the journey shorter and more efficient. The reliability needed for military service can't be less than the reliability required for home and business.

One thing is for sure. In my plan, it should be the consumer who decides how competition should unfold and not the regulator.

Financial

Financial Engineering Should Never Displace Systems Engineering

Infrastructure businesses simply don't play well as part of a transaction society fueled by financial engineering. In the 1920s and in the 1990s, the electricity industry saw financial engineering dominate systems engineering. In both cases, the business collapsed from the weight of fraud, mismanagement, greed, and laissez-faire political ideology. That's not to say that there isn't a prominent role for the private investor class. There is. The investment framework, however, must be consistent with the very long-term nature of this business. You don't want the same investment framework that guides and nourishes, for example, shampoo, governing a product that serves as the very foundation of modern society.

What this means is that electricity that is subjected to trading, to market forces, should be limited. Too much price volatility at the foundation of the economy isn't good for anyone. An artificially or naturally induced shortage of, say, corn or soybeans, or silver, resulting from market manipulation is disruptive, but not threatening. An artificially induced shortage of electricity, as was experienced in California in 2000–2001, unseats governors at best, and stirs revolutions in countries not as stable politically as ours at worst.

If greater oversight and government intervention is necessary in the electricity business, then it is in the trading and markets side of the house. Abuse can be avoided by either limiting the amount of electricity subject to trading, by making sure better tools are in place to manage flows (such as electricity storage), or by direct governmental oversight and intervention.

The financial dimension is a difficult one to manage currently. About 40 percent of generation assets are now owned by private entities. Private investment is taking more direct control of electricity assets through less regulated means such as hedge funds and private equity investment pools. No longer is financial control conducted through investing in the public equities or debt instruments of the companies, which are regulated through the SEC. I hope that I'm wrong, but I can almost see over the horizon the same train wreck that occurred with the merchant gas-fired business in 2002 (widely regarded as Enronitis) slamming the wind energy business: Generous government subsidies, financial engineering greasing up the performance and revenue projections, limited players, supportive public and regulatory framework seeking all things renewable, and new wind turbine technologies being introduced too quickly to serve a potentially overheating market.

At this point, I'm not sure what should be done, other than to appoint a commission to evaluate the role of private investment in electricity and determine whether it is being moved in a healthy or unhealthy direction.

Global

Secure All of the Supply Lines Affecting Our Domestic Electricity Infrastructure

To the extent that we generate electricity from indigenous sources of energy, we insulate the sector from global threats. However, at present, demand for all commodities, those for example that are required to build any kind of power station, whether nuclear or wind, is high around the world. We may have to rely on the global labor market for skilled workers and engineering talent. The supply lines for all of the "inputs" to our electricity value chain have become, or are becoming, global.

Currently, there is only one domestically domiciled supplier of wind turbines, and much of its manufacturing base is overseas. We haven't ordered a new nuclear unit in this country since 1978. The nuclear supply chain in this country has been decimated. A utility planning to build dozens of new coal units noted with pride recently that it scoured the world for low-cost manufacturing. That executive reported that they found plenty of opportunities, few of them on-shore. Most of our sector's supply chain is controlled by non-U.S.-domiciled parent companies. That doesn't mean we won't get what we need; it just means that those companies control how the profit and revenue is allocated, whether business in some other area of the world is more lucrative, and the extent to which our fortunes are linked through the international monetary system to everyone else's.

We potentially are embarking on a massive construction program here in the United States. However, meeting incremental electricity for 3 percent of the world's population pales in comparison to supplying electricity to the one-third of the planet's population that barely has any access to a grid. China is building one coal-fired power plant a week! It seems pretty clear that the world's manufacturing infrastructure will be located in Asia to serve this growth. The rest of the world will be served from this base as well. Power plant equipment will be shipped in large modules from Asia and "bolted together" at the sites. All we will do here is "assemble," Much like how cars are "manufactured" domestically.

We may want to think less in terms of securing fuel supply lines over the next 50 years, and instead of securing supplies of critical commodities for maintaining our electricity infrastructure, labor to keep costs reasonable, and the like. We may also want to adjust our expectations for just-in-time (JIT) inventory control and instead begin to stockpile critical components to have them ready.

Perhaps a simple way of underscoring the global issue is that we have lost much of our control over the technologies and supply chain for bulk electricity supply. We are far behind many other countries of the world—Japan, Korea, France, Germany, the countries of Scandinavia, and others. However, because we have the best-equipped and trained military in the world, we do maintain a high degree of control over the technologies and supply chain for distributed power generation suitable for retail electricity markets. Repurposing these technologies for the consumer electricity revolution, expanding the supply chain, manufacturing, and assembly of these components and systems; and encouraging their use in distributed systems surely will have a positive impact on our economy as well. Who knows, that once-trusted phrase, "Made in the USA," might again have real relevance to our electricity infrastructure.

Relying and encouraging use of our home-grown technologies and energy sources, vastly shrinks our electricity supply lines.

Social

Make Electricity Visible, Understandable and Part of Our Everyday Discourse

Electricity should be accorded the same respect as other parts of our society. Five years ago, people at social gatherings talked about their investment in the stock market. Last year, all I heard about at cocktail parties was the increase in home values. People are more than happy to talk about environmental issues. We should be talking about electricity when the lights are on, not just when the lights go out. We should be debating whether the lengthening supply lines that I keep referring to are a good thing or a bad thing, whether we can sustain reasonable electricity prices with little control over the global supply chain, whether our electricity infrastructure should be controlled by investment funds that are not overseen by the government, and what types of new power stations we should be building.

Mr. (or Madam) President, electricity needs to come out of the wall and into our lives, and you have the best bully pulpit to make sure this happens.

Postscript

Personal Accountability

In September 1990, my wife and I launched a publication called *Common Sense on Energy and Our Environment*. For my part, the inspiration came on Earth Day in April of that year—and one-sided arguments about the environment coming from both sides of the debate, which left me enraged.

It was like George Bush's edict after 9/11: "You're either with us or against us." If you didn't side with the environmentalists, then you sided with industry. And vice versa. Very little rational thought seemed to permeate the debate. Environmentalists cleverly exploited emotion and passion—and the public's general lack of understanding of science and technology. Industry, on the other hand, seemed always to resort to economic arguments. Cleanup is too costly. Jobs will disappear. Manufacturing will move offshore. Your electricity bills will skyrocket.

The editorial philosophy for *Common Sense* was to always explain science and technical issues in nonthreatening language and to provide both sides of the story. Environmentalists seemed to always gloss over economic realities or what the consumer would ultimately pay for environmental protection. On the other side, it seemed, industry also neglected the fundamental economic principle that emission and discharges were, in effect, wasted materials that imposed costs on the business paid for elsewhere. Another aspect of *Common Sense,* however, was the notion of individual responsibility and personal accountability.

For Americans and electricity consumption, this is a particularly important principle. We are not Europe. Europe faces energy costs that are twice ours, and Europe also favors governmental structures that are more socialistic than ours. Many European countries with "sound energy policies" are also more homogeneous than the United States. European countries are more urbanized, with denser population centers, than much of America. All of these characteristics mean that it is easier to impose an energy policy from the top down as social policy. Europe pays more for electricity and energy mostly because of higher taxes imposed to direct social policy.

As much as this book is about reforming our physical, market, legislative, and financial infrastructure to avoid looming threats to our electricity supply, mitigating those threats can't be done without a greater sense of individual responsibility.

President Carter was widely ridiculed, reviled even, especially by Republicans, for equating energy independence with "the moral equivalent of war" in 1977. But guess what? Today, the most prominent leaders running around the country stirring up support for energy independence are Republicans like ex-CIA Chief James Woolsey. Given that the Iraq War was prosecuted, among other reasons, to defend global petroleum supply lines, maybe energy conservation and independence really are the moral equivalent of war. It pays to remember that Carter's moral equivalent of war had no dead bodies. This latest escapade has cost the lives of more than 3,000 American soldiers at the time of this writing, along with estimates of at least 50,000 Iraqi civilians dead, and hundreds of thousands of Iraqis fleeing their country.

Sheer numbers about our consumption argue for some moral structure. America has less than 5 percent of the world's population, but we generate and consume approximately one-fourth of the world's electricity, with all the environmental impact that entails. Plus the rest of the world would rather live like we do, and many of their societies certainly appear to be making this goal a reality. Think about it. What happens to all of the issues we've been dissecting in this book if the other 95 percent of the world becomes just like us: inefficient consumers of electricity on a massive scale?

When my youngest daughter tells me she loses sleep over issues like global warming, I tell her that until she learns to turn off the lights in her room when it is unoccupied, I don't want to hear about it. In *Common Sense,* I railed against people who create fear in the minds of the public—and get people to open their purses and wallets for donations. That's because many of these same people have no problem ravaging the planet by patronizing skiing areas in pristine mountain areas or golf courses in the middle of the desert, or building and living in homes three and four times the size they need, or even protesting wind turbines because they ruin their view. But they want you to donate money to them because they're against global warming. The hypocrisy of it all astounds me.

In closing this book, as was my intent with *Common Sense,* I want you to associate every increment of electricity, every electron that is generated for your consumption, for your pleasure, for your comfort and convenience, for your health care and for extending your life in old age, with all of its other attributes: the molecules of carbon dioxide that are contributing to global climate change and reinforcing extreme weather events, the radioactive spent fuel rods that will have to be responsibly managed out to (effectively) the end of time, the global natural gas and petroleum supply lines that have to be defended to ensure that the lowest cost sources of energy are continually made available to us, the unsightly wind turbines obstructing someone's view into the horizon or out over the shoreline, and the thermal exhaust from your car, truck or SUV that is wasted energy that just heats up our urban areas even more.

I want you to associate your seemingly insatiable demand for electricity, or your insatiable desire for it (if you live in a developing country), with the power generating station, whether nuclear, wind, solar, coal, or gas, that you want built in someone else's backyard. I would like you to know that the new 5,000-square-foot home that you have for a family of four (or the big, rambling hundred-year-old home that I live in) requires that much more electricity than a smaller home or a modern home more sustainability built. The sprinkler system you use to water your lawn is driven by a pump. That pump is driven by an electric motor. The potable water you sprayed on your lawn just to keep it green required electricity and energy to treat it, only for it to flow right back into the ground probably laced with exces fertilizer.

The liquid-crystal-display television you just bought consumes four to five times as much electricity as the one it replaced. Microwaving your food instead of using a gas stove substitutes electricity for fuel. All of the computers and home entertainment equipment you leave on consumes a small but constant amount of electricity.

I would like you to ask yourself why we participate in reading groups and investment clubs to improve our understanding of the world and pad our retirement accounts, but no one joins a club about energy conservation. Think about it. Sharing ideas, tips, and, most importantly, providing a support network and social structure that emphasizes the importance of energy consumption to our well-being, and the well-being of our children, is simply something we don't do. Maybe your daughter isn't sleeping because of global warming, either. If so, maybe setting an example in energy conservation is a better life lesson than teaching her how to make more money to satisfy a higher-energy lifestyle?

Maybe you have a son or daughter that has chosen a career in the military. I think you need to understand that there indeed is a connection between the electricity we use in this country and strife we deal with overseas. This connection will strengthen if we begin to import larger volumes of liquefied natural gas from places like Nigeria, Russia, Algeria, Libya and, yes, Iran. But the connection must get beyond the simpleton rhetoric of "we invaded Iraq because of oil" or "we liberated Kuwait because we want oil." Military campaigns are based on intricate analyses and multiple goals and objectives. It is critical to understand, though, that defending our energy supply lines is a key element of our geopolitical and military posture, affecting both our offensive and defensive capabilities. It may be a small part, but it is certainly one we ignore at our peril.

For as long as I have worked on the supply side of the electricity business, I concede that starting with personal demand and personal accountability are truly the first way to avoid a *lights out* scenario. Today many people are arguing for the reinstatement of the draft or, at least, a period of national service that follows high school or college. As the rationale goes, it's a way of ensuring that all citizens contribute to the war effort or that they contribute to the good of the nation. National service could include time and effort understanding and applying energy conservation, *regardless of what the prevailing price is of gasoline or electricity.*

I also want you to understand that there are other important connections to make between the electrons you use and your health. Whether you have an electric car or a gasoline-powered one, riding a bike for the really short trips not only keeps you more fit but reduces your energy footprint. Walking outside and getting some fresh air avoids the impact of running an electric treadmill. I find it completely ironic that I will take one and a half hours twice a week to bicycle 20 miles in the summer. Then I will get in the car and go to the grocery store I passed on my way! It's crazy. I know better. But I'm a participant in this mess just as you are.

Of course, there is a time element to all this. Energy consumption saves you time now available to do other things, hopefully more rewarding and productive things. But if I rode my bike to the video store, or the grocery store, figured out how to carry stuff, I'd save those short-haul miles that, by the way, are the most polluting because the engine isn't yet warmed up. I may also put myself in greater danger riding a bike on roadways clearly designed for heavier, more powerful vehicles. Perhaps all the money and time invested in Rails-to-Trails programs could have been better invested in carving out a protected bike lane for people going to the store and back?

The moral or ethical imperative starts by working backward from the electricity that you consume. Consumer-driven demand has always been the hallmark of business in this country. In a short 10 years, something like 60 percent of the American population has regular access to the Internet and the valuable resources it provides. What do you think we could do as a nation if the value of electricity conservation was perceived to be as high as the value of the Internet? How much smaller of an environmental footprint would we make if we reduced electricity demand with the fervor that we invest in the stock market?

The moral or ethical imperative is enhanced when you get beyond dollars. The financial motivation to reduce energy use at times of high primary energy cost is not enough. The other costs which our accounting systems fail to include must be factored in as well. This is where morality and ethics truly play a role. They make up the gaps in our humanity when other incentives don't work, or don't work well. We are taught to do unto others as you would have them do unto you. We administer this edict even when there is no financial gain because there is a spiritual gain, a social gain. It is, after all, the Golden Rule that is, in some way, shape, or form, fundamental to every ethical tradition and religion on this planet.

Once personal responsibility is established, then accountability must follow. Get acquainted with your electricity bill. Start quantifying everything. If you don't have time, assign one of your kids to be responsible for the household energy accounting system. One of our daughters is responsible for recycling. It'll help them apply the math they learn in school. Keep a logbook. See if you can "see" the reduction in electricity use as you switch your bulbs to fluorescents. Find out if motion-detector-equipped lighting systems could make sense for your situation.

If you fervently oppose nuclear power or coal, fine. Find out what the percentage of your utility's generating capacity is nuclear or coal, and reduce your consumption by that much. If you are a proponent of wind energy, then go to your electricity provider and tell them you'll happily look at wind turbines out your back yard and put up with the annoying hum of the low-frequency noises. Get a coalition of your neighbors to do the same. Convert your monthly electricity consumption to an equivalent carbon dioxide discharge. Put it on the wall in the kitchen. Let your family know what your household contribution to global warming is and what your planetary footprint is.

Above all else, don't let the vagaries of electricity price escalations and declines interrupt your action plan. It can take a lifetime to change social behavior. Remember, there are social and environmental values that our price-driven accounting system neglect.

None of this is intended to make you feel guilty. Quite the opposite. It is intended to empower you, to make you understand that, just like every vote matters (though it does take time), every kilowatt-hour matters, when you trace it back and discover the footprint that increment of electricity has on your surroundings. What is the first step a financial advisor suggests if you are sinking deeper into debt each month? That's right. Make a budget and stick to it. "Running the numbers," as I call it in my house, instills fiscal discipline. An energy impact budget will instill energy discipline in your lives.

I just heard a utility executive at the industry's largest meeting say that he hopes that by next year, no one will be talking about electricity. We operate best when it is "in the background," he says. That is like politicians telling you, "Don't worry, we will take care of it." That's the kind of attitude that gives rise to fascism, by the way. As Bruce Springsteen cautioned in one of his concerts that I saw during the "Born in the USA" tour: "Blind faith in your leaders will get you killed." Well, blind faith in utility executives like the one I just quoted probably won't kill us. But it won't help us keep the lights on while sleeping, comforted in the knowledge that we're taking proactive steps to capitalize on the benefits of electricity without destroying ourselves in the process.

Keeping electricity "in the wall," so to speak, is exactly what we shouldn't be doing. It is the least visible of all the forms of energy we consume regularly. We see the price of gasoline every time we fill up the car. We see a fuel oil tank that has to be replenished if we use heating for home heating. We see natural gas burning in our furnaces and stove burners. We are far less engaged with our electricity production and consumption, and that needs to change. Today.

Bibliography

The following books, articles, technical reports and papers, either provided source material for *Lights Out*, or would be helpful for readers seeking more.

General

Anderson, J. 2006. "Problems in the Organized Markets: A Large Energy User Perspective," Indiana Energy Conference, Indianapolis, IN, September 27, 2006.

Bakke, D. 2005. *Joy at Work: A Revolutionary Approach to Fun on the Job*. Seattle: PVG.

Barnett, D., and K. Bjornsgaard. 2000. *Electric Power Generation: A Non-technical Guide*. Tulsa, OK: Pennwell.

Berenson, A. 2006. "The Other Legacy of Enron," *New York Times*, May 28, B1–B4.

Bodanis, D. 2005. *Electric Universe: The Shocking True Story of Electricity*. New York: Crown Publishers/Random House.

Crocker, D., and T. Linden. 1998. *Ethics of Consumption: The Good Life, Justice, and Global Stewardship*. Lanham, MD: Bowman and Littlefield Publishers Inc.

Federal Energy Regulatory Commission. August 2006. *Demand Response and Advanced Metering*, Staff Report. Federal Energy Regulatory Commission.

Hyman, L. 2005. *America's Electric Utilities: Past, Present, & Future*, 8th ed. Vienna, VA: Public Utilities Reports Inc.

Johnston, D. 2006. "Competitive Era Fails to Shrink Electric Bills," *New York Times*. October 15. A1–A27.

Johnston, D. 2006. "Grid Limitations Increase Prices for Electricity," *New York Times*, December 13. A1–C4.

Johnston, D. 2006. "Flaws Seen In Markets for Utilities," *New York Times*, November 21. C1–C4.

Makansi, J. 2002. *An Investor's Guide to the Electricity Economy*. New York: John Wiley & Sons.

Munson, R. 2005. *From Edison to Enron: The Business of Power and What It Means for the Future of Electricity*. Westport, CT: Praeger.

Nye, D. 1990. *Electrifying America: Social Meanings of a New Technology*. Cambridge, MA: MIT Press.

Parfit, M. 2005. "After Oil: Powering the Future." *National Geographic*, 208, no. 2: 2–31.

Patterson, W. 1999. *Transforming Electricity: The Coming Generation of Change*. London: The Royal Institute of International Affairs.

Perkins, J. 2004. *Confessions of an Economic Hit Man*. New York: Penguin Group.

Scientific American. 2006. "Special Issue—Energy's Future: Beyond Carbon," *Scientific American*, 295, no. 3: 46–114.

Seifer, M. 1998. *Wizard: The Life and Times of Nikola Tesla*. New York: Citadel/Kensington.

Sterman, J. 2000. *Business Dynamics: Systems Thinking and Modeling for a Complex World*. New York: Irwin/McGraw-Hill.

Sweet, W. 2006. *Kicking the Carbon Habit: Global Warming and the Case for Renewable and Nuclear Energy*. New York: Columbia University Press.

Talbot, D. "It's Not Too Late: The Energy Technologies That Might Forestall Global Warming Already Exist," *Technology Review*. 109, no. 3: 37–69.

Technology Review. 2002. "Special Issue: Energy." *Technology Review*, 105, no. 1: 32–80.

U.S. Government Accountability Office. August 2004. *Electricity Markets: Consumers Could Benefit from Demand Programs but Challenges Remain*. GAO-04-844.

Wald, M. 2006. "A Power-Grid Report Suggests Some Dark Days Ahead," *New York Times*, October 16. A14.

Value Chain: Nuclear Power

Nuclear Power: Technical and Institutional Options for the Future. Washington, DC: National Academy Press, 1992

Carey, J. 2005. "Maybe in My Backyard," *Business Week*, September 5.

Fialka, J. 2006. "Nuclear Power Revival Could Encounter Hurdles," *Wall Street Journal*, December 5, A4.

Gertner, J. 2006. "Atomic Balm?" *New York Times Magazine*, July 16, 36–47.

Gray, T. 2005. "Can Nuclear Power Become Just Another Business?" *New York Times.* November 20. www.newyorktimes.com.

King, L. 2006. "Going Nuclear: Demand for Electricity Requires New Plants," *Las Vegas Review-Journal*, August 20.

Murray, R. 1989. *Understanding Radioactive Waste*, 3rd ed. Columbus, OH: Battelle Memorial Institute.

Nealey, S. 1990. *Nuclear Power Development: Prospects in the 1990s.* Columbus, OH: Battelle.

Value Chain: Energy Storage

Baxter, R. 2006, *Energy Storage: A Non-technical Guide.* Tulsa, OK: Pennwell.

Makansi, J., and Baxter, R. 2003. *Energy Storage: The Sixth Dimension of the Electricity Value Chain.* St. Louis, MO: Pearl Street Inc./The Energy Storage Council.

Value Chain: Coal

Goodell, J. 2006. "Cooking the Climate with Coal," *Natural History*, www.naturalhistorymag.com. (May): 36–41.

Goodell, J. 2006. *Big Coal: The Dirty Secret Behind America's Energy Future.* New York: Houghton Mifflin.

National Coal Council. 2006. *Coal: America's Energy Future, Staff Report.* Washington, DC: National Coal Council.

Industrial Ecology

Makansi, J. 2003. "The E-Equity Index: The Use of Industrial Ecology Principles to Benchmark Sustainable Business Practices for Power Generation Facilities." In *Industrial Ecology for a Sustainable Future.* Ann Arbor, MI: International Society for Industrial Ecology's Second Conference.

National Research Council. 1998. *Industrial Ecology Approaches to Coal-fired Power*

Plants. Board on Energy and Environmental Systems Workshop, March, Washington, DC.

Odum, H. 1996. *Environmental Accounting: Energy and Environmental Decision-Making,* New York: John Wiley & Sons.

Vulnerabilities: Global Warming

Aston, A., and Helm, B. 2005. "The Race Against Climate Change," *BusinessWeek,* December 12, 59–66.

Begley, S. 2006. "Scientists Explain How They Attribute Climate-Change Data," *Wall Street Journal,* May 12. A15.

Burr, M. 2006. "Facing Global Warming." *Public Utilities Fortnightly,* 144, no. 8: 52–56.

Glick, D. 2004. "Global Warming." *National Geographic,* 206, no. 3: 2–75

Kolbert, E. 2005. "The Climate of Man-I," *New Yorker,* April 25, 56–71.

Kolbert, E. May 2, 2005. "The Climate of Man-II," *New Yorker,* May 2, 64–73.

Lindzen, R. 2006. "There Is No Consensus on Global Warming," *Wall Street Journal,* June 26.

Powicki, C. 2006. "Climate Policy Gets Down to Business," *EPRI Journal,* September, 16–39.

Supply Lines: Workforce

Burr, M. 2006. "Baby Boom Blues." *Public Utilities Fortnightly,* 144, no. 7: 28–35.

Krishnan, R. 2006. "Aging Workforce: A Challenge to the Industry." *Power Engineering,* 110, no. 6: 36–39.

Peltier, R. 2006. "The Future of Workforce Training." *Power,* 150, no. 5: 26–31.

Demand Management

Barker, B. 2006. "Turning on Energy Efficiency," *EPRI Journal* (September): 4–13.

Casten, T. 1998. *Turning Off the Heat: Why America Must Double Energy Efficiency to Save Money and Reduce Global Warming.* Amherst, NY: Prometheus.

Grant, P. 2006. "A Power Grid for the Hydrogen Economy," *Scientific American,* 295, no. 1 (July): 78–83. www.sciam.com

Romm, J. 2006. "Hybrid Vehicles," *Scientific American,* 294, no. 10 (April): 72–79.

Talbot, D. 2003. "Lightbulb." *Technology Review* (May): 31. www.technology review.com.

Supply Lines: LNG

Burr, M. 2005. "The Geopolitical Risks of LNG," *Public Utilities Fortnightly*, 143, no. 3 (March): 28–33.

Energy Information Administration. 2003. *The Global Liquefied Natural Gas Market: Status & Outlook*, Staff Report, December. Washington, DC: Energy Information Administration/U.S. Department of Energy.

Foss, M. 2006. "LNG Development in North America," *Fortnightly's Spark* (November): 1.

Krauss, C. 2006. "Not Afraid of Natural Gas," *New York Times*. October 4.

Makansi, J. 2006. "LNG: Will It or Won't It (Meet US Natural Gas Demand)?" *Combined Cycle Journal* (First Quarter): 58–62.

Nesbitt, D. 2005. What Will LNG Imports Do to North American Gas Prices?" *Natural Gas & Electricity*, 21, no. 8: 1–9

Insecurities: Transmission

Abraham, S. 2002. *National Transmission Grid Study*. Washington, DC: U.S. Department of Energy.

Altman, D. 2006. "Terror Proof, Except for All the Vulnerabilities," *New York Times*, August 20, 2006, Section 3, p. 3 (from www.nytimes.com)

Amin, M. 2004. "North American Electricity Infrastructure: System Security, Quality, Reliability, Availability, and Efficiency Challenges and Their Societal Impacts." In *Continuing Crises in National Transmission Infrastructure: Impacts and Options for Modernization*, 1–20. Washington, DC: National Science Foundation.

Center for Smart Energy. 2005. *The Emerging Smart Grid: Investment and Entrepreneurial Potential in the Electric Power Grid of the Future, Center for Smart Energy*. Washington, DC: Center for Smart Energy, Global Environmental Fund. www.centerforsmartenergy.com.

Edison Electric Institute. 2005. *EEI Survey of Transmission Investment: Historical and Planned Capital Expenditures (1999–2008), Staff Report, May*. Washington, DC: Edison Electric Institute.

Fairley, P. 2001. "A Smarter Power Grid." *Technology Review*, (July–August): 41–49.

Hirst, E. 2004. *U.S. Transmission Capacity: Present Status and Future Prospects*. Washington, DC: Edison Electric Institute.

Hyman, L. 2006. "Transmission Business Chicago Style." In *The Rudden Energy Strategies Report*, 1–2. Kansas City, MO: Black & Veatch.

Javetski, J. 2006. "Transmission Need an Emergency in PJM, the RTO Says," *Power News*, October 20, 1–2.

McNeal, G. 2005. "The Terrorist and the Grid," *New York Times*, August 13, www.nytimes.com.

National Security Telecommunications Advisory Committee, Information Assurance Task Force. 1997. *Electric Power Risk Assessment.* <http://www.ncs.gov/n5_hp/Reports/EPRA/electric.html>.

North American Electric Reliability Council. 1998. *Y2K Coordination Plan for the Electricity Production and Delivery Systems of North America, Staff Report, June 12.* Princeton, NJ: North American Electric Reliability Council.

North American Electric Reliability Council. 1999. *Preparing the Electric Power Systems of North America for Transition to the Year 2000, Staff Report, August 3.* Princeton, NJ: North American Electric Reliability Council.

North American Electric Reliability Council. 2006. *2006 Summer Assessment: Reliability of the Bulk Power System in North America, Staff Report, May.* Princeton, NJ: North American Electric Reliability Council (NERC).

Office of Electric Transmission and Distribution. 2003. *Grid 2030: A National Vision for Electricity's Second 100 Years.* Washington, DC: U.S. Department of Energy Office of Electric Transmission and Distribution.

U.S. General Accounting Office. 2004. *Critical Infrastructure: Challenges and Efforts to Secure Control Systems, Staff Report, March.* Washington, DC: U.S. General Accounting Office.

Vulnerabilities: Extreme Climate Events

Dean, C. 2006. "Surprises in a New Tally of Areas Vulnerable to Hurricanes," *New York Times*, October 10, D4.

Fell, K. 2006. *Technology Challenges and Future Direction.* New York: The New York Independent System Operator.

Hayden, T. 2006. "Super Storms: No End In Sight," *National Geographic*, 210, no. 2 (August): 66–77.

National Research Council. 2004. *Abrupt Climate Change: Inevitable Surprises.* Washington, DC: The National Research Council. <http://www.nap.edu/books/0309074347/html/>.

Revkin, A. 2006. "Updating Prescriptions for Avoiding Worldwide Catastrophe," *New York Times*, September 12, C2.

Insecurities: China and India

Bremner, B. 2005. "Reactors? We'll Take Thirty, Please." *BusinessWeek*, October 3, 52–53.

Central Electricity Authority. 2005. *Review of Growth of India Electricity Sector, Staff Report*. New Dehli: Central Electricity Authority. china.html>.

Das, S. 2005. "Indian Power Sector—Is it Recovering in a Real Sense—A Wider Scenario." *EnergyPulse.net*, July 18. <http://www.energypulse.net/centers/article/article_display.cfm?a_id=1053>.

Engardio, P. 2005. "A New World Economy," *BusinessWeek*, August 22, 52–58.

Kotkin, S. 2006. "Living in China's World," *New York Times*. November 5.

Kumar, S., A. Khetan, and B. Thapa. 2005. "Indian Power Sector-Emerging Challenges to Growth." In *World Power*, 1–5. Fairfax, VA: ICF International.

Larkin, J. 2005. "Indian's Energy Woes Go Deep." *Wall Street Journal*, July 11, 2005, A11.

Larmer, B. September 2006. "The Manchurian Candidate," *National Geographic*. 270, no. 3: 42–73.

Panagariya, A. 2005. "A Passage to Prosperity." *Wall Street Journal*. July 14, A14.

Prayas. 2005. *Indian Power Reforms Update*, Issue 10 (March): 1–26.

U.S. Department of Energy, Energy Information Administration. 2004. *Country Analysis Briefs: China*. <http://www.eia.doe.gov/emeu/cabs/.

World Energy Council. 2006. *World Energy in 2006*. London: World Energy Council.

Distributed Power

Borbely, A. 2001. *Distributed Generation: The Power Paradigm for the New Millennium*. Boca Raton, FL: CRC.

Brent, R. 2003. "A Blueprint for DG: Presenting a Fair and Simple Distributed Generation Plan for Utilities and Policy-Makers," *Public Utilities Fortnightly*, 141, no. 1 (January): 28–33.

Lesser, J. 2002. "Distributed Generation: Hype vs Hope," *Public Utilities Fortnightly*, 140, no. 11 (June): 20–28.

Lynch, J. 2006. "The Rise of MicroGrid Power Networks," *Energy & Power Management* (February): 16–21.

About the Author

J ason Makansi earned a bachelor of science in chemical engineering from Columbia University. He worked in power plants at the Tennessee Valley Authority during the summer of his junior year and after graduation and then at a refinery in New Jersey. In 1981, he joined *Power* magazine, one of the oldest and most successful industry trade publications in the country. There he became a leader and spokesperson for the industry and evaluated most every technology relevant to electricity generation. In 1994, he was appointed editor-in-chief and led the publication, launched new information products and platforms, and interpreted the industry's tortuous transformation for his audience.

Like many in 2000, Makansi took a millennium plunge into the dot.com pool, only to hurry back out, get his towel, dry off, and find more rewarding things to do. He then formed Pearl Street Inc., named for the famed power plant that launched an industry in 1882, which was built by his boyhood hero, Thomas Alva Edison. Pearl Street is a consultancy firm from which Mr. Makansi has launched several businesses, some of which he manages or collaborates with, intended to capitalize on the electricity production and delivery value chain. Information on these businesses, as well as Mr. Makansi's current and previous leadership posts in various industry and engineering organizations, can be viewed at www.pearlstreetinc.com.

Makansi considers himself a communicator within the industry and to professionals and nonspecialists outside of it. For example, from 1990 to 1996, he published as a moonlighting business the monthly newsletter *Common Sense on Energy and Our Environment* to educate the public about energy issues. In 2002, Makansi published *An Investor's Guide to the Electricity Economy* to provide better information and analysis to investors about the electricity industry.

Mr. Makansi pursues several passions outside the electricity business. He writes fiction, participates in online and offline writers groups, and has published several short stories. He hopes one day to get involved in the emerging field of applying systems concepts to sociology and social organizations. He plays viola and piano (neither well), makes feeble attempts at improvising and composing, and worships at the alter of music in almost all its forms. When mentally exhausted, he turns to bicycle riding, jogging, tennis, basketball, and other activities.

Mr. Makansi is the author of two other books, and hundreds of articles about the electricity industry in a variety of different publications. He has been a guest of CNBC's *Wake Up Call*, National Public Radio, and Financial News Network, and appears in a frequently running show on The History Channel, *Modern Marvels: Power Plants*.

Mr. Makansi grew up in Wilmington, Delaware, and Signal Mountain, Tennessee, and has lived more of his life in and around New York City than anywhere else. He currently resides in St. Louis with his wife, Kristina, daughters Amira and Elena, and two dogs who seem to always bark during teleconference calls.

Index

293

security. *See* Domestic electricity
   infrastructure
shrinkage, 139–141
usage, explanation, 6
Symbols, power, 243
Synfuels, usage, 181–183
Systems engineering, replacement,
   270–272

T&D. *See* Testing and development
Tectonic movement, 221–223
Telecommunications
   integration, 210
   stations, 213
Tennessee Valley Authority (TVA), 46
   example, 268
Tesla, Nikolai, 42–44
Testing and development (T&D)
   circuits, 229
   control centers, data (entry), 239–240
   infrastructure
      inadequacy, 232
      usage, 229–230
   system, 239
   total losses, average, 254
   utility expenditures, 84
Thatcher, Margaret, 54
Thermal energy, electricity conversion, 261
Thermotunneling, 216–217
Third world, private investment, 244–245
Third-world grid
   reasons. *See* First-world country
   usage, 7
      reasons, 73
      worry, 74
Thomas Edison State College, program
   initiation, 107–108
Three Mile Island (TMI), accident, 48, 69,
   188–189
   consequences, 190
Time of use rates, 208–209
Total electricity delivery capacity, 164
Traders, impact, 79–80
Traditional power systems, distribution power
   systems (contrast), 223f
Trained/skilled workers
   airlifting, consideration, 16–17
   supply shortage, 12–13
Transactions-based economy, 91

Transmission
   assets, roll-up. *See* Independent system order
   bibliography, 287–288
   facilities. *See* Merchant transmission
      facilities
   functionality, 7
   importance/respect, 260–261
   integration, 80–84
   investments, decline, 81f
   management, 87–88
   repair, 62
   weak link, 8–9
Transmission grid
   perspective, 62
   problem/loss, 8
   term, usage, 7
Turbines
   impact, 227–228
   usage, 20, 126–127
TVA. *See* Tennessee Valley Authority
Two-way meter, usage, 208–210
TXU Corp.
   construction program, 149–150
   size, increase, 152–153

Ugly American, impact, 245
Ultra-capacitors, usage, 170–171
Uninterruptible power systems (UPS), 213
United States, China economic parity
   (desire), 251
United States Enrichment Corp. (USEC),
   201–202
UPS. *See* Uninterruptible power systems
Uranium
   concentration, 204
   energy density, 202
   usage/percentage. *See* Electricity
U.S. Agency for International Development
   (AID), 248
U.S. electricity demand, growth, 57f
U.S. manufacturing, transfer, 250
USEC. *See* United States Enrichment Corp.
Utility
   assets, ownership, 148
   companies, purchase, 53–54
   executives, management consultants
      (impact), 37–38
   expenditures. *See* Testing and
      development